ETHICS AND PLANNING RESEARCH

Ethics and Planning Research

Edited by
FRANCESCO LO PICCOLO
Università degli Studi di Palermo, Italy

HUW THOMAS
Cardiff University, UK

LONDON AND NEW YORK

First published 2009 by Ashgate Publishing

Published 2016 by Routledge
2 Park Square, Milton Park, Abingdon, Oxon OX14 4RN
711 Third Avenue, New York, NY 10017, USA

Routledge is an imprint of the Taylor & Francis Group, an informa business

Copyright © 2009 Francesco Lo Piccolo and Huw Thomas

Francesco Lo Piccolo and Huw Thomas have asserted their rights under the Copyright, Designs and Patents Act, 1988, to be identified as the editors of this work.

All rights reserved. No part of this book may be reprinted or reproduced or utilised in any form or by any electronic, mechanical, or other means, now known or hereafter invented, including photocopying and recording, or in any information storage or retrieval system, without permission in writing from the publishers.

Notice:
Product or corporate names may be trademarks or registered trademarks, and are used only for identification and explanation without intent to infringe.

British Library Cataloguing in Publication Data
Ethics and planning research.
    1. City planning--Research--Moral and ethical aspects.
    I. Lo Piccolo, Francesco, 1966- II. Thomas, Huw, 1954-
    174.9'71-dc22

Library of Congress Cataloging-in-Publication Data
Ethics and planning research / edited by Francesco Lo Piccolo and Huw Thomas.
    p. cm.
    Includes index.
    ISBN 978-0-7546-7357-6 1. Social sciences--Research--Moral and ethical aspects.
2. Social sciences and ethics. 3. Research--Moral and ethical aspects. 4. Social scientists--Professional ethics. I. Lo Piccolo, Francesco, 1966- II. Thomas, Huw.
    H62.E764 2009
    174'.90014--dc22

                                    2009008829

ISBN 9780754673576 (hbk)

Contents

List of Figures and Tables	*vii*
Notes on Contributors	*ix*

1	Introduction *Francesco Lo Piccolo and Huw Thomas*	1

PART I   ETHICAL FRAMEWORKS

2	Consequentialism and the Ethics of Planning Research *Nigel Taylor*	13
3	Virtue Ethics and Research Ethics *Huw Thomas*	29
4	Pragmatic Ethics and Sustainable Development *Niraj Verma*	41

PART II   INSTITUTIONAL CONTEXTS AND CONSTRAINTS

5	Planning Research, Ethical Conduct and Radical Politics *Kanishka Goonewardena*	57
6	The Knowledge Business in Academic Planning Research *Rob Imrie*	71
7	Ethical Issues in PhD Research Training *Daniela Mello*	91
8	The Responsibility to Ask Questions: The Case of Bias in Travel Demand Forecasting *P. Anthony Brinkman*	107
9	Environmental Planning Research: Ethical Perspectives in Institutional and Value-Driven Approaches *Filippo Schilleci*	119

10	Ethics and Consultancy *Adrian Healy*	145

| 11 | Researching Planning Practice
Patsy Healey | 161 |

PART III   ETHICS IN THE PRACTICE OF PLANNING RESEARCH

| 12 | Toward a Naturalistic Research Ethic: Or how Mediators
must Act Well to Learn, if They are to Practice Effectively
John Forester and David Laws | 179 |

| 13 | Knowledge, Power and Ethics in Extraordinary Times:
Learning from the Naples Waste Crisis
Laura Lieto | 191 |

| 14 | Ethical Awareness in Advocacy Planning Research
Giovanni Attili | 207 |

| 15 | On Having Imperial Eyes
Libby Porter | 219 |

| 16 | Multiple Roles in Multiple Dramas: Ethical Challenges
in Undertaking Participatory Planning Research
Francesco Lo Piccolo | 233 |

| 17 | Conclusions
Francesco Lo Piccolo and Huw Thomas | 255 |

Index   *261*

List of Figures and Tables

Figures

6.1	The 'business-facing' orientation of UK planning schools	78
6.2	The significance of interdisciplinary research	80
10.1	The ECORYS Code of Business Ethics	147

Tables

11.1	Implementation matrix for South Staffordshire housing	168
11.2	The extent to which the strategic themes have been implemented	169
12.1	Research ethics in practice	184

Notes on Contributors

Giovanni Attili, Dipartimento di Architettura ed Urbanistica per l'Ingegneria, Università 'La Sapienza', Rome and School of Community and Regional Planning, University of British Columbia, Vancouver.

P. Anthony Brinkman, Department of Geography, University of Nevada, Reno.

John Forester, Department of City and Regional Planning, Cornell University, Ithaca.

Kanishka Goonewardena, Department of Geography and Planning, University of Toronto.

Patsy Healey, Professor Emeritus in the School of Architecture Planning and Landscape, University of Newcastle upon Tyne.

Adrian Healy, ECORYS.

Rob Imrie, Department of Geography, Kings College London.

David Laws, Department of Political Science, University of Amsterdam.

Laura Lieto, Dipartimento di Progettazione Urbana e Urbanistica, Università 'Federico II', Naples.

Francesco Lo Piccolo, Dipartimento Città e Territorio, Università degli Studi di Palermo.

Daniela Mello, Dipartimento di Progettazione Urbana e Urbanistica, Università 'Federico II', Naples.

Libby Porter, Department of Urban Studies, University of Glasgow.

Filippo Schilleci, Dipartimento Città e Territorio, Università degli Studi di Palermo.

Nigel Taylor, School of the Built and Natural Environment, University of the West of England, Bristol.

Huw Thomas, School of City and Regional Planning, Cardiff University.

Niraj Verma, Department of Urban and Regional Planning, The State University of New York at Buffalo.

Chapter 1
Introduction

Francesco Lo Piccolo and Huw Thomas

The Genesis of the Book

The book is the outcome of a developing interest of the editors in ethical issues in planning research. At the heart of this interest has been a realisation that what troubles researchers in planning is rarely some variant of a crude temptation of the flesh, as illustrated in the image on the book's cover. To be sure, it does no harm to be reminded that even Aristototle's focus on learning could be diverted at times (though we must also remember that diversion at an appropriate time is reasonable and commendable). But as much of the material in this book makes clear, the kinds of concerns which give rise to real anxiety among researchers in planning involve considerations more subtle, more all-embracing than a simple fight against an easily defined temptation. They revolve, often, around a search for clarity about what it is to do research that is worth doing – worth doing both intellectually and socially/politically.

The original ideas were pondered over some time ago, partly jointly and partly individually, as the editors reflected on their research experiences. Having conducted investigations over many years into the pluralistic composition of the city's social structure, the role and conditions of minority groups (not just ethnic ones) contained within it, the majority-minority ratio and the relative recognition of rights of citizenship in planning processes and policies, inclusive and excluding forms of (participatory) planning processes, and related legal and institutional aspects in these areas of research, all these experiences have forced us to question the ethical implications of our research time and again. The questions raised were both conscious and unconscious. And while our reactions were sometimes instinctive, we were aware of, and could draw on, the general social science literature on research ethics, which has become increasingly sensitive to the social context of research, not simply matters of individual probity. It is widely acknowledged that social researchers must be sensitive to the power relations within their research – those implicated in that which they are investigating (see Flyvbjerg 1998) and those power relations between the researchers and those with whom they have dealings. Thus Ladson-Billings (2000, 73) cautions researchers about the dangers of regarding poorer communities as 'data plantations', while Fine et al. (2000) point out the ways that social research can become caught up in consolidating social relations which are ethically/politically questionable.

There have been some discussions of research ethics in relation to disciplines cognate to planning – such as the built environment disciplines (Wilkinson and Morton 2007), or Geography (see Askins 2008), but there has been little which relates directly to planning. We believe that disciplinary-specific discussions can play an important role in furthering understanding and practice in relation to research ethics for two reasons. First, because the details of context are central in any discussion of what might be salient in a particular case. Of course, planning researchers can learn from discussions in Geography or surveying, but in the end they have to apply these lessons to a different kind of research setting, involving different institutions, histories, relations…The second advantage of disciplinary-related discussions is that they may draw upon, and indeed help create and consolidate, a practice community, a community in which members share a sense of purpose in relation to a shared endeavour, and a sense of what kinds of things might and should count as good reasons for action. They share a way of seeing things (see Wenger 1998; Lo Piccolo and Thomas 2008). We are not entirely sure that such communities exist in relation to planning research, but if they do, or if they might, then a book like this may help in their flourishing.

Though it is clear that there has been an increasing concern about social science research ethics among institutions and individuals (Israel and Hay 2006) which makes the book timely, our interest has also been fuelled by some relatively recent personal experiences which have induced us to think anew about the weight, relevance and importance of the sphere of ethics within the scope of our research activities and our daily relationships with colleagues, doctoral students and students more generally (Lo Piccolo 2008; Thomas 2005). Responses to these papers, and other kinds of discussions (such as academic gossip, story-telling or observations on a more structured theoretical basis) have led us to believe that our experiences, and concerns, are not unique within international planning education. This has led to the desire to try to draw on a wider range of experience than simply our own, to get beyond simple anecdote, and ideally begin to set out options for how experiences and issues in research ethics in planning can be understood and addressed systematically.

The awareness that we were exploring a little-investigated field, and that we could not address the research only through our own points of view, and consequently of the need to compare our observations with the experiences of other colleagues who may have encountered similar experiences and dilemmas (in different contexts) led us to establish a Thematic Group on 'Research Ethics and Planning', within the framework of the different Thematic Groups launched by AESOP.[1] This Thematic Group was based on the contention that research into planning raises ethical issues

---

1   As part of its duties and activities, AESOP (Association of European Schools Of Planning) established some Thematic Groups, in order to 'encourage and support the interaction among the Association's members in specific areas of research and teaching interest. The hope is that these Thematic Groups will flourish under the AESOP umbrella, to support AESOP's development. (…) The Thematic Groups are intended to be autonomous,

which are distinctive enough to warrant more attention than the routine references to standard social science discussions which are the usual responses given by research monographs and doctoral theses. Our purpose in this Thematic Group has been to explore a way of thinking about planning research that considers the social context of moral perception and behaviour; by doing this we hoped to shift the emphasis of discussion from individual probity to the circumstances which help researchers develop and use sound ethical judgement. In the initial proposal to launch the Thematic Group, we stated that:

> this approach has implications for the kinds of institutions within which planning research can be undertaken, and the likely source of the most potent threats to both excellence in research and ethical behaviour. The purpose of the Thematic Group is to build up a framework for considering ethical issues in planning research. Most researchers could list some of the ethical observations that they feel should shape the conduct of research; some will have personal experience of ethical dilemmas related to research. This Thematic Group would like to explore whether anything systematic can be said about how such ethical issues arise, hence how they might be understood, and addressed.

The Thematic Group on 'Research Ethics and Planning' was established in 2005, and has held regular meetings and debates during the association's annual conferences. In all truth, and this aspect will be taken up again later, participation in the Thematic Group on 'Research Ethics and Planning' was restricted to a limited number of scholars, in spite of general expressions of interest shown by many and stimulating discussions which took place during some of the meetings. Indeed, right from the beginning of our 'adventure', we sensed the difficulty, and at times embarrassment (if not discomfort) experienced by many of our colleagues in confronting this topic, without doubt delicate, arduous and at times embarrassing.

Despite such reservations, a round-table entitled 'Research Ethics in the Context of Racialised Conflict and Oppression' was held in Naples in the summer of 2007, on the occasion of the XXI AESOP Conference 'Planning for the Risk Society: Dealing with Uncertainty, Challenging the Future'; the round-table excited great interest, participation and an animated debate. Only some of those called to participate in the round-table in Naples[2] went on to contribute to this volume; others declined for various reasons. Just as many of the colleagues who, despite our invitation and their declared interest in the subject, subsequently forwent the opportunity to contribute

---

and will move into directions based upon the desires of their members. Outputs will include research, workshops, papers and books' (from the AESOP Yearbook 2004).

2   The round-table 'Research Ethics in the Context of Racialised Conflict and Oppression' was held in Naples on 12 July 2007, with the following participants: Yasminah Beebeejaun (Manchester University), Geraint Ellis (Queen's University Belfast), John Forester (Cornell University), Libby Porter (Sheffield University), Oren Yiftachel (Ben-Gurion University), Silvia Macchi (Università di Roma 'La Sapienza').

their papers and observations. We decided to mention these contingent events not, obviously, for anecdotal support; this aspect, although in some ways marginal and also linked to the fortuitousness of circumstances, highlights the difficulty involved in dealing with this topic, and the embarrassment and discomfort that it can evoke in every one of us when it must be faced, starting with our own personal experiences in research. This aspect increased our determination to pursue the project, and involve, eventually, a large number of colleagues, whose contributions are contained in this volume. However, the autobiographical approach has prevailed in a larger part of the volume's contributions, as explicitly requested by the editors.

The Purposes of the Book

The first purpose is to help planning researchers engage constructively with a working and policy environment in which research ethics has an increasing profile. In most advanced capitalist countries there has been increasing attention given in recent years within the governance of social research to securing ethical behaviour (Israel and Hay 2006). Within the UK university research ethics committees now have their own journal (*Research Ethics Review*). In most universities the fresh attention being given to research ethics in social research applies right down to undergraduate study. In addition, the Economic and Social Research Council (ESRC) has promoted its own policy on research ethics, sponsored training sessions, and has funded initiatives such as the research seminar series on 'the social relations of contract research'. It is clear from the overview provided by Israel and Hay that the UK is in line with developments elsewhere. Planning research – especially that within universities – is subject to this new, more vigorous (and possibly more rigorous) regime. Inevitably, it has raised the awareness of researchers (and students) about research ethics, and the issues and dilemmas associated with it. There are discussions of these matters in general texts on research methods, but this volume will provide a discussion with the circumstances of planning research in mind. It has been argued in different contexts – e.g. business ethics – that those teaching ethics to students need assistance in reviewing the ethical dimensions of their own circumstances (Chesley and Anderson 2003). This is a significant difference from general discussions because it is in the nature of ethical discussion that precise circumstances are central to ethical judgement (Campbell 2006; Flyvbjerg 2001). A book which has planning research specifically in mind, therefore, will be of great value to planning researchers and students of planning.

Secondly, the book provides an opportunity for researchers in planning to think about the implications for their work of the changes in governance and planning which have been both a spur for, and object of, some of their research. In large measure, these derive from a perennial set of ethical issues surrounding research which seeks to inform public policy. These are not unique to planning – even historians who seek to engage with public policy find that ethical issues then arise (Johnes 2007). In broad terms these concerns relate to:

- relations between the researcher and client (and the potential influence of the latter on the research project and outcomes);
- the 'life' of the research findings once they are released by the researcher (for example, the possibility of their being used to promote unjust or exploitative policies), and, related to this;
- the role of the research in a broader policy and political context and the possibility of its facilitating political projects which the researcher finds ethically troubling.

The way that these kinds of issues play out in a planning context has been explored a little by Healey (1991), but the changing context of governance, and the political economy of higher education within that,[3] makes it timely to have a comprehensive look at research ethics in planning.

Yet there are ethical challenges which are distinctive of the kind of research which at least some planning researchers undertake, and the book will address some of them. The definition and use of space is bound up with social justice in the broadest sense: issues of distribution of resources (Eversley 1973), and the construction of – and struggles over – identity and respect (Massey and Jess 1995). In thus involving both the politics of distribution and recognition (Fraser 1995) the appropriation, control and management of territory (all understood in the broadest sense) is central to the way power is exercised in society. Planning researchers are particularly likely to find themselves researching in contexts of social tension and/ or conflict, therefore, sometimes associated with clear oppression and injustice (see Bollen 2000; Gleeson 1999; Home 1994; Yiftachel 2006). These circumstances are only more extreme versions of the challenge to any planning researcher – that her/his work is enmeshed in struggles over the spatiality of the good society, and how this should be ordered, and that defining the field or terms of research inquiry, let alone undertaking the research and drawing conclusions about the world, is itself a contribution to those struggles. This book will have a section of reflective case studies by researchers of various planning locales about:

- how they came to recognise the ethical dimension of their work,
- how they addressed this dimension, and
- the implications of their experience for their own research practice and the training preparation of researchers.

These will be valuable in their own right to other planning researchers and planning students, and will also feed into the concluding chapter of the book where approaches to ethics will be re-visited in the light of the case studies, and conclusions drawn for research practice and research training in planning.

---

3   See the Interface section on Planning Education published in 2005 in *Planning Theory and Practice* 6:2, 235-253.

The Organisation and Contents of the Book

The book has three parts. The first considers some of the influential ways of thinking systematically about ethics in the Western intellectual tradition. While these are not drawn on explicitly in the case studies in part three of the book, they do offer the reader one way to interpret this material, and – indeed – their own lives as researchers. Consequentialism, the subject of Nigel Taylor's chapter, is an approach to ethics which emphasises the primacy of right action in the good life, and has a distinctive approach to understanding what constitutes a right action: that which has the best consequences. The utilitarian version of consequentialism has been extraordinarily influential in shaping public policy and private morality in Western countries, despite its having some obvious difficulties. Taylor examines some of these as they might relate to the work of planning researchers.

An increasingly influential alternative to consequentialism is virtue ethics, another very broadly defined approach with many variants. As Huw Thomas explains, what is distinctive about virtue ethics is its focus on the nature of a person's character (without necessarily ignoring actions, of course). Different theoretical frameworks often have different emphases in their view of topics. Within virtue ethics moral education assumes a significance as something which is perhaps more difficult to do properly than is commonly appreciated.

Major figures in the Pragmatist tradition – hugely influential in planning theory via the work of north American theorists – had important things to say about education and also about the socially engaged intellectual. Niraj Verma's chapter draws on Pragmatism to argue that ethical considerations are at the heart of research activity – because they relate to research as a cognitive activity, and are not simply about the management of desires.

The second part of the book discusses some of the institutional context within which research into planning takes place. Alasdair MacIntyre (1981) reminds us that ethics cannot be discussed in a social vacuum because sensible and worthwhile discussions of ethics should be about people as they are, in the world as it is, or could reasonably be expected to be. Discussions of research ethics need to understand the institutional context within which research is conducted and the factors which influence the mentality and behaviour of researchers. Three of the chapters – by Kanishka Goonewardena, Rob Imrie and P. Anthony Brinkman – discuss some of the pressures which researchers in planning schools can find themselves under. Both Imrie and Goonewardena highlight the ways in which Western universities are increasingly aligning themselves materially and philosophically with business. So, for example, university managers talk of the need for entrepreneurialism, academics at all levels think in terms of 'outputs', and competition is central to university life at all levels – between individuals, between schools, between universities, between national constellations of universities, and so on... Some of this is not at all new, but some is: in particular, the rigour with which competition along easily measurable dimensions of academic life has been enforced in academic life in very many countries. Its causes are in part sensitivity to the hegemony of neoliberalism in many countries, and in part an embracing of that political economy and its core values by many academics. The consequences for ethical research, argue Imrie and Goonewardena, are profound.

P. Anthony Brinkman's thesis overlaps with these kinds of considerations, but also has some different elements. The phenomenon that he discusses – a research silence in relation to potentially embarrassing topics – is not a recently discovered one. It pre-dates the new political economy of higher education, and according to Brinkman points to the significance of power relations within universities and academic disciplines. Brinkman's concerns resonate with some of those of Filippo Schilleci, who reviews the ineffectiveness and partiality of attempts to evaluate initiatives to manage protected areas in Sicily. He highlights the silence of institutionally-driven research (i.e. that commissioned by or done within governance agencies) on questions which are prominent within value-driven research.

Patsy Healey's chapter – a reprint of a 1991 paper for *Town Planning Review* – explores what happens when silence is broken. Reflecting on her experience of conflict with a government department which sought to persuade her how to present research findings from a project it had commissioned, she makes the important point that academics do many different kinds of planning research. The likelihood of being enmeshed in relationships with interests outside the academy will depend in large measure on the kind of research one does. The intellectual significance of the research can be irrelevant in this regard. Thus one of us was recently asked to divulge to a government body the results of a very straightforward small scale survey of users of the planning system that he had undertaken for a non-governmental client. The survey results might possibly have been mildly embarrassing for the government planners, and they wanted to have a preview of the results. In this case it wasn't difficult for the researcher to work out the right thing to do, but the case illustrates how some kinds of research can bring researchers to the attention of institutions and individuals who, in the cut and thrust of daily work, may perhaps temporarily lose sight of the significance of ethical behaviour.

As a consultant in planning and related fields Adrian Healy is very close to that cut and thrust. His chapter reflects on what kinds of issues he encounters and how he deals with them. For him, ethics in research is part of a broader set of considerations about corporate behaviour, and *research* ethics is underpinned by the broader business case for good corporate behaviour in general. In time, unethical behaviour will erode corporate credibility, and hence corporate viability. This is a consequentialist line of argument of the kind Taylor discusses earlier in the book. For Healy the range of terrain over which ethics ranges excludes the knowledge and skills deployed in the consultancy work itself. His view of consultancy is that it is a technical activity, the results of which play a part in a wider public life which inevitably bring with them ethical issues and dilemmas. But the technical core of his job is ethically neutral. This view of the research task will be challenged in some case studies in the book's third part, particularly those working within a Foucaultian perspective (e.g. Laura Lieto) and a more generally post-modern approach (e.g. Giovanni Attili).

Different perspectives on what a researcher is doing when doing research will have different implications for the appropriate training for researchers. The PhD is rapidly becoming globally accepted as the standard qualification for researchers in planning. It is important, therefore, to have some information about the way ethics features in doctoral programmes. Daniela Mello's chapter begins that process, with a case study of doctoral education in Italy. One novel aspect of her chapter is that it draws upon a questionnaire survey of students as well as documentary evidence and key informants among planning faculty. She found a variety of practices, and a variety of student views expressed about the desirability of including ethics in doctoral programmes. She argues that the variety of student views, at least, can be explained in terms of the way that the doctorate is perceived within the professional development of the student.

Discussions of values, including ethics, demand examples. For such discussions need to be grounded, as it is the complexities of real life that demonstrate what a person may mean by general terms, or principles. Moreover, it is in the flux of everyday life that it can become difficult to recognise the precise ethical (or, indeed, political) contours of what is going on around you. The third section of the book includes accounts, sometimes autobiographical, of how ethical issues arise in practice in planning research. In the autobiographical chapters – by Libby Porter, Giovanni Attili and Francesco Lo Piccolo – we see researchers grappling with the implications of the political contexts within which they are researching and within which their findings will be published. As editors we asked them to think about the kinds of ethical issues that arose in a particular research project they undertook, the way they became sensitised to the ethical issues, and how they addressed them. Their responses provide fascinating insights into research ethics in the planning field. Attili, Lo Piccolo and Porter describe the ethical issues which arise undertaking research with minorities, which are marginalised or excluded due to social, linguistic, cultural and economic disengagements. Their critical approach also considers the role and influence of emotions in the research process. This view of emotions as social is also fundamental to the 'ethics of care' of Carol Gilligan (1982), which calls for a situational ethics, wherein relationships with 'others' are of crucial importance. Consequently, in different ways and contexts, the chapters of Attili, Lo Piccolo and Porter can be framed in the light of situational ethics (Denzin 1997 and 2003), which implies a different commitment of the researcher in the relationship with the topic and subjects of her/his research.

The chapters by Laura Lieto and John Forester and David Laws look at some of the kinds of research work that is undertaken in planning – Lieto through a case study of 'technical' policy-related research in Naples, Forester and Laws by considering hypothetical examples of research related to mediation, drawing on their extensive research into the practice of mediation. In both cases, the idea of there being access to a realm of value-free technical knowledge is disputed (albeit for different reasons). The effective researcher in planning must be ethically and politically engaged, though the precise understanding of what that involves differs, as we will discuss in our concluding chapter.

References

Askins, K. (2008), 'In and Beyond the Classroom: Research Ethics and Participatory Pedagogies', *Area* 40:4, 500-509.

Bini, G. et al. (eds) (2008), *Fare Ricerca* (Florence: Alinea).

Bollen, S. (2000), *Urban Peace-building in Divided Societies* (Boulder, Colorado: Westview Press).

Campbell, H. (2006), 'Just Planning: The Art of Situated Ethical Judgment', *Journal of Planning Education and Research* 26: 1, 92-106.

Chesley, G.R.D. and Anderson, B. (2003), 'Are University Professors Qualified to Teach Ethics?', *Journal of Academic Ethics* 1:2, 217-219.

Denzin, N.K. (1997), *Interpretative Ethnography: Ethnographic Practices for the 21st Century* (Thousand Oaks, CA: Sage).

Denzin, N.K. (2003), *Performance Ethnography: Critical Pedagogy and the Politics of Culture* (Thousand Oaks, CA: Sage).

Denzin, N.K. and Lincoln, Y.S. (eds) (2000), *Handbook of Qualitative Research* 2nd edn (London: Sage).

Eversley, D. (1973), *The Planner in Society* (London: Faber and Faber).

Fine, M. et al. (2000), 'For Whom? Qualitative Research, Representations and Social Responsibilites', in Norman K. Denzin and Yvonne S. Lincoln (eds).

Flyvbjerg, B. (1998), *Rationality and Power. Democracy in Practice* (Chicago: University of Chicago Press).

Flyvbjerg, B. (2001), *Making Social Science Matter* (Cambridge: Cambridge University Press).

Fraser, N. (1995), 'From Redistribution to Recognition? Dilemmas of Social Justice in a "Post-socialist" Age', *New Left Review* 212 (July/August), 68-93.

Gilligan, C. (1982), *In a Different Voice: Psychological Theory and Women's Development* (Cambridge, MA: Harvard University Press).

Gleeson, B. (1999), *Geographies of Disability* (London: Routledge).

Healey, P. (1991), 'Researching Planning Practice', *Town Planning Review* 62:4, 447-459.

Home, R. (1994), 'Planning and Gypsies', in Huw Thomas and Vijay Krishnarayan (eds).

Israel, M. and Hay, I. (2006), *Research Ethics for Social Scientists* (London: Sage Publications Ltd.).

Johnes, M. (2007), 'Applied and commissioned histories: A cautionary tale of a researcher, a subject and a university'. Unpublished paper – available author at Swansea University.

Ladson-Billings, G. (2000), 'Racialized Discourses and Ethnic Epistemologies', in Norman K. Denzin and Yvonne S. Lincoln (eds).

Lo Piccolo, F. (2008), 'Questioni di Metodo, e di Merito, nella Ricerca dei Dottorati in Pianificazione e Urbanistica', in Giada Bini et al. (eds).

Lo Piccolo, F. and Thomas, H. (2008), 'Research Ethics in Planning: A Framework for Discussion', *Planning Theory* 7:1, 7-23.

MacIntyre, A. (1981), *After Virtue* (London: Duckworth).

Massey, D. and Jess, P. (eds) (1995), *A Place in the World?* (Oxford: Oxford University Press).

Thomas, H. (2005), 'Pressures, Purpose and Collegiality in UK Planning Education', *Planning Theory and Practice* 6:2, 238-247.

Thomas, H. and Krishnarayan, V. (eds) (1994), *Race Equality and Planning* (Aldershot: Ashgate).

Wenger, E. (1998), *Communities of Practice* (London: Sage).

Wilkinson, S.J. and Morton, P. (2007), 'The Emerging Importance of Feminist Research Paradigms in Built Environment Research', *Structural Survey* 25:5, 408-417.

Yiftachel, O. (2006), *Ethnocracy* (Philadelphia: University of Pennsylvania Press).

PART I
Ethical Frameworks

Chapter 2
Consequentialism and the Ethics of Planning Research

Nigel Taylor

Introduction: Consequentialism Explained

In this first section of this chapter I explain what consequentialist ethics is, giving examples of philosophers who have propounded the most popular version of ethical consequentialism, namely, utilitarianism. In the second section, I note the initial attraction of ethical consequentialism (and its utilitarian version in particular), but also note a number of criticisms that have been made of it. Not all of these criticisms bear directly on the ethics of scholarly research, which is the subject of this book. In the third section, therefore, I turn to criticisms that touch more directly on the ethics of research into environmental planning (and indeed, into any discipline) with a more extended discussion of the ethics of truthfulness and personal integrity in relation to the utilitarian version of ethical consequentialism. A fourth section concludes with a few remarks on the ethics of training would-be researchers.

I begin, then, with an account of what ethical consequentialism is.

In ethics, consequentialism is the position that the rightness or wrongness of actions depends on the consequences, effects or outcomes, of actions. A moral consequentialist is therefore someone who holds that, in deciding what, morally, we should do, or how we should act, we should identify and weigh up the probable consequences that would flow from alternative courses of action open to us, and then choose that action which seems likely to generate the most desirable consequences.

But *what* consequences? *Any* consequences? Clearly not. A consequentialist is also someone who has a view about the *kind* of consequences, or outcomes, it is morally desirable to bring about, and herein lies their substantive moral position or (as I shall shortly explain) their theory of the good. Over this, too, we find the possibility of different forms of consequentialism. For different consequentialists, whilst all agreeing that what is right or wrong depends on the consequences of actions, can differ about what consequences they think it is morally good to realise. For example, an evangelical Christian consequentialist would be in favour of bringing about (by actions such as street preaching, door-to-door visiting, leafleting, etc.) the consequence of there being more people converted to Christianity, whereas an atheist or agnostic consequentialist would be opposed to *this* consequence but might, instead, favour the consequence of increasing human happiness regardless of religious belief.

In all of its varieties, consequentialism is what philosophers term a teleological ethical theory because any version of consequentialism advances some desirable end state – some 'telos' (e.g. a world full of Christians, or a world full of happy people, etc.), and then actions are judged to be right or wrong depending on whether they yield consequences that lead towards or away from this desired end state. According to the American philosopher John Rawls, the two main concepts of ethics are those of 'right' and 'good' and, in teleological theories, 'the good is defined independently of the right' (Rawls 1971, 24-25). Thus, in teleological ethical theories, what is considered to be right (or wrong) is judged instrumentally in terms of what will best realise the good. In the case of consequentialism, the good is a desired end state, and what is right or wrong are actions, whose rightness or wrongness are judged in terms of whether they have consequences that lead towards, or away from, the end state defined as good.

A feature of consequentialism that emerges already from this account is its focus on the external world – on 'states of affairs' in the world – and hence, too, on action, and the effects (consequences) of actions on the state of the external world. Thus it is actions, and what these actions actually produce, that are judged right or wrong. Hence, for consequentialists, moral deliberation focuses on how things actually are, and might be made better, in the world, and on assessing the impact of our actions on how things are, and might be made better, in the world. Hence, too, the strong link in Britain between the most popular form of consequentialism, namely, utilitarianism, and political reform. With this emphasis on (reforming) action, it is possible for a person to be well intentioned and yet – from the point of view of consequentialism – do the wrong thing, if what he does makes the world a worse place. And equally, a bad person might, inadvertently, do the right thing, if what he does brings about good consequences. It is on this point that consequentialism contrasts with virtue ethics. For virtue ethics has an inner focus – a focus on the person, and his or her predispositions and intentions and whether, in particular, they act virtuously. And according to some virtue ethicists, it is possible for a person to do the right thing, morally, if they act with good or virtuous intentions, and yet for their action to result in a worse state of affairs in the external world.

In philosophy the most well-known and popular version of consequentialism is utilitarianism. In fact, utilitarianism itself can come in several different versions. However, for the purposes of this discussion I shall confine myself to what Rawls (1971, 22-27) terms classical utilitarianism, which is the same as what J.J.C. Smart (in Smart and Williams 1973, 9-14) terms 'act-utilitarianism'. Classical (or act-) utilitarianism holds that what is morally right is action that brings about (i.e. has the consequence of) an increase in the happiness of others who stand to be affected by our actions. The 'others' here could simply be one individual, or a large number of individuals, or even a whole community or society. But whichever is the case, the same moral rule – the principle of utility or 'happiness principle' – would apply. And, in considering how best to act, a utilitarian would advise us to examine whether or not an action is likely to generate an increase in the happiness of the relevant person or people, taken as a whole, and if it does seem likely to yield this consequence, then a utilitarian would say that that action is morally right.

Even in its classical form, we are straight away confronted by a matter that divided utilitarians, and that is over how to conceive the desired end state of 'happiness'. Arguably the first systematic statement of utilitarianism was made by the English philosopher Jeremy Bentham, in his *An Introduction to the Principles of Morals and Legislation* (Bentham 1789). In this, Bentham equated 'happiness' with 'pleasure', and so asserted that pleasure is what we should seek to maximise. And for Bentham, the opposite of pleasure was pain, so that, as well as acting to maximise pleasure, we should also act to minimise pain – an aspiration termed by J.J.C. Smart 'negative' utilitarianism (see Smart and Williams 1973). Bentham did not distinguish between different kinds of pleasures and, as he famously wrote (in *The Rationale of Reward*), if the quantity of pleasure gained from playing push-pin (a child's game of his time) was equal to that gained by listening to music or reading poetry then, morally, push-pin was as good as music or poetry.

It was this equation of happiness with simple pleasure, and with *any* kind of pleasure, with which another great classical utilitarian, John Stuart Mill, could not agree. For Mill held that there were qualitatively different kinds of pleasure and that some were of greater worth, or 'higher' pleasures, than others, and so these higher pleasures should be accorded greater weight in moral deliberation. In particular, Mill held that those pleasures which employed our 'higher faculties' of thought and reflection were richer pleasures than those pleasures which give instant and only superficial gratification. As he famously put it: 'It is better to be a human being dissatisfied than a pig satisfied; better to be Socrates dissatisfied than a fool satisfied' (Mill 1861, 260). For Mill, then, even to be unhappy *as a rational being* was still to experience a higher form of happiness than to be a contented pig which, whilst sentient, had no notion of what 'real' happiness is. Paradoxically perhaps, Mill held that to be human and unhappy was still to be 'happier' (i.e. to experience a higher level of happiness) than to be a dumb, yet contented animal. Mill also applied his distinction to human pleasures, claiming that some human pleasures are superior to others. Thus Mill held that the experiences of music and poetry (or at least good music and poetry) were higher pleasures, or higher forms of happiness, than the pleasures to be gained from playing push-pin or – we might now add – the pleasures of watching reality television, pornographic films, etc.

Some have taken exception to Mill's notion of higher pleasures as being 'elitist'. Yet, more recently, the American philosopher Robert Nozick (1974, 42-45) put forward a thought experiment which has certain affinities with Mill's position. Nozick asks us to imagine the possibility of being wired up to an 'experience machine' which, being an ingenious machine, would enable us ('at the push of a button') to have any experience – and therefore any pleasure – we wanted. And equally, this ingenious machine would enable us to avoid any painful experience, such as physical pain, mental depression, loneliness, sexual frustration, etc. Nozick then asks us to consider whether, if we had the choice, we would want to be wired up to such a machine for the rest of our lives. And he is confident that most of us wouldn't. For although, with this machine, we could live a life of unadulterated pleasure, and avoid any pain, in agreeing to be wired up to this machine we would forego our personal autonomy, and since this is central to our humanity Nozick reasons that most of us would wish to remain as thinking, autonomous human beings, even if remaining so continues to bring the pains, anxieties, and unhappiness that come with the human condition of being relatively autonomous. Rather like Mill, then, Nozick thinks that, for human beings, it is a greater happiness to be an autonomous and sometimes dissatisfied human being, than to be a satisfied non-human animal or a contented but non-autonomous human being.

But already I am running ahead of myself and getting into debates between different versions of utilitarian consequentialism. So let me return to the general moral stance of classical or act-utilitarianism as representative of ethical consequentialism. Under (classical or act-) utilitarianism, then, the rightness or wrongness of actions depends on whether they bring about greater happiness (however this is defined) for the person or persons affected by those actions. So, if an action A1 brings about an increase in happiness (call this H) to the people (call them P) affected by A1, then A1 is a morally right action. But now, what about an action (call it A2) that brings about an increase in happiness to P, but not so much happiness as A1; say, H-1 unit of happiness? From a utilitarian point of view such an act would still be morally desirable, but, because it produces less happiness than A1, it would be morally less desirable than action A1. Likewise for other lesser happiness-producing actions, such as A3, A4, etc. From this, we can see why a utilitarian consequentialist should aim, when possible, to bring about the *greatest possible* degree of happiness; he should seek to *maximise* happiness.

The foregoing evaluation of different degrees of happiness-producing actions also helps us to understand the utilitarian position in situations where no positive happiness-producing action at all is available. In such unhappy circumstances utilitarian deliberation and action can still apply, though in this case it would be directed to identifying and choosing the least-worst, or least 'unhappiness-producing', action. Consider the case of some people trapped by an enemy who – the people have good reason to believe – will subject them to gruesome torture before putting them to death, but where the trapped people have available to them the possibility of putting an end to their own lives quickly and 'painlessly'. One could hardly call either option available to the trapped people something that will increase their happiness; indeed, happiness in any meaningful sense is simply not available to these people. But, given that they are going to die anyway, they may at least minimise their unhappiness (minimise their pain) by killing themselves quickly rather than being caught by the enemy and undergoing gruesome torture before being killed. And so, on utilitarian grounds, this would be the best thing to do (this might, for example, have been the situation of the 1st century Jews besieged on Masada by the Romans). And likewise if we are considering how best to act towards some other person or persons for whom, sadly, there is no realistic possibility of positive happiness. In short, utilitarianism aims to minimise pain or unhappiness if the option of increasing (not to mention maximising) happiness is unavailable.

Utilitarian Consequentialism Reviewed

Bernard Williams (in Smart and Williams 1973) describes utilitarianism as the 'central case' of ethical consequentialism, and so I shall continue to use this example of consequentialism in the remainder of this chapter. And straight away it is worth saying that there is an immediate appeal to the utilitarian position. Indeed, we are all probably utilitarian consequentialists up to a point in that, in numerous situations – be they private or public/professional situations – in which we are faced with the need to act and we wish to act well, we instinctively seek to do that which will bring about a better, or happier, state of affairs. Who, indeed, other than a psychopath or megalomaniac, would seriously contemplate trying to do something that makes some situation *worse*, or some other person or group of people *unhappier*? There is, then, a certain common-sense-ness about utilitarianism. As many might ask, rhetorically: 'isn't it *obvious* that we should do whatever increases the happiness or well-being of others affected by our actions?'

Certainly, when asked to advance a view of how one should choose between alternative plans or policies, most students of urban planning suggest that ('obviously') one should choose that plan or policy which brings about the greatest good. And this 'common-sense' view of most planning students is mirrored by most urban planning textbooks on plan evaluation, which assume without question that some kind of utilitarian evaluation is the most appropriate method of identifying the best plan from the alternatives available (see e.g. Lichfield, Kettle and Whitbread 1975; Lichfield 1996). Amongst professional philosophers, too, utilitarianism is a widely favoured moral position. Indeed, W.D. Hudson (1980) claimed that utilitarianism is one of the two main rival positions in contemporary moral philosophy (the other being, on his account, various forms of intuitionism). The great classical utilitarian philosophers Bentham and Mill have already been mentioned, and with them stands the 19th century philosopher Henry Sidgwick (1874), whose *The Methods of Ethics* has been described by a modern utilitarian, J.J.C. Smart, as the 'best sustained exposition of act-utilitarianism' (Smart and Williams 1973, 4). Amongst modern philosophers, in addition to Smart himself, R.M. Hare (the former professor of moral philosophy at Oxford) and Philip Pettit have both put strong cases for utilitarianism (see Hare 1981; Pettit 1991; Pettit 1997; also Sen and Williams 1982).

However, in spite of its appeal, utilitarianism and, by extension, consequentialism more generally, have been criticised by non-consequentialist moral philosophers from both Kantian and virtue ethical points of view. Several of these criticisms, though important in themselves, do not bear directly on the ethics of scholarly work and research, which is the subject of this book. In the remainder of this section, therefore, I shall only briefly summarise the main criticisms of utilitarian consequentialism before turning, in the next section, to a more extended discussion of those criticisms that are more directly relevant to the ethics of planning research.

There are two criticisms of utilitarianism that we can deal with quickly because they are not strictly, or solely, external criticisms of utilitarianism, but arise as matters of concern and debate within utilitarianism.

First, if, as a utilitarian, one is committed to doing whatever will further and where possible maximise the happiness (or well-being, welfare, utility, etc.) of those likely to be affected by one's actions, then one needs to give careful consideration to the effects of alternative actions. And, in any situation of moderate complexity, it is rational to do this as precisely as possible, carefully estimating, weighing, calculating and, if possible, quantifying the effects of alternative courses of action. In fact, Bentham himself devised a not unsophisticated 'felicific calculus' for just this purpose, which is itself the precursor of more modern methods of plan and project evaluation such as cost-benefit analysis. But needless to say, putting a weight to, and even moreso quantifying the value of, the felicific effects of actions is highly controversial, and thus subject to debate, disagreement and criticism. In fact, there are three areas of possible dispute. First, over the very identification of happiness or unhappiness-producing effects; second, over the weighting of the degree of happiness or unhappiness, or benefits and harms (or costs), of individual effects of actions; and third, over the practice of aggregating or summing different happiness or unhappiness-producing effects of actions so as to arrive at some overall total of the happiness and unhappiness, or benefits and costs, of actions. Yet, controversial though all this is, the criticisms that arise here are not really external 'in-principle' criticisms of the ethics of utilitarianism as such, but rather methodological criticisms of operating utilitarianism in practice. And as such, these problems, and any criticisms of attempts to deal with them, arise equally within and amongst proponents of utilitarian consequentialism as they do externally from non-consequentialist critics.

Second, and a more relevant ethical criticism of any version of consequentialism, is the question of what end-state, and hence what conception of the good, is advanced as the criterion of consequentially right action. In the case of utilitarianism this is, obviously, 'happiness', or some variant of this such as 'well-being', 'welfare', etc. But again, there is inevitably controversy, disagreement, and thus criticism of proposals as to what this desired end-state should be, or over how this state should best be conceived and described. Yet this, too, is not just an external criticism of either consequentialism in general or utilitarianism in particular, for such controversy and criticism can arise within consequentialism, between different consequentialists themselves. As noted earlier, John Stuart Mill disagreed vehemently with Jeremy Bentham's characterisation of happiness as any pleasurable experience, maintaining instead that some pleasures, or forms of happiness, were superior in value to others.

An altogether more substantial external criticism of utilitarian consequentialism concerns the fairness, or justice of its possible outcomes. Imagine the following case. There are two alternative plans for a city, C, involving a new transport link. Call the alternatives P1 and P2 (plans 1 and 2). After a careful evaluation of the costs and benefits of each, it is clear that P1 will bring about more benefits (i.e. more happiness) to the citizens of C *taken as a whole* than P2. Accordingly, a utilitarian consequentialist would choose P1 over P2. However, there is a detail about P1 that causes some people disquiet when considering this outcome. Although P1 does, overall and by a considerable margin, bring about a greater *sum* of happiness for the citizens of C than P2, enacting P1 would mean making a significant minority of the citizens of C worse off with respect to the environment in which they currently live and, furthermore, these citizens already inhabit a relatively poor quality environment. In other words, enacting P1 will make a group who are already environmentally disadvantaged even more disadvantaged. For example, enacting P1 might cause these disadvantaged citizens, who currently inhabit an ugly environment, also to suffer the traffic noise and pollution that will be generated by the new transport link. By contrast, although P2 will generate a smaller amount of happiness for the citizens of C taken as a whole, it generates a more equitable distribution of benefits and costs (happiness and unhappiness) amongst the citizens of C and, in particular, it would not disadvantage the minority group that would be disadvantaged by P1. Because of this, some people would claim that, morally, P2 is preferable to P1, and specifically because it generates a fairer or more just distribution of environmental goods.

This criticism of consequentialism in terms of distributive justice has been voiced by the American philosopher John Rawls (1971). According to Rawls, justice is the 'first virtue' of a society, and utilitarianism does not necessarily result in the most just outcomes because, as Rawls says, it 'does not take seriously the distinction between persons' (ibid., 27). As he puts it:

> The striking feature of the utilitarian view of justice is that it does not matter, except indirectly, how (the) sum of satisfactions is distributed among individuals anymore than it matters, except indirectly, how one man distributes his satisfactions over time. The correct distribution in either case is that which yields the maximum fulfilment (ibid., 26).

Although the foregoing critique in terms of distributive justice is arguably, at least from a Kantian ethical perspective, the most telling criticism of utilitarianism, it does not necessarily have a direct bearing on the ethics of research into environmental planning. To be sure, we can imagine circumstances in which it could present a researcher into planning with an ethical dilemma. Suppose, for example, a planning researcher was himself a committed utilitarian, but that the government for whom he was working instructed him to undertake research to find that spatial plan or policy for an area or project that would result in the most equitable distribution of environmental benefits and burdens, rather than that outcome which, from the researcher's utilitarian viewpoint, would bring about the best overall outcome for the environment and the population in the long term. In these circumstances, our committed utilitarian researcher might be tempted to fudge his research findings so that they issued in the utilitarian outcome he favours rather than the supposedly more just outcome favoured by the government. However, if he were so tempted, then the real ethical dilemma for him would not be so much his disagreement with the more equitable distribution of environmental goods favoured by the government, but rather over the ethics of distorting his research findings so as to obtain the utilitarian outcome he favours. In other words, his ethical problem would be over the question of honesty and truthfulness in the handling of research findings. This may indeed be an ethical challenge for a utilitarian, and it touches on another area in which ethical consequentialism has been criticised. But the criticism here derives from the virtuous ethics of acting truthfully and with personal integrity, rather than from a Rawlsian view of distributive justice. It is therefore to this criticism, which does have a more direct bearing on the ethics of research, that I turn in the following section.

Utilitarian Consequentialism, Truth and Truthfulness, and the Ethics of Scholarship and Research in Environmental Planning

Let us imagine that we are ethical consequentialists, and more specifically, utilitarian consequentialists engaged in research into environmental planning. As such, we could find ourselves facing real ethical dilemmas and conflicts. Why might this be?

Consider, first, what kind of ethical commitment one enters into in scholarly work and research. In engaging in research (in any discipline), one is necessarily engaged in the search for knowledge (be it new knowledge or the re-examination, or 're-search', of existing knowledge), and one is thereby also engaged in the search for truth. And this already implies an ethical commitment. For sometimes the truth is not what one expected, or wanted, or hoped for. Sometimes the truth is uncomfortable, or unpopular, either with the public at large or with one's working colleagues. Sometimes the truth is unpalatable to constituted authorities, perhaps authorities who have themselves instigated the very research that one is engaged in. And, if the truth is unpalatable – if, that is, it is not the truth that the authorities *want* to hear – then sometimes authorities will seek to ignore the truths told them by researchers, or suppress these truths, or, even, suppress and silence the researching authors of these truths. And it is in all these kinds of circumstances that the ethics of engaging in research are exposed. For we can see, here, how the pursuit of knowledge is not only guided and governed by the search for truth, but also by an ethical commitment to adhere to and speak the truth. Not only are researchers engaged in the pursuit of knowledge and truth as a matter of fact, but also, ethically, this is what they *should* be guided and governed by, even when this is uncomfortable or unrewarding for them. And this ethical commitment to the truth should not only obtain in the quiet seclusion of their studies and 'ivory towers', but also when the going gets tough, as when, for example, one's search for or exposure of the truth brings one into conflict with others who might seek to stifle or suppress the truth. Thus it is that the ethic of genuine scholarship – the ethic of truthfulness – can sometimes demand courage, even heroism. Certainly, the commitment of scholars down the ages to the truth is the stuff of heroic stories, as in Galileo's struggle against the Roman Catholic church over his telescopic observations that led him to accept a Copernican, heliocentric view of the universe, or, in our own time, in the struggles of intellectuals and scientists against the truth-resistant authorities of the old Soviet Union, or 'communist' China, or Nazi Germany. The ethic of 'living in truth' can be a life-and-death matter (Havel 1986).

To be sure, there are philosophical problems with identifying and grounding claims of 'truth'. But first, these problems are not themselves ethical problems but rather epistemological ones, and second, however these problems may be resolved, the ethical injunction to scholars remains: one should seek and abide by the truth, as far as one can see it. In other words, whilst truth may be elusive, scholars and researchers should, ethically, seek to be *truthful*; truthfulness is the mark of the virtuous scholar (see Williams 2002).

But now, what is or might be the problem in all this for someone who is a utilitarian? It is this. To be an ethical utilitarian one should adhere to the moral rule or principle of doing whatever furthers, and where possible maximises, the happiness (or well-being, welfare, etc.) of others who stand to be affected by one's actions. And if this commitment comes into conflict with other moral principles that one may also subscribe to, such as telling the truth or being truthful, one must – if one is a strict classical or act-utilitarian – give priority to the principle of utility. But then this means that, as a researcher in pursuit of the truth, one might find that one should suppress the truth oneself, or cease to be truthful, if one sincerely believed that doing so would be to the greater good, or happiness, of humanity.

The possibilities here are various. One possibility, put by Bernard Williams, might arise for someone even deciding to become, or take a job as, a researcher:

> George, who has just taken a Ph.D. in chemistry, finds it extremely difficult to get a job. He is not very robust in health, which cuts down the number of jobs he might be able to do satisfactorily. His wife has to go out to work to keep them, which itself causes a great deal of strain, since they have small children and there are severe problems about looking after them. The results of all this, especially on the children, are damaging. An older chemist, who knows about this situation, says that he can get George a decently paid job in a certain laboratory, which pursues research into chemical and biological warfare. George says that he cannot accept this, since he is opposed to chemical and biological warfare. The older man replies that he is not too keen on it himself, come to that, but after all George's refusal is not going to make the job or the laboratory go away; what is more, he happens to know that if George refuses the job, it will

certainly go to a contemporary of George's who is not inhibited by any such scruples and is likely if appointed to push along the research with greater zeal than George would. Indeed, it is not merely concern for George and his family, but (to speak frankly and in confidence) some alarms about the other man's excess of zeal, which has led the older man to offer to use his influence to get George the job…What should he do? (Williams 1973, in Smart and Williams 1973, 97-98).

Although not an example from the field of environmental planning research, the structure of Williams's example could, and undoubtedly does, arise in cases of research into environmental planning. Imagine, for example, a research centre in a university school of planning considering whether to make a bid for a research project established and generously funded by central government to find additional land for private housing development in areas of green belt land or on sites currently designated for their great landscape or ecological value. Imagine, too, that this research centre stands a high chance of winning the research contract if it makes a bid, on the basis of the reputation of its researchers and its past record of research into housing land availability. But now imagine, also, that the researchers in the centre do not believe that the release of further land in green belts, or in areas of great landscape or ecological value, is to the greater good. What, then, should this university research centre do? Should it still go ahead and make the bid? If, because of the moral disquiet amongst its researchers, it doesn't, other university research centres will still make bids and the research will go ahead anyway. Indeed, because of their moral disquiet, if they obtain the research project, the researchers in the centre can at least try to minimise the loss of aesthetically attractive and ecologically sensitive sites, and in that way minimise the overall harm to the environment. The situation of the research centre is here analogous to that of George in Williams's example. Nor is this kind of case merely hypothetical. For this is exactly the kind of ethical dilemma faced by many researchers in planning nowadays, in an era when, in Britain at least, central government seems often to be guided primarily by the demands of private developers and market forces in ways which many professional planners consider not to be in the long-term interests of the environment or the public.

Mention, here, of 'professional' planners prompts a further point about the ethics of professionalism in planning. In the kinds of cases described above, the moral dilemma faced by planning researchers arises because of their adherence to a utilitarian view of what is most in the public interest. And many researchers may equate this sincerely held utilitarian position with what, if they are professional planners, should also govern their ethical judgements about planned action, even if this sometimes comes into conflict with certain factual truths. In other words, from the point of view of what they perceive to be their ethical commitments *as professionals*, such researchers might consider it their professional duty to adhere to the utilitarian aspiration of serving the greater good, even if this involves suppressing, or 'massaging', the truth. However, a central plank of the ethics of professionalism (in any established profession) is a commitment to integrity and probity, which in turn implies being truthful (Taylor 1992 and 1996). Professional planners involved in planning research who are sincere utilitarians, and who also believe that utilitarianism accords with what professional planning should aspire to, thus face the possibility of being caught on the horns of ethical dilemmas when their utilitarian beliefs about right action come into conflict with the ethic of professional integrity.

Certainly, personal integrity and truthfulness is central to the ethics of occupational professionalism. Thus, in advising others as professionals, and in our dealings with other professionals, a central part of what it is to act professionally is to act, and render advice and judgements, sincerely and truthfully. But again, if we are also sincere utilitarians, truth and truthfulness have to be weighed against, and may sometimes have to be subsumed under, the ultimate aspiration to act in whatever ways will, in our considered judgement, maximise human happiness or well-being.

Once again, Bernard Williams has spoken to this point in describing how utilitarian consequentialism can alienate a person from moral (or – as imagined above – professional) integrity. Williams's argument is that, in order to be a genuine moral consequentialist, one should reflect on the rightness or wrongness of one's actions solely in terms of their contribution to the consequence that one is, morally, committed to realising – this being, in the case of utilitarianism, happiness, pleasure, or some analogous notion of well-being. As Williams puts it:

> I take it that in any form of direct consequentialism, and certainly in act-utilitarianism, the notion of the right action in given circumstances is a maximizing notion: the right action is that which out of the actions available to the agent brings about or represents the highest degree of whatever it is the system in question regards as intrinsically valuable – in the central case, utilitarianism, this is of course happiness (Williams 2002, 85).

Starting from this premise, Williams invites us to imagine moral dilemmas in which agents are required to act and where, in doing so, they seek to act in ways they believe to be consequentially right. But Williams also asks us to imagine what he takes to be typical of at least anyone who is concerned with morally right action, namely, that agents are real people who will come to these situations with already developed beliefs and commitments about how, in the general course of their lives, they should act. Indeed, as morally serious people, they are likely to see themselves as trying to live their lives so as to realise some moral purpose, mission, or project. In the case of people who are scholars and researchers, and also (let us suppose) members of a profession such as planning, then that moral purpose is likely to be one in which adhering to the truth, and acting truthfully, is central to their moral mission or project.

However, as Williams points out, it is always possible to imagine situations in which, from a consequential point of view, it would be better not to be truthful –

where, in the case of utilitarianism, it would maximise human happiness, or at least minimise unhappiness, if a scholar or researcher in planning were *not* to adhere to the ethic of truthfulness. And, if the scholar or researcher in question also happens to be a sincere moral utilitarian,[1] then, as Williams observes, the fact that the researcher in question comes to a situation believing that it is right to be truthful is, from a strictly utilitarian point of view, irrelevant to the question of how he should act. Further, and again from a strictly utilitarian point of view, it is also irrelevant that other people or institutions, such as the government or market forces, have brought about (and are therefore responsible for) the situation in which the researcher finds him or herself; after all, this is a fact about most situations we find ourselves in where we are required to make moral choices. From a utilitarian point of view, one has to take the world as one finds it, and then undertake, as best one can, utilitarian calculations and act in whatever way seems most likely to bring about the best consequences or, in the case of very bad situations, the least worst consequences.

But now, what – according to Williams – is the ethical problem here? The problem is that, in discounting an agent's prior moral (and/or professional ethical) beliefs as irrelevant to how he should conduct himself in a given situation, consequentialism disregards a person's integrity as a moral agent. Consider, again, our imagined scenario. A scholar and a researcher into environmental planning finds himself in a situation in which it would bring about happier consequences if he were not to be entirely truthful in undertaking some research or in reporting his research findings. Accordingly, if this person is to adhere to a consequentialist ethic of doing whatever furthers human happiness, then his prior moral belief that it is wrong to be untruthful is, in this situation, irrelevant. At least, it is *morally* irrelevant. To be sure, the researcher's prior moral beliefs may be *psychologically* relevant to him, inasmuch as being untruthful may subsequently prey on his conscience (rather as, in more extreme circumstances, the killing of an innocent woman preyed on Raskolnikov's conscience in Dostoyevsky's novel *Crime and Punishment*). But, from the purely *moral* point of view, under a consequentialist perspective all that matters is how the calculation comes out, with the right action being whatever the calculation of consequences shows to be the best outcome. In the case of utilitarian consequentialism, whatever you happen initially to believe is morally right or wrong has to be set aside if the utilitarian calculation shows that setting these prior feelings and commitments aside will yield greater happiness. But to do this, argues Williams, effectively means setting aside one's moral integrity as a person. As he puts it:

> It is absurd to demand of such a man, when the sums come in from the utility network which the projects of others have in part determined, that he should just step aside from his own project and decision and acknowledge the decision

---

1   And surely we don't want to consider the case of someone who is *not* a sincere utilitarian, but just a 'fair weather' utilitarian, or a utilitarian when it suits them.

which utilitarian calculation requires. It is to alienate him in a real sense from his actions and the source of his action in his own convictions. It is to make him into a channel between the input of everyone's projects, including his own, and an output of optimific decision; but this is to neglect the extent to which *his* actions and *his* decisions have to be seen as the actions and decisions which flow from the projects and attitudes with which he is most closely identified. It is thus, in the most literal sense, an attack on his integrity (Williams 2002, 116-117).

Of course, the kinds of difficult situations envisaged here may not arise, and so a happy coincidence can obtain between the scholarly demands of truth-telling and the utilitarian injunction to maximise happiness (or whatever other consequence any other version of consequentialism favours). But then a person's moral position isn't tested in easy situations where, as it were, the person can have their cake and eat it. Rather, our moral beliefs, and our real ethical position, is challenged and exposed when we have to make hard moral choices in situations where different moral principles to which we subscribe come into conflict. And, as we have seen, if one is a scholar and researcher into planning and at the same time a sincere utilitarian, one may face situations when the hard choice one has to make is between, on the one hand, acting to do whatever one believes will be to the greater good and, on the other hand, adhering to the scholarly (and professional) ethic of telling the truth, whatever that truth may be.

Consequentialism, Truthfulness and the Ethical Education of Researchers

The potential ethical dilemmas described in the previous section between the demands of utilitarian consequentialism and truthfulness emerge starkly if we imagine ourselves in the position of initiating and training people to become researchers in environmental planning (or indeed, in any discipline). I shall therefore conclude by presenting, starkly and in summary form, two models of what one might say to new researchers about the ethical dimension of their work.

Model 1: Truthfulness

'I have been asked to say a few words on the ethics of doing research. It can only be a "few words" because I have been given only a little time to say something about this. But perhaps a few words is all I need. For what I have to say about this is really pretty obvious. What you will be engaged in is the pursuit – and the enlargement – of our knowledge and understanding. And if you think about it, this is an age-old and noble pursuit. To be sure, there will be days when, in the midst of some tedious piece of data collection or analysis, or in the middle of your 100th interview with yet another person, you may wonder what the point of it all is, whether it matters, what does it all mean or amount to. But even when you do have these natural thoughts, remind yourselves that, however puny your efforts may seem in the grand scheme things, you are engaged in nothing other than the pursuit and enlargement of human knowledge and understanding. And this is, I repeat, a noble occupation. Think of Galileo, gazing through his telescope at the stars every night (and the same old stars, night after night). Do you imagine that he, too, didn't sometimes wonder what his star-gazing was all about, whether his research was worthwhile or would lead to anything important. Of course he must have sometimes wondered!

There's something else. In pursuing knowledge, you are pursuing the truth; *that* is your goal. And this is where the ethics of what you will be doing is thrown into sharp relief. For, as scholars and researchers, it is your duty – your *moral* duty – to pursue and speak the truth as you see it, even if what you find out is uncomfortable or unpalatable to you, or unpopular with your colleagues because it is not what they believe or want to hear, or, even, if it is not what your employers or the government of the day want to hear or hoped you would say. Never mind all that. Your job is to tell the truth as you find it, regardless of the consequences. That is the ethical principle that should guide you, and only that. So really, I didn't need long to tell you this…'

Model 2: (Utilitarian) Consequentialism

'I have been asked to say a few words on the ethics of doing research. It can only be a "few words" because I have been given only a little time to say something about this. But perhaps a few words is all I need, since what I have to say seems pretty obvious and straight-forward to me. For I think it should be clear to you, and especially in a discipline like environmental planning, that our prime purpose in life is to make things better in the world – to improve, as the great utilitarian philosophers put it, the sum total of human happiness or well-being on this Earth. And this is exactly what should inform your work as researchers in this field. Always ask yourselves: is this research that I am engaged in going to – or does it seem likely to – contribute to some improvement in human happiness or well-being? To be sure, there will be days when, in the midst of some tedious piece of data collection or analysis, or in the middle of your 100th interview with yet another person, you may wonder what the point of it all is, whether it matters, what does it all mean or amount to. Those are natural thoughts and feelings, and it is easy, when immersed in what might seem to be tedious detail, not to see the wood for the trees. But that is the time to remind yourselves: what your work is all about – I mean, what, ethically, it *should* be about – is the enlargement of human happiness. And so, when the going gets tough, if you ask yourself whether what you are doing is contributing, in however small a way, to the improvement of the human lot, and you can answer "yes" to that, then that is what, ethically, justifies your research.

Some people standing here in my shoes might have talked to you about "truth" as the guiding torch of research. Well, in engaging in research, it goes without saying that you are trying to find out some truths, trying to push back the frontiers of human knowledge and understanding. I take that for granted. But what's the *point* of this knowledge, what is the *point* of truth? It is – at least in our field – to find out things that will, somehow, improve human well-being on this planet, and that, actually, is the main thing, not "knowledge", or "truth" for its own sake. We're not philosophers or cosmologists, interested in knowledge and truth for its own sake. Who, really, cares about that? For us, what is important – and I mean ethically important – is knowledge and truth that *matters*, and what matters is improving human happiness and well-being. In fact, because that is our ultimate aim, it is actually more important than "truth". I mean that. If you were, by chance perhaps, to discover some truths that would not in any way improve human well-being, then those truths would not be worth anything and should be ignored or discounted. Sure, you should be concerned with the truth, but only those truths that make for a better life on this Earth.'

References

Baron, M.W., Pettit, P. and Slote, M. (eds) (1997), *Three Methods of Ethics: A Debate* (Oxford: Blackwell).

Bentham, J. (1789), *An Introduction to the Principles of Morals and Legislation*, edited by W. Harrison, 1948 (Oxford: Basil Blackwell).

Hare, R.M. (1981), *Moral Thinking: Its Levels, Method and Point* (Oxford: Clarendon Press).

Havel, V. (1986), *Living in Truth*, edited by J. Vladislav, 1987 (London: Faber and Faber).

Hudson, W.D. (1980), *A Century of Moral Philosophy* (Guildford and London: Lutterworth Press).

Lichfield, N. (1996), *Community Impact Evaluation* (London: UCL Press).

Lichfield, N., Kettle, P. and Whitbread, M. (1975), *Evaluation in the Planning Process* (Oxford: Pergamon).

Mill, J.S. (1861), *Utilitarianism*, reprinted in: Mill, J.S. *Utilitarianism*, edited by Mary Warnock, 1962 (London: Collins Fontana).

Nozick, R. (1974), *Anarchy, State and Utopia* (Oxford: Basil Blackwell).

Pettit, P. (1991), 'Consequentialism' in Peter Singer (ed.).

Pettit, P. (1997), 'The Consequentialist Perspective', in Marcia W. Baron, Philip Pettit and Michael Slote (eds).

Rawls, J. (1971), *A Theory of Justice* (Oxford: Oxford University Press).

Sen, A. and Williams, B. (eds) (1982), *Utilitarianism and Beyond* (Cambridge: Cambridge University Press).

Sidgwick, H. (1874), *The Methods of Ethics*, reprint of the 1907 edition, 1981 (Indianapolis: Hackett).

Singer, P. (ed.) (1991), *A Companion to Ethics* (Oxford: Blackwell).

Smart, J.J.C. and Williams, B. (1973), *Utilitarianism: For and Against* (Cambridge: Cambridge University Press).

Taylor, N. (1992), 'Professional Ethics in Town Planning: What is a Code of Professional Conduct For?', *Town Planning Review* 63:3, 227-241.

Taylor, N. (1996), 'Professionalism and Monitoring CPD: Kafka Revisited', *Planning Practice and Research* 11:4, 379-389.

Williams, B. (2002), *Truth and Truthfulness: An Essay in Genealogy* (Princeton: Princeton University Press).

Chapter 3

Virtue Ethics and Research Ethics

Huw Thomas

Introduction

This chapter discusses the strengths of an approach to research ethics which is framed by virtue ethics. Virtue ethics – a general approach to understanding ethics – has a number of variants (see, e.g. Darwall 2003; Welchman 2006, xix-xxiii). These differences will be mentioned only where appropriate for our purposes as the chapter is a contribution to a discussion of research ethics in planning, not a contribution to discussions of virtue ethics. In addition, the chapter will not give a list of, or attempt to justify, key virtues for researchers. The chapter will try to show that a concern for the character of the researcher, rather than a focus on actions alone, is essential for securing ethical conduct in research. This has implications for the education and training of researchers, and the institutional context within which it is desirable that research take place. This leads to a brief consideration, in the chapter's final section, of the notion that if researchers are not to feel that their conduct, while judged ethical is still in some sense arbitrary and/or simply blind rule-following then they need to think more about the practice of research, in its institutional context and within their own lives, rather than about ethics as such.

Ethical reflection can take many forms. For example, at times we might be concerned about the right thing to do; at other times we may struggle to get a sense of perspective on things – a feeling for what is really important in our lives or those of others. If we take the question of 'what kind of person should I be?' seriously then virtue ethics will have some attraction, because it places a particular kind of person – the virtuous person – in a central place in understanding what it is to be ethical. This is an ancient approach to ethics, but one which was overshadowed in English speaking philosophical circles for much of the 20th century by a focus on action, on doing the right thing. Thus arises the tension between whether the primary focus of ethics (and moral education) should be becoming a good person, or should it be doing the right thing. Of course, any plausible moral outlook will accommodate discussion and reflection on both matters; the issue is whether either is – in some sense – more basic or fundamental than the other. So, for example, if one is struck by the force of a concern for right action, then one will define a good person as one who (usually) does the right thing, and will identify the right course of action independently of any reference to the character or goodness of persons. A very influential answer to the question of how right action might be identified has been the injunction to look at their consequences (and only their consequences). This is an approach termed 'consequentialism'. The significance of consequentialism in influencing Western thought (and public policy) over the last century and a half leads Welchman (2006, ix) for example, to identify it as one of the main traditions in moral thought. A later section of this chapter will suggest reasons for thinking virtue ethics more attractive than a consequentialist approach to research ethics.

Virtue Ethics: A Sketch and some Implications

Within virtue ethics, the key to understanding what it is to live properly is the virtuous person. Faced by questions about what we should do in a particular set of circumstances, or indeed how we should regard something or other, then we should think 'how would a virtuous (i.e. good) person respond?'. As Statman (1997, 8) puts it, what is essential to virtue ethics 'is the idea that…judgements about character are prior to…judgements about the rightness or wrongness of actions.' There can be variants of virtue ethics depending on how priority is understood, and whether is allowed that at least some judgements of actions may be made independently of judgements of character. This chapter will concern itself with a very basic characterisation of virtue ethics. In practical terms, the expectation of a virtue ethics approach is that we might often think in concrete terms about a particular virtuous person, and use that person's hypothetical response as a guide. This approach certainly has a some everyday resonance: there can't be many of us who at sometime or another haven't thought 'how would my [hero, mother, father, religious leader, or even (research) mentor/project leader…] respond to this?' We shall come back to what is going in these kinds of cases, but at least some influential virtue ethicists would say that when we do this we are not simply slavishly copying our parents or mentor. Rather, we are using our knowledge of how they see things in order to help us get a grip on the salient aspects of the situation we find ourselves in; i.e. we are developing our cognitive capacities.

Virtue ethics emphasises the importance of a person's character as the key to a good life; and moral education, therefore, is centrally about character development. That is not to say that it is an exercise in looking inward, or in solipsism. On the contrary it is an exercise in learning 'how to…' (Alderman 1997, 148), where what one is learning is appropriate behaviour in the broadest sense. Working on one's character, on the kind of person one is, typically involves a number of distinctive methods. One is the use of examples (van Hooft 2006, 18), where one is guided as to appropriate things to look for – i.e. what is worthy of response – and what kind of response is appropriate (literature can have an important role to play in providing examples of this kind). Responding in the appropriate way to examples is a mark of having the right kind of character, and Hursthouse (1997) and others have argued that having the correct emotional response is an important part of moral development. Why emotions may be significant will be discussed later in the chapter. Finally, character development can often benefit from homilies, or

– in their modern incarnation – self-help manuals. As Annas (2006) points out, Seneca, a Stoic and, she argues, a virtue ethicist remains an influential source of self-help guidance for contemporary professionals. The nature of this moral education highlights one of the characteristics of virtue ethics' understanding of moral life, an understanding in which the unpredictability, uniqueness (and constantly unfolding depth) of individuals and social life is emphasised. A moral education based on homilies and examples would be a curiously convoluted way of teaching a comprehensive list of moral principles or rules (though examples might be used to illustrate some of the rules). In virtue ethics there is a place for rules of thumb to help people begin to appreciate the claims of morality, what it is to be moral: don't steal, don't tell lies and so on. But rules of thumb are just an early part of the process of moral development, a development which involves ultimately appreciating what it is to be a virtuous person. Stories, homilies, and examples are ways of getting people to see things a certain way, a way of building an understanding which goes beyond the examples themselves and allows people to cope with new, perhaps unique, circumstances. Later we will discuss the implications of such a view for how research ethics might be regulated.

Plausibility and Implausibility in Relation to Virtue Ethics

This section can do little more than sketch the outlines of some strategies for making virtue ethics appear attractive. The first is associated with an ancient Western ethical tradition labelled 'eudaimonic' which includes Aristotle. In this approach, virtues are defined in terms of dispositions which contribute to the flourishing of a person. We can talk of the attributes of a good knife – one which is fit for its purpose. And, in a slightly different vein, we can talk of the attributes of a flourishing plant – one which is reaching its potential, perhaps, in terms of growth, fruitfulness (e.g. flowering, seeding and so on). In both cases there is a teleological dimension which is central to the characterisation – knives and plants are primarily for this or that. If it were possible to think of people in the same way then we should be able to specify attributes which define a good person. So – what are persons for? Or, put differently, what constitutes the flourishing of a person? Seneca (2006), for example, answers forcefully that a person flourishes when he or she is rational: it then requires him to show that the virtuous life is the rational life (what rationality might consist of in this context is not something we need pursue in this chapter – it is Seneca's approach which is of interest). A modern, and influential, exponent of virtue ethics, such as Philippa Foot (2003, 113), would claim to be neutral between views of what constitutes a good life, and argues that virtues 'can be seen as correctives in relation to human nature in general', dispositions, then, which allow humans – in general terms – to live lives which pursue their version of the good.

An approach such as Foot's allows a sidestepping of an apparent difficulty with the idea of human flourishing – namely, that it appears that the notion – certainly in relation to people – can only be understood and specified within a given set of cultural norms. Yet it may be argued that some things surely cross all cultural barriers – physical integrity, for example, might be claimed as at least a necessary basis for flourishing, or perhaps an aspect of flourishing. But on closer examination this contention appears less persuasive. Whether physical integrity is part of human flourishing, and how it is part of it, will surely depend upon the circumstances of an individual life; and there may be many circumstances in which it may not be regarded as part of, or necessary for, human flourishing. It seems to me that there is no reason to be pushed into a position of having to say that 'in principle' physical integrity constitutes flourishing, though one may agree that as a matter of fact human flourishing often involves physical integrity and good health. The reason for this vagueness is precisely that the notion of 'flourishing' is only understandable within a cultural frame, a set of values and beliefs. The significance of physical integrity may well differ between different cultural outlooks (understanding 'cultural' here to encompass religious/spiritual outlooks). If this is at all persuasive then it leads to the idea that what counts as a virtuous life or character will make sense, and be justifiable, only within a given cultural context. Cultures are ways of life, which is to say that they are associated with, and dependent upon, collective life with a certain degree of structure and persistence. Virtuous behaviour, then, makes sense only within the confines of a certain kind of communal life. If that life breaks down or disappears then the moral ideas associated with it lose their purchase, lose their original sense. It is something like this that MacIntyre (1981) believes has happened in relation to contemporary Western morality, which uses terms which made sense inside a certain Judaeo-Hellenistic tradition, part of and supported by particular form of social organisation, but makes no sense now that tradition and its associated social form have disappeared.

It may appear that this approach is relativist – different cultures leading to different virtues and moralities. It depends what one means by relativist. The approach says what it says. But it need say no more: for example, it need not be pressed further to the view that any moral claim is as good as any other one; or the claim that the different cultures create their own worlds, including moral worlds, and that these are the only worlds there are. Indeed, a prominent supporter of a form of virtue ethics, John McDowell, is a moral realist (Thornton 2004). McDowell's (1979) discussion of virtues suggests a way in which we might understand moral education, ethical rules, and also how to avoid relativism. McDowell characterises moral development as the acquisition of a cognitive capacity, a sensitivity to morally salient characteristics of the world. This capacity is developed through supervised practice and example (and, indeed, by rule of thumb); but there comes a point where example gives out, where a person confronts a novel situation and is asked to carry on 'in the same way' – in this case to act as a virtuous person would. McDowell argues that going on in the same (virtuous) way is explicable in the same (Wittgensteinian) terms as rule-following in relation to mathematics, language and social practices generally. Rule-following does not involve learning (perhaps by induction) a principle which is then referred to (even unconsciously) and applied in new circumstances; it couldn't, because properly novel circumstances in the form we are interested in them are those which go beyond examples and rules we have ever encountered and imagined. It follows that any rule we may try to use in such circumstances is compatible with an infinite number of ways of 'going on'. So, in going on we can not be simply applying a template. Rule-following which is deemed generally correct is, rather, a mark of inclusion in a set of social relations, a form of life. It is this which is the insight in MacIntyre's (1981) use of the idea of a social practice as a way of explaining how virtues can be defined, and developed. We might say (if we wish – and I would) that a form of life understood as a practice provides the existential basis for developing certain cognitive (including moral) capacities. These considerations will help us reflect later on the value and limitations of codes of ethics for researchers.

One reason for feeling that virtue ethics might be incomplete as an approach to ethics is thinking that what one does, rather than what one's character is like, should be the primary focus of the moral life. The over-riding concern for actions (and their consequences) has many roots. The significance of social reform is, perhaps, one consideration which can make action seem central – the pressing importance of improving an all too obviously imperfect and unjust world has struck as many philosophers as it has intellectuals in general. It is clearly important that any plausible account of ethics, and moral education and training, places appropriate weight on action, on helping create a particular kind of world. On the other hand, accounts of ethics should also be able to explain the significance of contemplation and reflection in the moral life. A consequentialist approach has an account of contemplation, but we may feel that it is a rather thin account. In essence, moral contemplation, for the consequentialist, amounts to a kind of fact-finding and checking of calculations (for example, 'has some kind of personal animus influenced my evaluation of the likely consequences of action "A"?'). This kind of reflection is important, but there is another kind of contemplation – undertaken, for example, by monks (or their equivalents) in most religious traditions, and also by 'lay' people who may also meditate, go on retreats, or – less glamorously – lose themselves in contemplation of art. In this chapter we needn't explore what this kind of contemplation might be about; for now it's enough to suggest that it is a recognisable part of moral life, and prima facie one might expect an account of ethics to explain its role in the moral life. Virtue ethics, like any character-based account of ethics, can account for the role of contemplation in the moral life: it is one way of getting a sense of perspective, of (for example) reducing the way that concern for self can obstruct our view of the world as it really is (Murdoch 1970).

Another reason that stressing the primacy of action might appear attractive can be a particular picture of persons in which action is what it is which makes an individual distinctive, particularly in a moral sense. If we are attracted by the idea that freedom of will is best exemplified in choosing to act in a given way (and hence it is in those actions that an individual most clearly expresses what is distinctive about him or herself) then that aspect of the person which connects directly to action will have a particular significance. Many have supposed that wants/desires are the motive force, as it were, of action. At least some of a person's wants or desires are brute facts about any given person (others might be cultivated); and the significance of desires is that they are the well-springs of action, restrained (on occasion) perhaps by the capacity of reason or cognition, but not fundamentally influenced by it. Action might typically issue from a combination of belief/knowledge and desire, but the cognitive element of this combination is, in itself, powerless to induce action. So, the really significant part of the moral characters of people is that they have certain kinds of desires and 'passions'. To the extent that they can be schooled and trained, they need to be. But this kind of approach to understanding a moral life takes no account of the character of the person, independently of that person's actions – there is no point in doing so – so, for example, will pay little or no regard to whether a particular action is done grudgingly or not. It is the thinness of this approach to ethics which Iris Murdoch (1970) highlights in her famous example of a woman who has always 'done the right thing' in relation to her daughter in law, but whose view of her changes over time. Because the mother in law's actions have always been proper, there is no outward change to mark a change in cognition; she now simply sees her daughter in law differently. If this change is one in which the daughter in law is seen more accurately, more clearly and fairly, then Murdoch – and many others of us – would want to say there has been a significant moral improvement. It matters what kind of person we are – how we see things, indeed how we feel about things – not just what we do. In the context of research it is to my mind obviously preferable that a researcher genuinely abhor the possibility of exploiting vulnerable research 'subjects' than that she or he act out of fear of being caught out if they do engage in exploitation. But such a consideration is perhaps not the most significant one in relation to moral character and research activity.

The connecting of goodness with a certain clarity of vision – seeing people or things as they really are – suggests the idea that goodness and cognition are intertwined. Seneca, for example, compares a person's capacity for self-delusion to the ignorance of a simple-minded person who suddenly becomes blind. Murdoch's inspiration is Platonic, but the idea that much or all vice is some kind of insensitivity to reality, including a fantasising about what one wishes to be the case rather than what is, is wholly consistent with a virtue ethics approach. This would lead to the view that good research has to be ethical in the sense that only virtuous people can see the world clearly. There is an obvious, and significant, problem with that thesis in that there appear to be plenty of counter-examples of flawed people who undertake celebrated research, and some apparent advances in knowledge which were arrived at in arguably unethical ways. However, it's important to be clear about what is being claimed. Some kind of understanding of the world is, clearly, possible by all but those entirely caught up in a fantasy world; after all, we all pretty much get by after a fashion. The claim is that virtue helps deepen understanding, all else (notably, native intellectual ability) being equal.

The line of thought in the previous paragraph is unlikely to be attractive to many without considerably more support. Flyvbjerg (2001) has provided an extended discussion which concludes that in the social sciences, at least, the character of researchers is significant, in that they need the Aristotelian quality of phronesis, practical wisdom (Flyvbjerg 2001, 57). Phronesis combines what we would today classify as intellectual and ethical considerations inasmuch as it involves judgement (which, clearly, is an intellectual capacity), but based on a conception of what constitutes the good for a person. The spine of Flyvbjerg's thesis is that social science depends upon an understanding of people and the meanings they find in the world, its enchantment; such an understanding, by definition, requires phronesis. Yet Flyvbjerg's illustrations of a phronetic approach to social science appear thin – essentially, a matter of asking a certain limited range of questions. From his own argument, however, it would appear that the phronetic approach isn't defined by overt questions (which, after all, can be articulated by anyone, however naïve, or indeed evil, they may be) as much as by a constant awareness of the enchantment (i.e. the meaning-infused nature) of the world and the true nature of people in it. (We may speculate that the thinness of Flyvbjerg's account stems from his still being in thrall to what MacIntyre (1990) has labelled a liberal approach to knowledge-acquisition and scholarship which, by default, has come to emphasise technique over content.) Be that as it may, Flyvbjerg's contention about the importance of phronesis can be held by those who reject the eudaimonistic approach that Flyvbjerg himself works within: we might hold that social science, inasmuch as it seeks an understanding of people, inevitably requires wisdom to be performed at its best (i.e. for a more complete understanding), but that wisdom does not involve some kind of appreciation of what is good for a person, but rather has as its basis possession of a sensitivity to the kinds of meanings people find in the world and how these motivate them. This sensitivity to people, to seeing what there is to see of them, is what a virtuous person has.

Virtue Ethics and Research Ethics

The previous section has gestured at a case for arguing that planning research might only be properly conducted by virtuous persons, and in that sense research ethics would take care of itself. However, even if this position is not adopted, there are many implications of taking a virtue ethics approach to research ethics. The first is that a virtue ethics approach will stress the importance of developing the moral characters of researchers as the key measure in securing ethical behaviour (Lombardi 1980). On this approach, codes of ethics, and ethical approval procedures, are secondary measures which may or may not be useful in particular circumstances. It is essentially a practical matter as to whether – and in what form – an ethical approval procedure may help achieve better ethical standards among researchers (for example, having a procedure may help researchers anticipate potential issues; and this is helpful for any researcher, however good his or her character). But researchers of good character would think ahead, and good character is a necessary and sufficient condition for achieving ethical behaviour in any circumstances encountered once the research is underway.

This latter consideration is one of the more persuasive arguments for a virtue ethics/character based approach to research ethics: whatever safeguards, procedures, mechanisms there are to monitor or review research before, during or after it is undertaken there will still be times when researchers are on their own. Because the complexity of life cannot be captured or anticipated in codes or procedures or questions on a form, the sensitivity of the researcher to the morally salient characteristics of whatever he or she encounters must rely on the development of such a capacity by the researcher, rather than reference to an external source of guidance. Such a sensitivity is precisely what being virtuous consists in according to McDowell (1979).

The virtue ethics approach to research ethics also involves a distinctive approach to research training, an approach which has parallels in education more generally (Dunne 2000). Broadly speaking, a virtue ethics approach would try to develop an idea of what kind of person a virtuous researcher is, rather than simply a listing of 'dos and don'ts'. Such an approach assumes that in relation to their work, at least, virtuous researchers have a characteristic stance or set of attitudes (ones which will, of course, be expressed differently because the characters and temperaments of researchers are different). It might be difficult, if not impossible to describe this set of attitudes in detail, but for someone like Iris Murdoch a key component might be a certain disregard for self and the aggrandisement of self, a humility in the face of the reality and autonomy of the world. It is this non-self-regarding aspect of virtue which is captured in MacIntyre's discussions of how virtues, or perhaps more properly proto-virtues, may be inculcated through social practices (Lo Piccolo and Thomas 2008). Whatever it is that distinguishes the virtuous researcher, we get on to it through examples (Lombardi 1980), and through instruction and correction, and discussion, in practice. Supervisors – of PhD students, and in the workplace – have an important role, therefore, in developing ethical sensitivity in researchers, and the relationship of the educator to the person being trained is an integral part of the process of training/education. Research ethics, on this outlook, is not something which can be conveyed equally well by a book as by the right kind of personal guidance and instruction; and that is not because of some technical deficiency in books, but because the relationship and nature of the educator is part of what is to be conveyed.

For all researchers, including more experienced researchers, periodic reflection and discussion with peers who are themselves serious about ethical behaviour is a necessity. It is ridiculous to ask that researchers continually ponder on ethical matters – as Lovibond (2006, 269) points out, to seek moral significance in every incident in our life (cooking sausages, checking addresses…) is morally pretentious. Yet, it is important that there are mechanisms which remind us, in some way or another, of morally salient circumstances, and also – as necessary – provide a forum for discussion of ethical concerns. After all, it is very well to have a virtuous person as an exemplar, but in the thick of research (or life) one might not realise that now is the time to reflect on that example. In addition, in an imperfect world, exemplars may sometimes be thin on the ground. It is collegial life which provides a context which can help keep us sensitised to ethical considerations of our work, and can help us do this by engaging in a common endeavour within which a certain sense can be made of ourselves and the world in which we are working/researching. There is no single template for the form that ethically supportive collegial life may take, for we live in many overlapping and intersecting social networks, even as researchers. Set within an appropriate context of shared understandings of research and learning, mundane processes such as ethical approval for research projects may play their part; informal discussions – such as talks at the water cooler – are clearly important too. In an electronic age, perhaps internet-based relationships can also play a part.

On this approach to research ethics, it is clear that understanding what constitutes a virtuous person can only be done within a shared form of life, or set of social practices. If these break down then the conditions for making ethical sense together disappear. MacIntyre (1990, 216-236) has argued that the dominant understanding of what constitutes systematic intellectual enquiry (and hence what constitutes a proper role for a university) has been impoverished in modern 'liberal' universities by a lack of sensitivity to their own pre-suppositions, and any proper acknowledgement of the seriousness of rival traditions of intellectual enquiry. Central to these rival traditions are views of what it is to be human and what it is to have knowledge of the world. Within these traditions what constitutes appropriate conduct for a researcher will be broadly defined, and disputes over individual episodes will take place against a background of shared beliefs about – inter alia – the purpose of university-based research. While holding out the possibility that some kind of coherent role for a university can be re-constructed (as 'a place of constrained disagreement' (pp. 230-231)) his verdict on the contemporary university is that it is floundering, an institution which accepts de facto a moral relativism working in a world of multiple and diverse beliefs and cultures. In these circumstances it cannot generate or sustain a coherent vision of its role and purpose, leaving it prey to pressures and fashions which suggest that 'old' ideas and practices can be re-worked and re-thought for a changing world. Radice (2001) summarises some of these changes in relation to British universities. Other authors have pointed to ways in which they have implications for research ethics.

Nearly thirty years ago Lombardi (1980) speculated that there were signs of corrosion of any sense of moral community in higher education in the United States, citing the effects of commercial pressures on universities and their researchers. More recently, Lo Piccolo and Thomas (2008) have suggested that this process has developed apace in relation to the university context of planning programmes in many countries, broadening the discussion of pressures from just narrowly commercial ones to an appreciation of the political economy of higher education (including its unevenness across space). In these circumstances, it may well remain possible for fairly small groups of researchers to develop a shared understanding of the requirements of being a virtuous researcher, setting this within a shared understanding of what the role of knowledge is – and what constitutes knowledge – in the life well lived. But for institutions like universities – which are often all too aware of their internal tensions and fragmentation in relation to purpose and ethics – a focus on virtue is simply impossible for they no longer have a shared life and sense of purpose; for universities in such circumstances, codes and procedures of ethical approval may be all that can be done to identify a kind of lowest common denominator of ethical behaviour. Of course, it is important that researchers don't fabricate results, and don't unreflectively harm anyone involved in the research process, staples of such codes. But only a rogue would wilfully engage in such behaviour, and he or she is immune to the persuasiveness of a code. Faced with questions such as what kinds of research questions are worth asking (let alone less central ones like when one might engage in deception in order to gain research results, or how one might interpret what might constitute respectful behaviour in the field) it becomes clear that many researchers within universities – and specifically within planning schools – share no view of what it is that is important in life, research and the connection between the two. Hence a framework for addressing these kinds of issues – or even identifying what constitutes an issue – is often missing in individual researchers' workplaces (and lives).

Conclusions

This chapter has sketched an approach to understanding what may be important in research ethics, how it might best be introduced into and sustained in the life of a researcher, and some of the obstacles to these processes. It has not said a great deal about what kinds of virtues a researcher might deploy, or what behaviour should be engaged in. In relation to virtues, how virtues are defined and given content will depend upon the nature of the shared forms of life within which people (researchers) are making sense of their activity. I will admit, here, that I have no real sense at present of such a shared purpose or community; I do feel somewhat bereft, my work in some ways simply a matter of going through particular routines. I have little to offer as a personal guide to the virtuous researcher, therefore. Virtue ethics is a way of understanding how we might understand the nature of ethics in our lives; one thing it teaches is that ethical behaviour is not about following a universal decision rule which can be specified in full prior to its application in any case. What it does say is that virtuous behaviour involves engaging in practices which are based upon and help sustain a shared conception of 'what matters'. I believe, with MacIntyre (1990) and many others, that 'what matters' – in relation to life and specific practices within it, such as research and scholarship in universities – is something which can be discussed and debated rationally; it is not simply a case of plumping for a set of views and sticking to them. That, however, is a complex, and separate, matter.

References

Alderman, H. (1997), 'By virtue of a virtue', in Daniel Statman (ed.).

Annas, J. (2006), 'Seneca: Stoic Philosophy as a Guide to Living', in Jennifer Welchman (ed.).

Darwall, S. (ed.) (2003), *Virtue Ethics* (Oxford: Blackwell).

Dunne, J. (2000), *Back to the Rough Ground* (Notre Dame, Indiana: University of Notre Dame University Press).

Flyvbjerg, B. (2001), *Making Social Science Matter* (Cambridge: Cambridge University Press).

Foot, P. (2003), 'Virtues and Vices', in Stephen Darwall (ed.).

Hursthouse, R. (1997) 'Virtue Ethics and Satisfying Rationality', in Daniel Statman (ed.).

Lo Piccolo, F. and Thomas, H. (2008), 'Research Ethics in Planning: A Framework for Discussion', *Planning Theory* 7:1,7-23.

Lombardi, L.G. (1980), 'Character versus Codes: Models for Research Ethics', *International Journal of Applied Philosophy* 5:1, 21-28.

Lovibond, S. (2006), 'Practical Reason and its Animal Precursors', *European Journal of Philosophy* 14:2, 262-273.

McDowell, J. (1979), 'Virtue and Reason', *The Monist* 62:3, 331-350.

MacIntyre, A. (1981), *After Virtue* (London: Duckworth).

MacIntyre, A. (1990), *Three Rival Versions of Moral Enquiry* (London: Duckworth).

Murdoch, I. (1970), *The Sovereignty of Good* (London: Routledge and Kegan Paul).

Radice, H. (2001), 'From Warwick University Ltd to British Universities Plc', *Red Pepper* March, 19-21.

Seneca, L.A. (2006), 'Extracts from "On the Happy Life" and "Moral Letters to Lucilius"', in Jennifer Welchman (ed.).

Statman, D. (1997), 'Introduction to Virtue Ethics', in Daniel Statman (ed.).

Statman, D. (ed.) (1997), *Virtue Ethics. A Critical Reader* (Edinburgh: Edinburgh University Press).

Thornton, T. (2004), *John McDowell* (Chesham: Acumen).

van Hooft, S. (2006), *Understanding Virtue Ethics* (Chesham: Acumen).

Welchman, J. (2006), 'Introduction', in Jennifer Welchman (ed.).

Welchman, J. (ed.) (2006), *The Practice of Virtue* (Indianapolis: Hackett Publishing).

Chapter 4
Pragmatic Ethics and Sustainable Development[1]

Niraj Verma

As someone trained in the systems tradition I am attracted to concepts that help to integrate other concepts. In academic research, which is the context for this chapter, integration is often seen as collaboration between researchers who are trained in different fields and who typically reside in different departments. A university provost or a senior foundation official, for instance, might put aside research funding to encourage proposals that are authored by investigators from different fields. Or, an institution might promote the short or long-term gathering of experts from different fields. Underlying these initiatives is the recognition that discipline dominated research has systematically left gaping holes in research that an interdisciplinary approach might address. Interdisciplinary questions are particularly relevant to the professions and in this chapter I will be interested in ethical questions that arise as part of interdisciplinary research.

Typically, ethical challenges in interdisciplinary research have to do with the management of human failings. So, for instance we might ask how researchers maintain their integrity in the face of temptation. What do they do when pressured by grant agencies towards specific outcomes? How do they handle political pressure? What of inter-personal issues within research teams? These questions demand a theory of ethics that provides normative guidance. But, for the most part, the situations represented by these questions are morally – but not cognitively stressful. This is an important distinction that bears some explanation. Morally demanding situations will often cast one set of interests against another. Loyalty to a professional core versus loyalty to one's country or state is an example. The role of ethics is to resolve this dilemma. In this sense morally demanding situations tax the heart but are easier on the mind. Even when some mind-work may be required, for example when the problem demands some savvy in negotiating political terrain, the ethical question is typically about maintaining one's moral rectitude by taking the higher ground. Figuring out the available paths – high, low, or other – is seen as relatively trivial and an ethically neutral exercise.

---

1 The second part of this chapter is adapted from a previous article that I published in the German journal *Trialog* (*Zeitschrift für das Planen und Bauen in der Dritten Welt*), 48, pp. 6-11, 1996.

Such an approach can be called an 'ethics of volition' because the ethical question is about being ethical (morally upright) in the exercise of our volition. But, however important an ethics of volition, it leaves unaddressed a whole set of human failings that are more cognitively than morally demanding. These include 'falling in love with pet ideas,' 'too accepting of conventional wisdom,' 'being seduced by rigor,' 'disregarding relevance,' 'ignoring problems that one is not trained to handle,' and other similar concerns. These are issues of particular concern for social science and planning research. Researchers are not susceptible to these issues because of malice or graft. Even when greed plays a role, it is greed in the form of eagerness for results, not the lust for profit. Sometimes researchers may not even know that they are being overzealous or that any other kind of problem exists. Yet the problems are far from idiosyncratic and can wreak havoc on outcomes.

In this chapter I will argue that American pragmatism provides particularly relevant guidance for these cognitively demanding human failings. Unlike the ethics of volition which admonishes us against the temptation to take advantage of discretion, pragmatic ethics is concerned about involuntary actions that can benefit from ethical deliberation. If the ethics of volition poses moral challenges, pragmatic ethics poses cognitive challenges. I will develop this line of argument in the context of a discussion on sustainable development because it represents an idea without borders, demanding of interdisciplinary inquiry. At the same time, despite its wide moorings and its impressive reach, sustainability is a particularly suitable arena for pragmatism because it demands some closure given its concern for application and implementation. Moreover, given the many calls to follow a 'precautionary principle' or the need for an 'imperative of responsibility' (Jonas 1984) a cognitively demanding ethics is particularly germane to sustainable development. The chapter is divided into two parts followed by a concluding summary. The first part concerns pragmatism and cognitive ethics. The second part applies this to sustainable development.

The Ethics of American Pragmatism

Consider the example of someone shouting 'Fire' in a crowded auditorium. The implementation is instantaneous and the auditorium is empty. According to the early pragmatists, particularly William James and Charles Peirce, this effect of the utterance is the most useful meaning of 'Fire' in this context. At other times fire may mean the ability to cook a meal or to layoff an employee; here shouting fire means 'emptying the auditorium.' In this kind of pragmatic thinking, propositions and their implementation go hand in hand. There is no separate phase marked 'implementation.' To associate meanings with consequences is to privilege consequences in a way that does away with the divide between propositions and implementation.

This idea of tying meaning to consequences is called the pragmatic theory of meaning. William James and Charles Peirce saw this is a way of challenging analytic philosophy's inadvertent proclivity to disregard action or application. They rightly surmised that a concern for implementation and action must pervade inquiry from its very outset. Disregarding concerns of action, even as a proviso while we make some headway in our inquiry, is so vested a process that it becomes a losing proposition.

I first encountered this general sensibility of American pragmatism in my conversations with C. West Churchman, my mentor at Berkeley. Churchman was a philosopher and logician and was trained in the formalism and rigor of logic and also in the applications of philosophical thinking. His teacher, Edward Singer, had been a student of William James. Singer took the pragmatic position to mean that the pruning that we do to our concepts weakens our inquiry and challenges its relevance. His example was the science of surveying, where he used Jamesian ideas to show that even the simplest measurement involved wide-ranging philosophical presumptions about the nature of the world and of intellectual inquiry. West Churchman took James and Singer's stance much further, moving beyond surveying to operations research, management science, and planning. For these fields Churchman (1994) showed that we needed a systems approach that in Singer's language 'swept in' other values that didn't at first blush seem related.

This brief intellectual history certainly helps to identify the tradition of American Pragmatism within which I am operating. But, that is not my purpose in introducing it. Rather, I want to show that the systems approach is not driven by a vapid or mechanical desire to 'be comprehensive,' whatever that might mean, but as a way of responding to the pragmatic idea of meaning. In other words, the systems approach is not pursuing the goal of bringing more and more under its purview nor is its goal one of finding similar theoretical structures between various systems, as for instance, some proponents of general systems theory interpreted it. Instead its role is one of righting wrongs. If implementation is the casualty of an analytic process the systems approach endogenises implementation into inquiry. If 'sentiments' are missing it adds them to 'reasons' (Verma 1998). If normative questions cannot be raised within an inquiry the systems approach makes it possible to include them. Elsewhere (Verma 1998) I have called this version of the systems approach the 'new comprehensiveness.' It is different from the old comprehensiveness in its critical defence of the necessity for comprehensiveness. This discussion also tells that ideas such as 'bounded rationality' are germane to the old comprehensiveness but not to the new comprehensiveness, where every expansion of the terrain is prompted by felt need rather than some directive to include more and more.

Moral and Cognitive Human Failings

Many planners are familiar with the term 'wicked problems.' Horst Rittel coined the term (Rittel and Webber 1973) to denote planning problems that lack neatly defined boundaries and consequently evaded attempts to solve them. Rittel brought the insight that in the act of defining problems we implicitly illuminate possible solutions.

The pragmatic idea of associating meaning with consequences offers a particularly nifty way of thinking through the consequences of wicked problems. Consider the following example. In the current economic climate opinion in the United States is sharply divided over what role the government should play in economic recovery. Should the taxpayer bailout American corporations, such as General Motors, or do such large scale interventions undermine the capitalist enterprise by creating long-term inefficiencies? While there will always be divergent responses to such questions, the idea of wicked problems suggests that these differences are not idiosyncratic. Some wicked problems may be traceable to human failings that are morally demanding while others may be the result of cognitively demanding failures. For example, there are allegations that the former NASDAQ Chairman, Bernard Madoff, started a Ponzi scheme that cheated its investors out of their life savings. If true, this would be a moral failing of someone who certainly knew better. On the other hand the near bankruptcy of the giant insurance and finance company, AEG, thus far appears to be a cognitive failing. AEG should have known better than to make such risky loans with little or no expectation of return.

Pragmatism's theory of meaning – the idea that the meaning of concepts lies in their consequences – exposes our particular take on problems and solutions. If wicked problems are susceptible to interpretation, the theory of meaning exposes this susceptibility to scrutiny and, in case of normative underpinnings, opens the way for the application of a cognitively demanding ethics for planning.

Structural and Purposeful Categories

Suppose we lean in favour of a broad territory of sustainable development, how might we organise this territory so as to suggest how action becomes possible? One way of organisation is through categorisation. It is useful to distinguish between purposeful and structural categories. Purposeful categories, as the label suggest, are those which deal with purpose; all other categories are structural. For instance, categories which separate ideas or artifacts according to the methods used in reaching them are structural. Examples of this might be categories such as rational, irrational, intuitive, deductive, inductive, etc. Disciplinary categories, which divide the world into sets of approaches, are also structural. Examples are categories with labels like 'sociological approach,' 'economic approach,' etc.

Structural categories are enormously efficient – perhaps too efficient. Their power comes from an analytic tradition of dividing the subject-matter so as to be able to make fine and insightful distinctions. But insight, in this tradition, is defined by a curious mix of surprise and logical conviction. So long as the logic is maintained, the more unexpected a hypothesis, the more desirable it is considered to be. In scientific inquiry, the most famous structural categories are those of objectivity and disinterestedness and they apply to the validation process. Surprise, on the other hand, is a sign of interestedness; it is not a part of validation but a function of the expectations of an intellectual community.

Purposeful categories, on the other hand, are not particularly efficient to analyse. They include such elusive and hard to measure categories as motivation, satisfaction, morality, and even, life, death, and consciousness. Attempts to impute measures for these categories on anything more than a nominal scale become problematic. For instance, economists talk of 'willingness to pay' or of 'contingent valuation' to measure concepts such as satisfaction or to assess the pleasure derived from natural resource conservation. The so-called 'existence value' (Krutilla 1967), for instance, is a measure of the satisfaction that one derives from knowing that something, such as a species or a habitat, exists. But, although the goal is to measure 'satisfaction,' this is rarely a psychological measure and the term is often simply a euphemism for the measuring of manifest choices.

The case for a purposeful, or what philosophers call a teleological, view of the world, can be made in many different ways. One way is proposed by German philosopher, Martin Heidegger (1966, 45), in *Discourse on Thinking*. Heidegger cautions against the pervasiveness of 'calculative thinking,' and tells us that it results in a 'flight from thinking.' To understand calculative thinking, Heidegger tells us, contrast it to meditative thinking which has to do with meaning and not with instrumental calculation. The distinction is similar to teleological (meditative) thinking and structural (calculative) thinking. However, both these distinction are problematic: they are easier to justify philosophically than to apply practically. For example, everything; i.e. every plan, every instrument, every artifact, every human, can be considered to be purposeful. Elsewhere, I have dealt with this question in detail (Verma 1998) and have shown that categories such as 'who is a beneficiary of a plan,' and 'what are the motivations of the participants,' should be given the label of purpose while measure of costs, benefits, efficiency, etc., are structural. I do not want to repeat that argument; in this chapter I want to add to the discussion on purpose by suggesting that calculative thinking over-estimates our freedom from constraints and mistakes the logic of analysis for logic of implementation.

The Ethics of Sustainable Development

The difficulties in a substantive definition of sustainability have not stopped its popularity. Some see it as being about energy efficiency while for others it is about clean fuel. At other times sustainability is about smart growth or green buildings. Indeed, the pervasiveness of the field is felt in areas as wide as sustainable markets and sustainable economies. Methodologically, however, it is easier to see the message of sustainability as advocating the integration of two or more opposing forces. Development versus conservation, present versus future, and renewable energy versus fossil fuels are some examples. In each of these cases, the message of sustainability is attractive because it aims at a balance between doomsday scenarios and notions of progress and development.

Such a message would be wonderful, except that our track record of 'striking a balance' is woefully inadequate. We have rarely done well when reconciling competing objectives. And just when we think we have, aspects of the problem we ignored come back to haunt us. Take, for instance, the perennial debates on the appropriate balance between public and private enterprise. Despite the end of the Cold War and the movement of many governments towards market-oriented reforms, there is little consensus on the right mix between public and private initiatives, an idea that is on renewed interest amidst talks of government help to rescue private enterprise even in unabashedly capitalist states.

So what should a pragmatist do? One strategy in the quest for a stable balance is to lean towards a 'comprehensive solution'; i.e. to include more and more aspects so that there are no surprises. The philosophy of holism and other such ideas support such a strategy. But, since the total list of relevant issues is virtually limitless, a comprehensive approach can become a process with no end in sight. After all, isn't everything which goes on our planet – and elsewhere! – relevant to the concept of sustainable development? The pragmatist 'meaning' of this is to focus on the purposes of sustainable development rather than its extent. Sustainable development, I will claim, belongs to a class of concepts which are teleological and for which conventional reductive measurement techniques may be less appropriate. That is, we should tie our justification of sustainable development to ends, intentions, and goals rather than to modes, costs, indicators, and methods.

There are two reasons for such a stance. First, an agreement on purposes keeps our options open on methods, approaches, and subject-matter. Purposeful thinking allows us to reach closure without pruning our terrain or prematurely declaring some issues as being irrelevant or less important. And seen this way, the alternative would be capricious: waffling on goals while being fixated on and decisive about methods! The second reason has to do with consequences and implementation. While technical justifications of sustainable development – such as those which use contingent valuation techniques or willingness-to-pay arguments – are logically convincing, they pass the burden on the implementation process. This is because technical reasoning is enormously powerful in an intellectual sense but exceedingly limited when confronted with the psychological, social, political, and ideological forces which play a dominant role during implementation. Reliance on technical reasoning amounts to endorsing the separation of planning and implementation. Moral and ethical justifications, on the other hand, are likely to provide greater inspiration. Since morality takes issues of personal and social behaviour head on, a convincing moral argument is likely to align political and social forces in ways that facilitate implementation. Using some works by Hans Jonas and my own recent work on ethics in planning, I will argue that we must think of ethics of sustainable development as an instrument to implant the idea of sustainability, and not merely as a normative guide to decide which course of action is the best one.

The Rhetoric of 'Balance'

The balance metaphor pervades all discussions of sustainable development. The balance can be sought on many fronts: between optimism and caution, present and future, private and public, individual and collective, long-term and short-term, and other such tensions. For instance, one views of sustainable development tries to ameliorate development (as in real-estate or economic development) with conservation (as in historic preservation). Here, one force suggests change; the other advises caution. Sustainable development, in this example, suggests that a judicious mix of preservation and change is more desirable than biasing in favour of one or the other extreme. Consider another example, when the tension is between present and future consumption. We know that fertilisers bring about green revolutions but they also interfere with long-term soil fertility. The philosophy of sustainable development suggest that neither present nor future have primacy and it is through a blend or a balance what we are likely to develop better social and economic policy. In this sense, sustainable development can be contrasted with the partisan philosophies of unmitigated consumption or overcautious preservation. Unlike them, it aims to bring a dual message of hope and caution.

More generally, we can usually identify two opposing concepts and the notion of sustainability suggests that a judicious balance between these extremes can be reached and should be reached. American architect Peter Calthorpe (1986, 2) attests to this in no uncertain manner: 'In all cases the goal is balance: a balance between uses, between climate and the needs of the building, between the community and the individual.' Or, as the Aalborg Charter of the European Commission (1994) declares, 'sustainability is neither a vision nor an unchanging state, but a creative, local, *balance seeking process* extending into all areas of local decision-making' [emphasis added]. Similar ideas, which posit the search for a balance as the corner stone of sustainable development, can be found in virtually all fields which comprise the scholarship on sustainable development.

But do we know how to implement such a balance? Unfortunately, at all levels (local, national and global), our track-record of satisfactorily reconciling competing considerations is rather undistinguished. And this is particularly so when these considerations address important constituencies in our decision-making apparatus, in our self-images, and in our knowledge and belief systems, Indeed, we can say with some confidence that if an issue can be reconciled easily it is not important and if it is important it can't be easily reconciled. The difficulties in adjudicating private and public systems, automobile and rail, fossil fuels and renewable energy, low and high density development, are examples. Although philosophy, from Kant to Hegel to Marx, tells us that a dialectical synthesis emerges from opposing forces – and that this is the way knowledge grows – such a synthesis has proven hard to reach. Take, for instance, the problem of air pollution in Los Angeles County – a topic that has attracted widespread scientific attention – and at least a partial solution to the problem in the form of car-pool lanes. We know that automobile exhaust in Los Angeles is the most important mobile source for

NOx and carbon monoxide pollution and we can calculate reasonably reliable levels of car-pool ridership to mitigate these influences. But all fails because we can't motivate our clients to use car-pool lanes. Is motivating the public part of the transportation planner's duties? Or is this part of implementation, separate from planning? Moreover, unless we are able to motivate the public to use car-pool lanes, how accurate is it to say that we have balanced the need for transportation with the harmful effects of automobile exhaust on the environment?

Systems and Sustainability

One demand of a balance is that we try to include more and more into our planning. Certainly, there is more than one precedent for this kind of expansion of the territory of planning. The systems approach that we encountered earlier and the idea of comprehensive planning are two examples. But as every realist knows, there is a downside to increasing the scope of our work. Planners have a professional obligation to act in a timely manner and every extra bit of research, every foray into an unknown area, comes at the cost of the timeliness of our actions. The quest for unlimited knowledge may be well justified, but what use is this quest if it incapacitates us into inaction?

There are strong arguments for broadening the terrain of knowledge and there are equally persuasive reasons for restricting its domain. The strongest arguments for a broad and capacious knowledge base come from epistemology, which tells us that since our problems are interconnected, anything less than an unbound idea of professional knowledge might exclude important aspects of our problems. Like the lost airline pilot who was happily making good time, we might end up solving the easiest but the wrong problems. At the same times, practicality and common sense emphasise closure of our terrain. Like Buridan's donkey that died of starvation while deciding which stack of hay to eat, we, too, run the risk of getting incapacitated by the extent of our concerns.

In previous work (Verma 1995), I have argued that this tension between narrow and wide, and between contemplation and action is – to borrow Thomas Kuhn's pithy phrase – an 'essential tension' for the professions; i.e. it is a recurrent and defining problem for professional inquiry. I suspect that most scholars will not disagree with this formulation. But the implications of this tension – the operational meaning – will certainly be controversial. The tension implies that if we factor a broad understanding of professional knowledge, we also have the burden of proposing an organisation of the territory so as to make action possible. And if we favour a more contained approach, we have the burden of showing that what is left out isn't relevant or isn't crucial. This is, as I see it, a new perspective on an old problem. If we agree that the tension of expansion and closure is an essential tension, we can no longer argue that sustainable development is about ecology or economy, about population or the physical city or the social milieu. It is all of these and more, and if we choose one aspect, we have to show how we account for the omission of the others.

Allow me to illustrate with an example. One definition of sustainable agriculture might link it to the production of food to meet needs but without serious harm to the environment. We might say that this calls for a balanced fertiliser policy. Fertiliser increases food supply but it also causes loss of long term soil fertility. So, is that the issue? Should we be seeking a balance between short-term and long-term fertility? Not quite! Fertiliser production is not a clean technology. Phosphate mining for fertiliser production, for instance, causes significant erosion of top soil and negatively affects air quality. In the Aqaba region of Jordan, for instance, which is the home of some of the best deposits of phosphate in the world, air quality is a known casualty of the increase in phosphate production. So, are we being comprehensive if we add air quality in our balancing act? What about pollutants which get transported by wind and other carriers and end up seriously interfering with the hydrological cycle? At least since Rachael Carson's *Silent Spring*, we cannot pretend that the atmospheric transport of contaminants is not a serious environmental and ecological hazard. Add to this the jobs lost by closing down fertiliser plants, and the domain for our balancing act becomes larger and larger. We don't have to belabor the point. The question of balanced fertiliser use is accompanied by several other attendant issues and tensions.

Connecting Ethics with Logic

How are the two logics, the logic of analysis and the logic of implementation, different? To examine this, consider an example of a logically convincing argument from transportation engineering. The traffic signalling system is built on a logic which says that when the light turns amber before a driver is in an intersection the driver must slow down and stop. But this disarmingly simple logic has exactly the opposite effect on many drivers: it prompts drivers to speed so that they might just cross the intersection before the signal turns red. How do we explain this? Why does such a reasonably-sounding logic fail? Traditionally, we have explained such failures of logic by invoking categories like politics, selfishness, greed, or defiance, or in scientific terms, by attributing the problems to NIMBYism, Prisoner's dilemma, or the difficulties in the inter-personal comparison of utilities. The problem, however, is that the meaning of these terms is far from clear. Take 'politics,' for instance. We use it in a 'catch-all' sense; i.e. as a residual category which shows our failure to analyse rather than as a category which displays serious understanding. After all, if politics, greed or defiance is sufficient to ruin the precise calculations of transportation planners, shouldn't transportation planning be researching precisely these themes?

More generally, the logic of argument is described using an inferential rule, such as *modus ponens, modus tollens*, etc., of Aristotelian logic. Inferential rules have two premises, typically a major and minor premise, followed by a conclusion. All cars use fuels; the Volkswagen is a car; *therefore* the Volkswagen uses fuel. In this example, if we accept the major and minor premises we accept the conclusion. But let us ask the obvious: What is the power behind the 'therefore' in the deduction?

For many this power is intuitive and not in need of justification. But epistemology, or the science of knowledge, has worried precisely about such questions so that our knowledge is put on a secure footing. The recognised ways of validation are many but the most popular ones are validation by appealing to our powers of reason, by empirical observation, or by both. But, there is a class of deductions where these methods of validation seem grossly inadequate. And this is the class that concerns us the most.

Consider this example: 1. non-biodegradable material is harmful to the environment; 2. no one wants to harm the environment; 3. therefore, non-biodegradable materials should not be used. This is also an example of a deduction, but it differs significantly from the previous example. One difference might be that the latter is explicitly normative while the former less. Logicians have analysed these kinds of deductions where one premise is explicitly normative. A key finding of their work is that normative deductions presuppose normative premises: i.e. at least one of the premises must be normative for a deduction to be normative (Bochenski 1974). Now, is this true of our example? The conclusion: 'therefore biodegradable materials *should not* be used,' is clearly normative. But is there a normative premise? One can argue that the proposition, 'No one wants to harm the environment,' is a tacitly normative premise: it is not a description of the case but a statement of what should be the case. Or, we might say that it signifies what people intend, not what they do. This would allow us to retain our logical schema. If we exercise this option, we are in effect using the separation between intention and implementation to keep our logic intact while simultaneously developing a contingent explanation for a phenomenon which might not have otherwise fit our schema. In the context of experimental science, the noted philosopher Karl Popper has called such contingent explanations 'auxiliary hypotheses,' which buttress hypotheses which might otherwise fail scrutiny.

Most importantly, however, a separation, such as that between intention and implementation, creates a demand for a theory of ethics. Once we accept that at least one of our premises is normative, the validity of our conclusion is no longer only a matter of logic; it is also a matter of ethics. But the more insidious result is that the demand is for a theory of ethics which is removed from the science of logic! In the last century two attacks on such separations have been made. One comes from Charles Peirce, one of the founders of American Pragmatism. For Peirce logic is the science of ethics. That is to say, the power of 'therefore' in a logical conclusion is derived from ethics; there is no logic without ethics. A second attack on the separation comes from a philosopher and ethicist Hans Jonas (1984). In a perspective not unlike the cognitively demanding ethics we have discussed, Jonas claims that ethics, as we know it, has highlighted intentionality to the exclusion of competence. Arguing that the nature of human action has changed in a technological world, Jonas tells us that all conventional ethics – including the much-celebrated Kantian and Rawlsian imperatives – are developed around volition and intention. In a technologically constrained world, says Jonas, the possibilities of human action have changes so dramatically – we have so much technological power at our finger tips – that an ethics of intentionality is insufficient as a tool which provides normative guidance. Instead, claims Jonas, we need an ethics for an endangered future – where competence and responsibility, not intentionality, occupy the pride of place.

Pragmatism's science of logic or Jonas' ethics for an endangered future can be fruitfully used to separate 'ordinary' ethics from 'professional' ethics. That is to say, while the defensible exercise of volition may be the ethics for a lay person, for a researcher or an advanced professional to be ethical is to practice one's craft with a high degree of knowledge, skill, and responsibility. And in the case of planning or design, the most relevant knowledge is that of the consequences of actions: What is the likely result if we declare some part of the forest as a natural reserve? What will happen if we reduce the budget for the Environment Protection Agency? Would a more integrated European Union provide a better organisational context within which to handle questions regarding the environment? Becoming knowledgeable about these kinds of questions is to be an ethical planner of sustainable development.

A Systemic Theory of Ethics

If Jonas rightly recognises the dangers that technology poses for our environment, he does not pay equal attention to the effects of technology on our educational system and on our cognitive powers; he does not heed Heidegger's warning of the 'flight from thinking.' Evidence of this flight is, however, all around us. Easy access to technological gizmos – a television programme designed for distance learning is an example – is supposed to make learning easy; it makes kids intellectually lazy. Higher education ends up making students so specialised that it breeds a gap between academics and practitioners. Worse, our educational system imposes on us what Andre (1992), writing in the context of medical education, has appropriately termed 'moral blindness.' But, these developments should not come as a complete surprise. After all, as Jacques Ellul warned us so many years ago, technology has an enslaving character about it: be it the technology of the automobile which reduces – and sometimes replaces – the demand for walking, or the technology of computation which focuses attention on data processing to the exclusion of fundamental questions about our subject-matter. Jonas is right, but only partially so. We need – as he points out – imperatives of responsibility for an endangered species; but we also need the cognitive wherewithal to treat our problems systemically.

Seen this way, ethics has three simultaneous roles to perform, and each role demands a particular kind of knowledge. *First*, in the tradition of Kant and Rawls, a plan is ethical only if the volition associated with its action is also associated with the exercise of 'duty' or 'good-will' by a planner or a group of planners. This understanding of ethics may be said to demand deontological knowledge; i.e. knowledge of the world as it ought to be. Preparation for such a task demands what

Jon Elster (1983) has called 'character planning,' rather than formal intellectual training. *Second* – and this is the cognitively demanding ethics that comes from pragmatism – an ethical sustainable development plan must not only contain a proposal for action but it must also include an explicit prediction of its short-term and the long-term consequences. The knowledge demanded here is predictive: it involves the tracing of 'what-ifs' on a long time horizon. To train ethical planners in this tradition would be to teach them to understand the social effects of technology, its risks, and its potentials. *Third*, ethics should become the bearer of a systemic meaning. That is to say, the measure of performance of sustainable plan may include aspects outside its immediate vicinity and may extend far into the future.

The consequence of systemic ethics is that we can no longer treat tunnel vision and compartmentalisation as just academic oversights; they are moral failings and bring with them all the sanctions that a confident morality can impose. The cognitive demands of systemic ethics are high: empathy and the ability to link seemingly disparate areas of inquiry; to think relationally; and to act in a way that overcomes the tendency to fragment, are demanded equally. Unlike methodologies which are dependent on the analytic tradition of inquiry – hypotheses testing is an example – systems approaches do not buy into the premise that knowledge grows by partitioning the planning domain such that fine-grained and insightful propositions can be asserted with confidence about smaller and smaller segments of the domain. Systems approaches oppose this and call instead for an inquiry where similarities are valued over differences and purpose is valued over method (Verma 1993 and 1996). A systemic ethics as proposed here, however, differs from traditional systems approaches by tying its justification to ethics rather than to pure epistemology. It is not content to merely propose an integrative methodology; it is concerned with how such a methodology might be implemented. To this end, it takes an instrumental view of ethics and uses the power of moral and ethical argument to cut through the psychological, political, and ideological forces that come in the way of implementation.

References

Andre, J. (1992), 'Learning to See – Moral Growth during Medical Training', *Journal of Medical Ethics* 18:3, 148-152.

Bochenski, J.M. (1974), *Was Ist Authoritat? Einfuhrung in die Logik der Authoritat* (Freiburg, Germany: Herderbucherei).

Calthorpe, P. (1986), 'The Urban Context', in Sim Van der Ryn and Peter Calthorpe (eds).

Churchman, C.W. (1994), 'What is Philosophy of Science?', *Philosophy of Science* 61:1, 132-141.

Elster, J. (1983), *Sour Grapes* (Cambridge, UK: Cambridge University Press).

Heidegger, M. (1966), *Discourse on Thinking*, translated by John M. Anderson and E. Hans Freund (New York: Harper and Row).

Jonas, H. (1984), *The Imperative of Responsibility* (Chicago: The University of Chicago Press).

Krutilla, J.V. (1967), 'Conservation Reconsidered', *The American Economic Review* 57:4, 777-786.

Rittel, H.W.I. and Webber, M. (1973), 'Dilemmas in a General Theory in Planning', *Policy Sciences* 4:2, 155-69.

Van der Ryn, S. and Calthorpe, P. (eds) (1986), *Sustainable Communities: A New Design Synthesis for Cities, Suburbs and Towns* (San Francisco: Sierra Club Books).

Verma, N. (1993), 'Metaphor and Analogy as Elements of a Theory of Similarity for Planning', *Journal of Planning Education and Research* 13:1, 13-25.

Verma, N. (1995), 'What is Planning Practice? The Search for Suitable Categories', *Journal of Planning Education and Research* 14:3, 178-182.

Verma, N. (1996), 'Pragmatic Rationality and Planning Theory', *Journal of Planning Education and Research* 16:1, 5-14. Translated into Italian by F.D. Moccia and reprinted (1996) as 'Rivisitare la razionalità: una teoria pragmatica della pianificazione', *CRU.Critica della razionalità urbanistica*, 5, 65-75.

Verma, N. (1998), *Similarities, Connections, and Systems: The Search for a New Rationality for Planning and Management* (Lanham, MD: Lexington Books).

PART II
Institutional Contexts and Constraints

Chapter 5

Planning Research, Ethical Conduct and Radical Politics

Kanishka Goonewardena

Wrong life cannot be lived rightly.

Theodor Adorno (1978/1951, 39)

Questions concerning ethics in planning research confront me routinely nowadays, when students request my signature on their 'ethics review' forms now required by our university for studies involving 'human subjects'. I have to confess that we – my students and I – have had mixed feelings about the institutionalisation of ethics in this way. Such feelings spring spontaneously not out of some postmodern nihilism; on the contrary, the worry for us is precisely the inability of ethics to be ethical. Yes, I can certainly see the moral import of considering the welfare of would-be human subjects in the very design of research. The first chapter of Naomi Klein's *The Shock Doctrine*, where she recounts the horrors of Dr. Ewen Cameron's CIA-funded experiments on shock therapy conducted at the University of Montreal in the 1950s, is sufficient to convince any skeptic of the need for subjecting what we call research to guidelines minimally capable of avoiding the reduction of the human to the animal and the object (Klein 2007, 23-55). Some may in this context even argue for the rights of not only animals but also objects – as did Walter Benjamin (1999) in the *Arcades Project*. Yet the same book – which suggests a shocking link between nefarious scientific experiments with humans and the politico-ideological genesis of neoliberalism – also points to the limits of such guidelines, at least in their typically existing form: that is to say, the *inadequacy* of ethics.

The bureaucratic zeal of the ethics questionnaires in question is the least of my complaints here, even if it seems symptomatic of deeper problems. When students vent their frustrations about the ethics questions they have to address, I sometimes remind them that they were in the first place drafted mostly with bio-medical researchers in mind, not so much progressive planners and critical theorists like themselves – or, for that matter, pharmaceutical companies. And I agree with them that their lingua franca betrays less a concern with anything as substantive as the cultural-politics of research methods; but more a will to avoid lawsuits. I have on occasion urged the disgruntled student to regard this exercise as a necessary formality, and hold their fire for adversaries more worthwhile than ethics review committees. For my part, I continue to be struck by the gap between our expectations of such ethical processes and what they can actually accomplish. The simple question that detains me here is this: what can we do by means of such protocols of ethics and what can we not do by means of such protocols of ethics? And how is the distinction between the two dictated by the wider world of socio-spatial relations within which planners and academics of various descriptions do their work? If the University of Montreal had a meaningful ethics review committee in the early 1950s, then surely Dr. Cameron's shocking experiments for the CIA would have been prevented. Yet the most basic question posed by this exemplary case for progressive planners is this: how could we have prevented the onslaught of neoliberalism with recourse to ethics?

It is when we are planning in the face of such powers as neoliberalism that our familiar ethical standards and protocols – in research as much as practice, as both are increasingly professionalised and corporatised – leave much to be desired. Or they do worse. By drastically narrowing the scope of the questions to be addressed, while stamping on them the 'economic-corporate' (Gramsci 1971) form assumed by planning firms and entrepreneurial universities as much as the omnipotent figure of the 'client', actually existing ethics in effect leave open the fundamental political challenges confronting urban planners largely to the laws of the concrete jungle of real estate development. The niches of ethics so carved out of the broader socio-political structure, amenable by design to rigorous policing in academic and professional worlds, in turn interpellate a peculiarly ethico-political subject engaged in planning research and practice – one who knows how not to cheat, and be loyal to the client, the clan, and the university, especially when these mutually beneficial alliances clash with even liberal definitions of the public good, let alone radical ideas of justice.[1] Is this not the well-groomed subject we routinely encounter in boardrooms corporate and academic? Is this not the resourceful subject who arranges the marriage between real estate capital and the ever more entrepreneurial university in the 'creative city', presiding over what now goes on in the education of planners?

Intending to be polemical but not pessimistic, I want to note right away that from a radical political standpoint there exists much of value in the diverse endeavours of planning schools today, and a lot of that in spite of the commonplace conceptions of ethics. For the effective limitation of such ethics largely to the concerns of clients and corporations, and the concomitant exemption from its scope of the political questions that really matter in social struggles over planning, results in a typically overblown assessment of the little that is left in it. The exaggerated import of ethics so restricted provides for our ethico-political subject of planning a useful

---

1   Here I must thank Stefan Kipfer for reminding me that planners define the public good variously, and that a sizeable liberal as well as a neoliberal tradition sees it more or less as the aggregate outcome of rational individual choices. In much of such thought, we find no tension between the ideal and the real to mount an immanent critique; rather, ethical doctrines of this neo/liberal sort amount to little more than justifications of the *status quo*, by collapsing norms unto facts and vice-versa.

moral shield – to be wielded against any perspective on planning that may reveal the gap between his liberal-humanist values and economic-corporate interests. It is no secret that he may fully be ethical, professionally and academically, while being involved with a resilient conscience in all kinds of dubious planning – gentrification, international development, even 'urbicide'. In every institutional formulation of planning ethics that I have seen – professional codes of conduct, ethical guidelines for research, and so on – the systemic contradictions that define the nature of political struggles over planning issues are avoided like the plague. Yet they inevitably raise their persistent heads, in the form of eminently practical dilemmas built into these ethical codes.

From the standpoint of research in planning, challenges facing ethics may be even more intractable, given the increasingly intimate embrace between universities and corporations. For as universities become more and more dependent on corporate funding for research, and corporations continue to exploit public funds still granted to universities for their own research and development endeavours, the profit motive asserts itself over the public good. 'We are all "entrepreneurial" academics now and few more so than planners', writes Huw Thomas in a perceptive survey of British planning education – suggesting that the trends of corporatisation we are witnessing are transatlantic, if not more global (Thomas 2005, 239). In this regard, my own institution provides an exemplary case involving Dr. Nancy Olivieri, a University of Toronto haematologist employed concurrently by the affiliated Hospital for Sick Children in Toronto, who discovered adverse side-effects in a drug she was studying during the course of industry-sponsored clinical trials with patients suffering from thalassemia – a potentially fatal blood disease (Thompson et al. 2005). But Apotex, the pharmaceutical company that sponsored this research, responded to Dr. Olivieri's findings in 1996 by promptly terminating their funding and threatening her with legal action should she make them public. The disclosure of research in this case was subject to the discretion of the sponsor – according to the contract entered by Apotex and Dr. Olivieri, who admitted with hindsight her error of judgement in signing it. Notwithstanding her compromised legal situation, however, Dr. Olivieri informed the patients involved of the risks associated with the drug-on-trial and published her research in a leading scientific journal in 1998 – at which point she became the target of smearing attacks by Apotex, the Hospital Board of Trustees and a few individuals attempting to publicly discredit her, even calling into question her medical practice license and academic credentials. According to the authors of an independent inquiry into this case commissioned by the Canadian Association of University Teachers (CAUT), 'the University [of Toronto] publicly acknowledged an obligation to defend her academic freedom, yet provided no effective support to her until more than two and a half years after Apotex first issued legal warnings to her'(Thompson et al. 2005). And they also note that 'in 1998, when the Olivieri case became public, the University and Apotex had reached agreement in principle to what would then have been the largest donation ever received by the University – $20 million for the university and an additional $10 million for affiliated hospitals' (Thompson et al. 2005).

This instructive story ends with some justice for Dr. Olivieri, who was completely vindicated on the basis of several independent inquiries. In 2002 she reached a mediated settlement with redress from the University and the Hospital over her grievances against unfair treatment – thanks in no small measure to the advocacy of CAUT, the University of Toronto Faculty Association (UTFA) and the two leading authorities in the world on thalassemia. In tandem with these proceedings, Dr. Gideon Koren, an award-winning professor at the University of Toronto and a pioneering researcher at the Hospital for Sick Children, was reprimanded in 2000 by the University and the Hospital for providing false testimony against Dr. Olivieri; and by the University again in 2002 for 'research misconduct in connection with an article he published favourable to Apotex's drug', before being publicly disciplined in 2003 by the College of Physicians and Surgeons of Ontario (CPSO) for professional misconduct (Thompson et al. 2005). The Olivieri case also led to a progressive revision of the policy on industry-sponsored research held by the University of Toronto and affiliated teaching hospitals. In addition, recommendations made in the CAUT report on this case were taken up by the three Canadian government research granting councils – SSHRC (Social Science and Humanities Research Council), NSERC (Natural Sciences and Engineering Research Council), CCA (Canada Council for the Arts) – in the drafting of their *Tri-Council Policy Statement: Ethical Conduct of Research Involving Human Subjects*. Such silver linings around the clouds of commodification gathering over academic research suggest that progress remains a limited possibility within the realm of ethical codes regulating university research, by means of which progressive academics may fight to safeguard academic freedom and even promote a progressive conception of the public interest.

Yet it would be a mistake to consider the Olivieri case – which inspired John Le Carre's *The Constant Gardener* – to be 'Canada's worst research and academic scandal in decades', as conservative correspondent Margaret Wente put it in the op-ed page of *Globe and Mail*.[2] For seeing it that way as an exceptional case places the blame on a few proverbial bad apples, diverting attention away from the more systemic forces at play in this ethical debacle. Recounting it in 2005, the authors of the CAUT report quoted earlier note that 'although the case itself has led to settlements, the problems it illustrates have not yet been satisfactorily resolved across the country or elsewhere'. And they urge us to understand their context in broad but precise terms: 'the changing international political economy of the past quarter century; the rapid growth of the pharmaceutical industry; the deteriorating financial circumstances of universities and hospitals; the failure of government agencies and universities to revise their research policies and address these new circumstances'. In a nutshell, 'the general background for events of the case is the neo-conservative political economy that became dominant from the 1980s onward, first in the US and UK and then in much of the rest of the world...'. Arguably less egregious but no less profound manifestations of more or less the

---

2   Wente (1999); see also Forsdyke (2005/2006).

same ensemble of contextual forces have been observed in planning schools. Their form and content in North America have not been immune from especially the real estate development industry and its affiliates in the world of planning consulting – from which flows the greatest share of private funds into planning education (in the form of research grants, scholarships and subsidised adjunct professors), and which also provides employment to the greatest number of planning graduates. On a more global terrain, one cannot here ignore the role played in 'international development' by especially the leading planning schools in the US – which routinely supply the influential cadres of organic intellectuals of neoliberalism to the World Bank, IMF and WTO. The latter rank among the most generous sponsors of much planning research instrumental in the terrors documented in Klein (2007), and continue to offer some of the most lucrative career paths for planners both academic and professional. As planning ethics travel back and forth through such swiftly revolving doors between powerful corporations, high offices of global governance and enterprising universities, what kind of justice can we expect them to accomplish?

In a pioneering paper on professional ethics in planning, Peter Marcuse suggested over three decades ago that the *contradictions* we routinely find in them derive from our doomed 'effort ethically to fulfil unethical tasks'.[3] It is a pity that this crucial insight, in arguably the most profound sentence on planning ethics ever written, has been all but ignored in the subsequent scholarly literature on the topic, contributions to which often begin with ritual parenthetical-citational homage to its author. Unlike much recent writing on planning ethics, Marcuse (1985/1976) did not concern himself overmuch with arcane moral philosophy, an ageing small branch of western thought well known for its endless search for the good life in abstraction from real life. His argument ran rather in exactly the opposite direction – away from the abstracted insularities of ethical discourse, through the telling contradictions of ethical codes of conduct, towards a critique of professional planning ethics. Beginning with five quasi-fictional case studies, he proved beyond doubt that in the real world of planning there exists no harmony between the demands of the public, the client, the employer and the profession, so long as planning remains a social praxis grounded in a world of antagonistic social relations, even if a small but vital portion of what counts as planning – radical planning – has as its objective the overcoming of these oppressive social antagonisms. Without dismissing entirely the honourable intentions of interventions in planning by ethical means, Marcuse (1985/1976) then offered a decisive judgement on the political function of codes of conduct in planning, from a radical political standpoint that made the case not for getting more and more abstracted in moral philosophy, but for going 'beyond professional ethics' to address the social origins of what I should like to call *ethical injustices*, that

---

3   Marcuse (1985/1976, 17). This article was originally published in the *Journal of the American Institute of Planners* 42.3, July 1976, 264-274. For an overview of the literature on ethics in planning, see also Hendler (1995) and Howe (1994).

is, injustices that are consistent with if not resultant from the proper observation of ethical standards of professional planning. Precisely what is obfuscated by the disproportionate amount of attention demanded – and commanded – by the latter informed his lucid conclusion of this chapter, which brought us back to the most fundamental question concerning the practice of planning, namely, the nature of its relationship to the social order: 'Planning in most jobs today is in practice clearly a system-maintaining activity', he noted, underlining that '[p]rofessional ethics facilitate that activity' (Marcuse 1985/1976, 19). His punch-line is clear: planning ethics acts in the final analysis as a support rather than a critique of the system.

Now, we can find in the world of planning a distinction to be made between professional practice and academic research. The peculiarities of each generate their own challenges for ethical thought in general, and attempts to draft codes of conduct in particular. Yet the lessons to be drawn from the Olivieri case and the questions posed by Marcuse (1985/1976) here suggest that there are also problems shared by both professionals and academics attempting to be ethical. To the extent that their origins are social, they cannot be resolved within the abstracted scope of ethical codes. Here we confront therefore the untranscendable gap between the realm of ethics as constituted by their institutional codifications and the realm of the social that is the testing terrain of radical politics. If the greatest merit of Marcuse's (1985/1976) original intervention on planning ethics has been the revelation of this disjuncture, then it must be a matter of prime import for critical minds in the field to ask how is it that we manage to live and die in this no man's land between the ethical and the social. In fact, he calls for precisely such an inquiry by locating our attempts to define planning practice as a *professional* practice rather than a *political* practice at the heart of the most intractable ethical dilemmas. Indeed, what does it mean for the self-consciousness of planning to be that of a profession rather than of a politics? And what are the political consequences of planning being conceived above all as a profession?

A useful political and historical perspective on these questions comes to us from Hegel's *Philosophy of Right* (1991/1821), the greatest attempt to address the contradictions of capitalist modernity before Marx. In this work, which is symptomatically absent from the discourse of ethics in the field of planning, Hegel develops his celebrated concept of *ethical life* (*Sittlichkeit*) as the actualisation of freedom in a rational organisation of society at the levels of family, civil society and state. While civil servants of the state assume the leading role in this system of ethics, the urban trades and professions also play a vital role in it. Hegel calls these *corporations*, that is, professional associations or guilds recognised by the state (Hegel 1991/1821). As they are rooted in the productive activity of civil society, which is understood by him as the level of the social that is essentially constituted and conditioned by the capitalist economy, he charges them especially with the responsibility of overcoming the systematic contradictions of market society: above all, its inherent tendency to produce extremes of wealth and poverty, by virtue of the competitive and atomising behaviour that drives it. *Philosophy of Right* is often credited, and rightly so, for ascribing to the state the duty of *policing* civil society, 'from which on the whole', says Hegel, 'poverty arises necessarily' (Wood 1991, xxi); less frequently acknowledged are the specific tasks he assigned to corporations in this context. According to Allen Wood's excellent editorial introduction to Hegel:

> Hegel...calls for the organization of civil society into 'corporations'...A corporation provides its members with a collective responsibility and aim within civil society: to look after the special business of their profession, to train new people to work in it, and to set standards for the work it does. Corporations also look after their own interests, providing assistance to members who are out of work...In Hegel's state...corporations are also the chief vehicles of popular political representation...Above all, corporation membership provides individuals with a sense of concrete social identity (Wood 1991, xix-xx).

Just as the meaning of corporation has changed between Hegel's time and ours, so has the practice of professional ethics. To wit: *Philosophy of Right* (§238-241) explains clearly the intent of the above-mentioned prescriptions – which is to ensure that the otherwise self-interested economic activity of civil society is channelled through professional associations into forms of self-fulfilling labour capable of serving the interests of society as a whole. And the premise of this intent is an equally clear recognition – of the fact that 'poverty in civil society is not an accident, or a misfortune or the result of human error or vice', but an essential aspect of it (Wood 1991, xxi). It is Hegel's solution to the latter problem by means of a 'rational system of social institutions' (Wood 1991, xii) that bears the name of ethical life, which involves a subsumption of the (limited and particular) rationalities of family and civil society into the (higher and universal) rationality of the state. The mediation of corporations in Hegel's ethical life therefore cannot be conceived apart from the crisis tendencies of civil society; indeed, the former's *raison d'être* is none other than reformatting the latter's structural dynamics, and with them, the totality of society. In Hegel's *Philosophy of Right* there exists no ethics of corporations that is not fully aligned with the ethics of a society worthy of actualising freedom.

One searches in vain, however, for such an articulation of the rationality (or ethicality) of the profession with the rationality (or ethicality) of the social totality in contemporary conceptions of ethics, whether in planning theory or practice. To measure the distance between Hegel and us on this issue, Marcuse (1985/1976) is again helpful. For he demonstrates how the range and depth of ethical tasks prescribed for corporations by Hegel – from those directed towards society at large to those focused on 'their own interests' – has been effectively narrowed and watered down in our professional codes of conduct to guild loyalty.

> Guild loyalty includes two types of ethical obligations assumed by professionals: one to fellow professionals, the other to the profession as a corporate body. The obligations to fellow professionals produces the bulk of the rules of

discipline...[of APA, CIP, etc.]: 'thou shalt not advertise', 'thou shalt not steal thy fellow's client', 'thou shalt not cut thy fees', and so on. [...] To a minor extent these may be justified as contributing to a strong profession better able to fulfill its social role, but primarily they are traditional guild-type rules primarily benefitting members of the profession...[H]istorically they stem from that guild membership which lies at the root of what constitutes a profession...They have been the most carefully explicated and vigorously enforced of all the canons of ethics (Marcuse 1985/1976, 12).

Which is not to say that professional codes of conduct of our time do not wax eloquent on the ethics of 'collective responsibility'. To be sure, they do a lot of that; but with rules that can hardly be enforced, and with words rarely backed up by deeds. It is too easy to note how much incredulity is inspired by these feeble dissertations on the public good replete with ubiquitous moral platitudes; but more important to think through the form of their essential contradictions, which Marcuse was the first to pinpoint. (Re)reading him in the light of Hegel and Marx, we cannot help but note how our veritable 'moral dilemmas' are nothing more nor less than the products of social relations underlying planning; and that so long as their contradictions and attendant political struggles provide the untranscendable horizon of liberal as much as neoliberal planning, no attempt to reformulate ethical codes in and of themselves can overcome their expressive inconsistencies. This much must be evident from Hegel and Marx. For Hegel's *Philosophy of Right* is nothing if not a radical response to the contradictions of civil society that attempts – ultimately unsuccessfully, as Marx's (1975/1843, 57-198) earliest writings argued – to overcome them in an ethical life. And historical materialism is nothing if not the realisation that real contradictions cannot be resolved in theory. Has planning theory responded to its ethical dilemmas, then, by rushing to deal with their social origins? Not al all. Neither Hegel nor Marx has been invited to stroll through the popular avenues of ethical discourse in planning. Instead, a motley crew of 'moral theorists' has cleared the rubble of social struggles off these pseudo-philosophical streets, paving the way for the eviction of politics by ethics.

The prime formal feature of the resultant discourse of ethics can therefore be named in a word as *pastoral*.[4] For although much of liberal planning theory betrays an acquired taste for ethical *dilemmas* formulated at various levels of abstraction from society, it has no stomach for their real basis in social and spatial *contradictions*. Notwithstanding appearances to the contrary, more than a mere resemblance exists between the abstract-formalism of such ethical thought and the technocratic nature of what used to be called 'rational-comprehensive planning'. As exemplars of the modern pastoral, both demand a habitus of *harmony*, guaranteed by the logic of analytic philosophy in one case, instrumental

---

4   For a suggestive account of the modern pastoral as defined by the absence of contradictions, see Hilde Heynen (1999, 13-14). The classic accounts are Leo Marx (1964) and William Empson (1974).

reason in the other; and both betray the perils of *limited* – abstracted – (ab)uses of reason, but not of reason *per se*. The lazy dismissal of 'rational comprehensive planning' by post-modern planning theory as yet another oppressive manifestation of occidental reason thus misses the point. More pertinent would be to critique it as a particular manifestation of not modernity as such, but the best modern example of pastoral ideology – the ideology of modernisation.[5] For conceptions of science and technology devoid of social content or historical context play the impossible role of legitimation in this discourse that is undertaken by notions of 'virtue' and 'good' in similarly cocooned ethical thought. The recent popularity of the idea of 'conflict resolution' in planning offers yet another example of this tendency to insulate the basic challenges confronting our field of practice from fundamental social antagonisms – in advancing the myth that conflicts in planning can indeed be resolved by learning the proper techniques from the relevant authorities, rather than by reformatting the social conditions that in the first place produce such 'dilemmas'. True, game theory as much as Jürgen Habermas can be useful to combatants on all sides engaged in this or that conflict to negotiate the best possible outcome from one's own standpoint under the given circumstances. But a radical approach to planning intends exactly to change those circumstances, a task not so much of ethics as politics.

We have come a long way from Aristotle, who believed that human beings can be virtuous only in community with others, and so tied ethics to politics – albeit with an ahistorical conception of human nature. The current non-relation between ethics and politics follows the modern opposition between value and fact, 'ought' and 'is' – which is symptomatically theorised in David Hume and especially Immanuel Kant, but produced in the first and last instance by bourgeois society.[6] Given the centrality accorded to a radical conception of freedom and equality in his thought, Kant has of course inspired generations of revolutionaries, including Marxists, but also countless defenders of capitalism and liberalism, for whom he provides a no less uplifting way of being moral without having to change the world. Although himself a progressive on some political issues, Kant's radical disjunction between value and fact prevented him from securing a social basis for his admirable ethical ideals. It is the fact that much the same could be said about many an attempt to propose some kind of ethics for planners in the wake of Marcuse's paper that makes the thought of Hegel and Marx in this regard especially noteworthy. As Paul Blackledge writes in his incisive essay, 'Marxism and Ethics':

> Developing…[an] ethics that goes beyond the limits of liberalism by drawing together individual and social conceptions of the good requires that we indicate some socially and historically specific practices through which non-egoistic forms of human relations might emerge. It was Hegel who first pointed towards

---

5 For a brief but pungent review of modernisation theory and its contemporaneity in imperialist ideology, see Harry Harootunian (2004).

6 See the founding text of Western Marxism by Georg Lukács (1971/1968, 121-149).

a solution to this dilemma by suggesting a historical model of human nature...
[His] great contribution to moral theory started from a historical comparison
of...[the classical and modern] contexts [of Aristotle and of Kant]: asking how
and why we (or more precisely Germans at the turn of the 19th century) are
different from ancient Greeks. By doing this he began a process, later completed
by Marx, of synthesizing and overcoming the limitations of both Kantian
morality and Aristotelian ethics.[7]

If the originality of Hegel and Marx here lies in *historicising* and *socialising*
ethical questions in order to render them irrevocably political, then the current
world-historical conjuncture of planning explains the apparent disjuncture we
are presented with in our own field and beyond between ethics and politics. For
we are still suffering from the consequences of the 'end of history' proclaimed by
Francis Fukuyama, unable to imagine systemic alternatives to liberal capitalism,
even if we are routinely urged to do so by the punctuality of global economic
crises and imperialist wars.[8] The 'end of history' in this sense represents not
only the end of politics as Hegel or Marx conceived it; it also marks at the
same time the *re*birth and re-entry of ethics, alongside the revived bourgeois
categories of civil society and democracy, with primary reference to difference
and human rights, into the spaces of our radical political consciousness vacated
by socialism.[9] After the displacement of politics by ethics, we have every reason
to be ever more vigilant about both professional practice and academic research
in planning, not least because of the extent to which the former is now dictating
the latter under the auspices of capital. The profession is required by its own
codes of ethics to educate future planners – to serve the 'public' interest, which
is increasingly subject to the interests of planning firms operating in the world
of 'private' practice, serving clients bureaucratic and corporate. And this they
do, not only by playing a considerable role as adjunct professors in planning
schools, but also by contributing to the public dialogue on planning. Much of
what I over-hear from professionals of planning discoursing on What Is To Be
Done in my own city reminds me of GM President Charles Erwin Wilson's
legendary testimony to the US Senate Armed Services Commission before being
confirmed as President Eisenhower's Secretary of Defense: 'For years I thought

---

7   Blackledge (2008). This lucid account benefits from the early Marxist writings of
Alasdair MacIntyre – who also wrote one of the best introductions to ethics: *A Short History
of Ethics*. See MacIntyre (1966).

8   On the concept of 'end of history', see the magisterial survey by Perry Anderson
(1992, 279-375).

9   For a devastating critique of the 'ethical turn' in contemporary theory, see Alain
Badiou (2002/1998). This work also includes his formulation of an alternative 'ethics of
truths', an explication of which lies beyond the scope of my means on this occasion. I
thank Andrew Shmuely for helpful discussions on this and other issues that have informed
this chapter.

that what was good for our country was good for General Motors, and vice versa'. Can what is good for Toronto not be what is good for its top planning firms and consultants, and vice-versa?

What about research in this context? Unsurprisingly, planning research serves planning practice: in fact, much of it occurs not in universities but planning firms too firmly immersed in what they do in order to obtain some critical distance from their vocation and location; and even the research undertaken by university faculty tends to follow the same trend to serve practice. Day-to-day exigencies – in the form of research grants, consulting opportunities, various demands for so-called 'excellence', etc. – rule over the more qualitative need to step back and ask basic questions about the aims of research in the university and reflect on the rationale for academic freedom. Theodor Adorno was fond of noting that the critical value of art lay in its autonomy and uselessness; whereas practical thought invested in reality risks sinking to the level of its object: 'economics is no joke, and merely to understand it one has to "think economically"' (Adorno 1978/1951, 132). The Olivieri case serves as an illustration for us of the pressures brought onto academic research by the thought of capital. And if ethical planners think that our virtuous discipline is somehow immune to such vices rampant in the fields ruled by the pharmaceutical industry, then they ought to read a warning sounded by Marx to his German readers in the preface to *Das Kapital*:

> What I have to examine in this work is the capitalist mode of production, and the relations of production and the forms of intercourse that correspond to it. Until now, their *locus classicus* has been England. This is the reason why England is used as the main illustration of the theoretical developments I make. If, however, the German reader pharisaically shrugs his shoulders at the condition of the English industrial and agricultural workers, or optimistically comforts himself with the thought that in Germany things are not nearly so bad, I must plainly tell him: *De te fabula narratur!*[10]

From my fifth-floor University of Toronto office facing the southern sun, I enjoy a fine view of the embourgeoisment of downtown Toronto. Halfway between its towers of finance capital surrounded by glittering new condos and myself is a cluster of buildings belonging to the medical sciences and hospitals affiliated to the university – the very site of the Olivieri case. Among them lies also the $120 million Martin Prosperity Institute of the Rotman School of Management – whose director holds a cross-appointment in my own Program in Planning and calls himself the 'World's leading public intellectual' on his own website. A recent article in *Globe and Mail* on 'academic rock stars' quoted this compulsively celebrated colleague of mine, Richard Florida, on the irresistible 'need in this world for public intellectuals' – which explains according to him why in less than twenty years 'star professors are going to be making a seven-figure salary' (quoted

---

10   'This tale is told of you!' See Marx (1976/1867, 90).

in Allemang 2008, F1). I begin to wonder: when planning professors start making ten million dollars, who might really afford to have them on their payroll? Looking out from my window, they are not too hard to see.

References

Adorno, T. (1978/1951), *Minima Moralia: Reflections from Damaged Life*, trans. E.F.N. Jephcott (London and New York: Verso).

Allemang, J. (2008), 'Academic Glam: Meet Professor Ziggy, Chair of Stardust', *Globe and Mail*, 2 February.

Anderson, P. (1992), 'The Ends of History' in *A Zone of Engagement* (London and New York: Verso).

Badiou, A. (2002/1998), *Ethics: An Essay on the Understanding of Evil*, trans. P. Hallward (London and New York: Verso).

Benjamin, W. (1999), *The Arcades Project*, ed. R. Tiedemann, trans. H. Eiland and K. McLaughlin (Cambridge, MA: Harvard University of Press).

Blackledge, P. (2008), 'Marxism and Ethics', *International Socialism* 120 <www.isj.org.uk> accessed 10 October 2008.

Empson, W. (1974), *Some Versions of the Pastoral* (New York: New Directions).

Forsdyke, D. (2005/2006), 'L'affaire Olivieri' <http://post.queensu.ca/~forsdyke/peerrev5.htm> accessed 10 October 2008.

Gramsci, A. (1971), *Selections from the Prison Notebooks*, ed., trans. and intro. Q. Hoare and G.N. Smith (New York: International Publishers).

Harootunian, H. (2004), *The Empire's New Clothes: Paradigm Lost, and Regained* (Chicago: Prickly Paradigm Press).

Hegel, G.W.F. (1991/1821), *Elements of the Philosophy of Right*, ed. and intro. A. Wood, trans. H.B. Nisbet (Cambridge: Cambridge University Press).

Hendler, S. (ed.) (1995), *Planning Ethics: A Reader in Planning Theory, Practice and Education* (New Brunswick: NJ: Centre for Urban Policy Research).

Heynen, H. (1999), *Architecture and Modernity: A Critique* (Cambridge, MA: The MIT Press).

Howe, E. (1994), *Acting on Ethics in City Planning* (New Brunswick: NJ: Centre for Urban Policy Research).

Klein, N. (2007), *The Shock Doctrine: The Rise of Disaster Capitalism* (Toronto: Random House Canada).

Lukács, G. (1971/1968), *History and Class Consciousness: Studies in Marxist Dialectics*, trans. R. Livingston (Cambridge, MA: The MIT Press).

MacIntyre, A. (1966), *A Short History of Ethics* (London: Routledge).

Marcuse, P. (1985/1976), 'Professional Ethics and Beyond: Values in Planning' in Martin Wachs (ed.).

Marx, K. (1975/1843), 'Critique of Hegel's Doctrine of the State' [1843] in *Early Writings*, ed. L. Colletti (London: Penguin).

Marx, K. (1976/1867), *Capital: A Critique of Political Economy*, vol. 1, intro. E. Mandel, trans. B. Fowkes (London: Penguin/New Left Review).

Marx, L. (1964), *The Machine in the Garden* (Oxford: Oxford University Press).

Thomas, H. (2005), 'Pressures, Purpose and Collegiality in UK Planning Education', *Planning Theory and Practice* 6:2, 238-247.

Thompson, J., Baird, P.A. and Downie, J. (2005), 'The Olivieri Case: Context and Significance', *Eclectica* <http://www.ecclectica.ca/issues/2005/3/index.asp?Article=2#_ednref17> accessed 10 October 2008.

Wachs, M. (ed.) (1985), *Ethics in Planning* (New Brunswick: NJ: Centre for Urban Policy Research).

Wente, M. (1999), 'Medicine, Morals and Money', *Globe and Mail*, 23 December.

Wood, A. (1991), 'Editor's Introduction' in Georg W.F. Hegel.

Chapter 6
The Knowledge Business in Academic Planning Research

Rob Imrie

...of resisting...the course
of the world, which continues
to hold a pistol to the head of
human beings.

Adorno (1992, 79-80)

Introduction

Adorno's (1992) observation can be related to contemporary social and political contexts in which the production of knowledge, and its dissemination, appears to be increasingly tied into universities serving the interests of corporate, business, government, and policy interests (see also, Bourdieu 1990 and 1998; Clark 1986 and 1998). For Adorno, the emergent feature of the academe in the 20th century was the creeping corporatisation of knowledge, and the cooption and capture of systems of knowledge production by vested, usually private, interests. By the early part of this century, such was the scale and pace of change in the academe that a mini industry of writings had emerged, seeking to understand what Ylijoki (2003, 308) describes as the decline of the public university, and the alleged replacement of 'the traditional mode of academic research' with 'a new post academic culture' (see also, Allen and Imrie 2010; Clark 1986, 1987 and 1998; Deem 2001; Reay 2004; Rhoades and Slaughter 2004; Slaughter and Laslie 1997).

The shift from traditional to post academic modes of teaching and research has been described as a subsumption of universities to market activity, and the acquisition of behaviour not dissimilar to that found in private sector business organisations (Slaughter and Laslie 1997). A key feature is universities' search for external funds to plug funding gaps brought about by partial state withdrawal from financial support of higher education. This is leading to increasing reliance by universities on contracts with a range of government and business sponsors as key to fiscal propriety. A consequence is the internal restructuring of the academe as part of its objective to develop its resource base, with much more emphasis on 'selling the university' by adopting market-like behaviour. A feature is use of mission statements and branding by university managers, and the development of products to increase markets, including new degree programmes and flexible forms of course delivery to capture a broad student base.

Such changes proceed hand in hand with government directives that require universities, as a condition of continued state funding, to demonstrate the usefulness and utility of their teaching, and to orientate what they deliver towards the requirements of the customer (or consumer). Knowledge is to be packaged and parcelled in bundles or subject to modularised forms that provide, ideally, a one-to-one correspondence with what is required in the labour market. A consequence is that teaching form and content is, allegedly, more prescribed than hitherto, and its delivery is subject to closer monitoring and checks to ensure that there is a fit with the customer's requirements (see Allen and Imrie 2010; Deem 2001; Worthington and Hodgson 2005). A new stratum of university administration is overseeing such processes, and providing the requisite delivery mechanisms and modes of discipline to ensure that the academe conforms to the structures of the customer focus (Deem 2001).

The reorientation of teaching, and its policing by a new set of administrative and disciplinary procedures, is part of a broader utilitarian turn in the academe. It is particularly pronounced in relation to the conduct of research, and a context whereby university staff are exhorted by government ministers to make their research relevant to the needs of society. Relevance is usually defined in relation to orientating the universities towards solving the major practical and policy concerns of the day, and enabling the alleged gaps between the academe and wider society to be bridged through knowledge transfer, and other, activities. Part of the changing context is an onus on the academe developing closer ties with business, third sector organisations, and government, with a view to contributing to economic development and betterment. David Sweeney, the research director of the Higher Education Funding Council for England, has recently restated this message, by noting that the universities need to contribute to 'the things that benefit the economy and society in the widest sense' (quoted in Lipsett 2008, 6).

This (perennial) observation chimes with the objectives of university managers' intent on using academic staff to increase resources through contract based research with external organisations. It is part of what some call the emergence of the entrepreneurial university, or what Rhoades and Slaughter (2004, 49) characterise as university managers viewing the academe 'as an added source of revenue' (see also, Glaser and Bero 2005; Hessels and van Lente 2008). Academics are encouraged to develop relationships with commercial organisations, and to orientate, narrowly, the production of ideas to contracts specified by sponsors. For some observers, this has potential to displace long term, basic, research with short term, profit seeking, ventures, and to truncate the exploration of ideas (Deem 2001). Akerlind, et al. (2007, 9) suggests that the 'entrepreneurial turn' in the academe is encouraging no less than the reorientation of the social sciences towards the production of 'social and political utility, capable of commercial or political exploitation'.

While such claims are open to debate, there is little doubt that planning schools, as part of the broader academic system, are subject to pressures to respond to the 'new realities' of the universities. These realities are transforming part of the rationale of planning schools, so some allege, from the production of knowledge for public good to private benefit, and thus raising a range of moral and ethical questions about the point and purpose of research (see Lo Piccolo and Thomas 2008; Thomas 2005). For Krimsky (1995, 125), the scale and pace of change has been so severe as to require 'a new public examination of the moral status of science'. This status is such that observers note that the transparency, quality, and integrity of research are threatened by market-orientated values. In this scenario, it is posited that commissioned projects will become ever more short term, public access to outputs will be subject to tighter controls by clients, and the production of knowledge will be no more than a pragmatic programme of work seeking to fit ideas to clients' pre-defined expectations of outcomes.

In the next part of the chapter I develop the observation that academic planning research is part of a broader process of the commodification of knowledge and ideas and, as such, it is, in Howie's (2005, 2) terms, 'antithetical to the examined life, to the values of mindfulness'. In its broadest terms, the planning academe, like the academe more generally, has been shifting from what Slaughter and Rhodes (2004, 28) characterise as a 'public good knowledge regime' to an 'academic capitalist knowledge regime'. I develop the argument that the moral-ethical context for the conduct of research, under the emergent regime, is increasingly bound into institutional-regulatory relationships, in which different forms of legal and quasi legal contracts seek to define and delimit the roles, responsibilities, and conduct of academics. Such contracts are an internalisation of external demands on the academe, from business, government, and others, and are manifest through a range of governance instruments and techniques that are core to the propagation of a knowledge production process orientated towards the imperatives of market expansion.

Such instruments range widely in form and type but typically include, amongst others, performance management, intellectual property rights, quality auditing, and patents, governed by a stratum of management and administration seeking to impose the values and practices congruent with the objectives of 'bringing the academe to market' (see Clarke and Newman 1997; Krimsky 1995; Slaughter and Rhoades 2004). Managerial governance has, however, the capacity to extract 'modes of activity from their context' and to create what Howie (2005, 7) refers to as 'a distance from political and moral analysis'. This observation is developed later in the chapter, noting that the managerial-contractual nature of much academic work may neutralise moral-ethical debate or issues. It is complicit, potentially, in creating contexts whereby the members of the academe may well fail to acknowledge, or engage with, the moral and ethical dimensions of the social and political contexts of (their) research practices.

Academic Research, Contractualism and the Utilitarian Turn

One of the core functions of the university is the conduct of inquiry into social and political life, and the generation of data and information that provides the possibilities of enhancing the understanding of the world that we live in. While this statement seems self evident and uncontroversial, there is much debate about the *raison d'être* of higher education, with emphasis being placed by government ministers on getting the academe 'to become business-facing' (Brooks 2008, 8). A recently published government report has suggested that British universities need to 'restructure to operate more flexibly...and that government funding should support flexibility' (HM Treasury 2006, 3). For one vice chancellor of a British university, flexibility is responding to 'the challenges to remaining competitive within a global knowledge economy' (Brooks 2008, 8). This is to be facilitated by employer-led lifelong learning, work-ready graduates, and the (re)orientation of research to enable the private sector to 'exploit the advantage that can be derived from knowledge' (Brooks 2008, 8).

This market orientation of the academe is, allegedly, displacing the traditional values and norms of universities, in a shift from what some describe as mode 1 to mode 2. The former reflects, arguably, an idealised understanding of university research that has its origins in Robert Merton's (1942) codification of the ethos of science. This ethos revolves around four dimensions of what Merton regarded as the moral and ethical basis of good academic practice. The first is communalism and the understanding that the results of academic research should be the common property of all, and not the preserve of a private interest. A second is universalism or the importance of detachment of academics in the pursuit of truth (claims). The third is disinterestedness and exercise of personal integrity by academics in purging emotional and financial attachments to their research. The final is organised scepticism and the refusal to accept the 'taken for granted', or evidence that is partial, particular, or incomplete.

Merton's schema contrasts with mode 2 that some characterise as the rise of a post academic culture in which, for Scott (1997, 12), not only are 'the priorities of universities being challenged...but its leading values, even its essence'. There is, however, conjecture about what precisely the universities are becoming, with one school of thought suggesting that they have capitulated to partisan and private interests, or what Reay (2004, 37) describes as 'individualistic and competitive' and lacking 'any intrinsic ethic of care'. Others concur in noting the capture of academic science by commercial interests that, for Krimsky (1995, 125), has potential to undermine 'the ethical standards of research and diminish public confidence in its results' (see also, Allen and Imrie 2010). Likewise, May and Perry (2005) refer to aspects of mode 2 academic research as 'short term expediency', in which projects have quick turnaround, are output driven, and likely to have limited applicability beyond the brief provided by the sponsor or client.

Such views are not uncontested and can be contrasted with those who see much diversity in universities, where counter trends to academic capitalism are evident

(Prichard and Willmott 1997). Thus, for Ylijokic (2003, 310), market forces in the academe provide options for 'alternative practices and values', a point emphasised by Farkas (1999) who notes that university partnerships with community organisations can counteract market pressures. Others argue that academic-industry links are complex and not reducible to a type, and that academics can maintain a critical distance for critique and reflective behaviour (Prichard and Willmott 1997; Scott 1997). It is also suggested that the extent of change is exaggerated and that universities have always interacted with commercial and government sponsors to capitalise on knowledge production. For instance, Feller (1997) argues that up to 60 percent of scientific innovations in universities, prior to 1700, were developed in response to business and government contracts, while noting that the 19th century college system in the US was funded by applied research sponsored by commercial patrons.

Notwithstanding these observations, much evidence points towards a significant shift in the focus of universities in recent years, towards what Slaughter and Rhoades (2004, 29) describe as 'knowledge privatisation and profit taking'. Part of this process is that the relationship between universities, government, and private sector organisations is evolving to interlink knowledge production much more directly to the challenges of global competition. There is significant documentation of this trend and, for Howie (2005, 1), it signifies the alignment of the academe to specific political values that are converting 'education from process to product'. Here, the emphasis, by academic institutions, is what they can do for their clients or customers, and what the tangible outputs or outcomes will be (see Deem 2001). Thus, the web sites of planning departments variously suggest what the products are or will be, with one department highlighting the significance of 'knowledge as a product': 'the Centre aims to provide, through research, an evidence and knowledge base for policy makers, practitioners'.

Slaughter and Rhoades (2004) suggest that this product orientation is illustrative of a new era of business-government-university linkages (see also, Allen and Imrie 2010; Reay 2004; Ylijoki 2003). Vavakova (2008) concurs in noting that what is emerging is no less than a new social contract between the respective sectors, in which the academe is being put to work to produce one of the essential raw materials of global competitiveness, knowledge (see also, Brooks 2008). Part of the process is connected to the development of institutional-regulatory systems, or what one might refer to as contracts that specify and (de)limit, often in legal and quasi-legal terms, the scope and form of academic enterprise and its engagement with customers (see Davis et al. 1997). In this context, the development of legal instruments and agreements, such as copy right and intellectual property rights (IPR), is paramount in a context whereby the clientele is seeking to ensure the supply of knowledge, and to attain rights of use over it.

This is overlain with systems and procedures to facilitate the development, management, and regulation of knowledge production. These include the means of diffusion, exchange, and delivery (i.e. knowledge transfer), and the use, by university managers, of surveillance and disciplinary techniques and procedures to ensure the appropriate research conduct by academics. The latter occurs most commonly through the scrutiny of research proposals and ideas by research ethics committees, and by research partners' specification of the contents of legal contract governing the conduct of the research process. In a context whereby university managers are aware of litigation, and are seeking to manage contracts to avoid disrepute, an outcome is the possibility of risk averse behaviour by academics. Research that broaches difficult, perhaps controversial, moral and ethical issues may be discouraged or side-lined by university managers, and not even countenanced by academics who know that their work may not proceed beyond the scrutiny of the committee systems.

In this respect, the contractualisation of research relationships, through formal regulatory mechanisms, is part of a process to (re)define academics' rights and responsibilities and their freedom to act.[1] For Davis et al. (1997), commenting on the rise of the 'contractual society', contract discourse revolves around a notion of (self) responsible agency that emphasises the 'freedom to choose'. It prioritises the individual over the collective and may be conceived as symptomatic, and cause, of what Thomas (2005) regards as the decline of collegiality in the academe (see also, Deem 2001; Reay 2004; Slaughter and Rhoades 2004). The recourse to the self is also akin to Foucault's (1977) conception of 'governing at a distance', in which the techniques and instruments of control, such as written codes and ethics committees, provides a basis for self disciplinary behaviour to emerge in ways whereby it is possible, and usually probable, that the goals of the organisation become translated into the goals of the (individual) academic.

The deployment of a contractual culture is also interconnected with conceptions of risk to the organisation, and the understanding that the broader, and diverse, constituencies of (customer) interests that are part of the expanding market pose potential costs or risks to the academe. There is, therefore, much more emphasis by organisations on issues of risk and its regulation and management (see also, Imrie and Street 2009; Power 2004). For planning schools, the shift towards a customer-contractor relationship with clients opens up multiple risks relating to project development and delivery, and meeting the obligations and terms of the specified contracts. An aspect of this is reputational risk management, that is, the management of risk objects, including academics and their research practices, to ensure that the reputation of the academe is maintained and enhanced as part of the process of seeking to secure competitive contracts with commercial clients (see Power 2004).

The implications for planning research of the alleged turn towards a client-focused, contractual, research environment in the academe, is the focus for the rest of the chapter. I discuss two interrelated parts of the process. First, I outline

---

1   The emergent relationships are, therefore, increasingly formal, legal, quasi-legal, and contractual, although there is nothing distinct or unique about this to the academe. A number of observers note that the relationships between different strata of society have become increasingly contractual since the late 20th century (Akerlind et al. 2007).

some of the ways in which the product orientation of the planning academe is shaping the form and content of research practices, and its governance. There is much emphasis, problematically, on the formation of new collaborations based on inter or trans-disciplinary research programmes, and a de-emphasis on the value of single or sole scholarship that, so it is alleged, has less likelihood of expanding the market or product base of the academe. Second, I develop the observation that the emphasis by university managers, on managing and policing risk in relation to the conduct of research, is implicated in the production of, potentially, docile researchers. What I argue here is that one is witnessing, in part, the alienation of academic labour from the process of knowledge production, and the significance of the policing and disciplining of the academe as part of a broader approach to securing (the legitimacy of) commercial contracts and the quiescence of academics.

Developing the Product Orientation of the Planning Academe

A rationale of the academic capitalist model is to develop the capabilities of the universities to increase their market potential and presence (see Allen and Imrie 2010; Deem 2001; Slaughter and Rhoades 2004). This is characterised by university managers putting into place programmes of product enhancement and enlargement, and the development of research infrastructure to support income generation. A consequence is that the academe is mimicking, in part, corporate and business behaviour in ways not dissimilar to those outlined by Marx and Engel's (2005) analysis of the 19th century capitalist system. As they observed, 'the more capitalistic production develops, the more it is forced to produce on a scale which has nothing to do with the immediate demand but depends on the constant expansion of the world market' (Marx and Engels 2005, 101; see also, Reay 2004). This is an apposite observation in relation to the contemporary academe, and particularly its emphasis on the re-scaling of activities to incorporate global and world markets.

The re-scaling of universities' operations is reflected, in part, through strategies to create a 'business-facing' profile and focus. It is commonplace for planning schools, like academic departments more generally, to highlight their business links, and the contributions that they make to teaching and research (see Figure 6.1). Thus, for one UK planning school, the business focus is paramount, or, as it is claimed: 'The School works closely with industry, public sector partners and community organisations to develop research and consultancy services tailored to their needs'. This is echoed by others, with another School's website proclaiming that close 'links are maintained with the needs of industry and practice through scholarship, research, consultancy and the provision for lifelong learning. These links support course development and ensure that all teaching is up to date and well embedded into industry and professional practice'. Here, a message being conveyed is of the academe helping to facilitate the development of industry's product base, through the deployment of useful and relevant knowledge.

> 'Our mission is to continue to provide high quality teaching, scholarship, research and enterprise activities to help generate business success and to create a generally more sustainable built environment. The School caters for the needs of government, industry, local communities and professional practice...'.
>
> 'We pride ourselves on combining academic rigour and sector expertise tailored to the individual needs of our diverse client base; whilst remaining competitive, flexible and business focused'.
>
> 'The centre seeks to engage clients and users, the property sector, the building design professions and the construction industry'.
>
> 'Collaborating widely with key individuals and research groups, the School develops theory and conducts empirical analysis, thus contributing to more informed public policy and private practice'.
>
> 'We have a long experience of many programmes which are highly valued by industry and practice. Our courses reflect and predict industry requirements and are fully up to date through our close links with employers and professional bodies and, of course, by our highly experienced academic staff'.

Figure 6.1   The 'business-facing' orientation of UK planning schools

Such relevance is defined as the academe orientating its knowledge to (product) applications of utility or usefulness in relation to serving the practical needs and demands of corporate clients. The propagation of the user-orientation in academic research is part of government policy, and it is administered by the research councils which are a significant part of the institutional and regulatory landscape of the planning academe. Increasingly, the research councils require academics to enter into contracts that demand a demonstration of the practical contributions of the research to the economy and societal well being. An example is provided by the major funding organisation of planning research, the Economic and Social Research Council (ESRC 2008), whose ambition is 'to advance knowledge and provide trained social scientists which meets the needs of users and beneficiaries, thereby contributing to the economic competitiveness of the UK, the effectiveness of public services and policy...'. One reading of this is that the research councils are perpetuating knowledge as a means to an end, and as serving a narrow, instrumental, view of the world.

Implicit in the research councils' agenda is assigning relative weighting to what constitutes 'more useful' from 'useful' knowledge, and 'useful' from the 'useless' (and irrelevant and fatuous). The underlying product approach is such that the understanding of 'useful' might easily be read off as a rejection of knowledge 'as an end in itself', and a call to the academe to adopt an unquestioning servitude to their clients (who are, in this formulation, best able to judge what 'knowledge' is). Such servitude is encouraging the corporatisation of knowledge or what some regard as the production of 'useless' knowledge (Slaughter and Rhoades 2004). This is knowledge that is captured and controlled by private customers, and characterised by its fragmentation from other forms of knowing and its specific, single use, orientation. It signifies a world driven by partisanship, wherein the packaging of ideas, and the circumventing of some concepts and the deployment of others, renders the production of knowledge as part of a force-fed process.

Such observations have resonance with Adorno's (1974, 196) views about the changing role of intellectual activities, or a shift towards a knowledge reductionism in which 'thought has by now been perverted into the solving of assigned problems' (see also, Bourdieu 1990). The danger with this is outlined further by Adorno (1974) who observe the ways in which government and the 'forces of reaction' divide the indivisible, and create a knowledge base that reduces understanding, potentially, to a lowest common denominator (see also, Imrie 2004; Reay 2004). To quote Adorno (1974, 125) at some length, he suggests that 'the division of the world into important and unimportant matters, which has always served to neutralize the key phenomena of social injustice as mere exceptions, should be followed up to the point where it is convicted of its own untruth. The division, which makes everything objects, must itself become an object of thought, instead of guiding it'.

However, the evidence suggests that academics do not have the capabilities or capacities to offer effective resistance, in a context whereby the inexorable trend is product development and enlargement supported, increasingly, by new organisations that provide members of the academe with training to ensure acculturation into the market place. Thus, a conference held in London in November 2008, entitled, *Making the most of your university's intellectual property*, advertised itself with the following headlines: 'Discover how to create a return on research investment; Gain an insight into industry partnering through case studies; Understand how to spin out an idea; Hear from the world's leading experts on intellectual property issues; Network with peers and industry leaders; Identify opportunities for growth'.[2] The sponsor was the law firm, Morgan Cole, supported by other parts of the higher education industry, including the Leadership Foundation for Higher Education, British Universities Finance Directors Group, UNICO, a knowledge transfer organisation, and the Association of University Administrators.

These emergent organisational forms are part of a broader socio-political context seeking to encourage the globalisation of the academe, and to use academics as means and instruments of realising such ambitions. This can take many forms, and one of the most common is the creation of inter-university research networks and collaborations that cross-cut national borders. Academic planning departments are subject to increasing demands by university managers to contribute to strategic initiatives to facilitate expansion into global markets. One of the keys to the process

---

2   The advertisement appeared in the issue of 6 November 2008 of the *Times Higher Educational Supplement*, p. 52.

is the propagation of inter and trans-disciplinary working as a 'good thing'. The web sites of planning schools outline the virtues of such linkages (see Figure 6.2). For instance, one School suggests that an objective is 'to foster interdisciplinary research in urban studies and planning...to act as a focus for interdisciplinary research...to undertake contract research for both the public and private sectors'.

For academics, one implication is loss of control over determination of research and is akin to Marx's notion of the alienation of labour or the separation of mental from manual labour. Academics are often unaware of strategic initiatives being set up 'in their name' until presented with a fait accompli to carry out the university's mission. In one example, academic staff in a constituent part of a UK university were informed by a senior manager of their forthcoming involvement in a research and teaching collaboration with other international institutions. The initial e-mail from the manager stated that 'the collaboration will enhance our international standing', a message reinforced by a line manager, the dean of a School, and Heads of departments, and conveyed to a group of academics sequestered to be part of the initiative. One academic wrote to a senior manager and asked, 'What puzzles me slightly is the origin of the programme. Who has prepared it and do we get to make any input into it given that it is meant to be a three way institutional interchange? Who is the lead player so far?'

The subsequent development of the collaboration was beset by underlying tensions, in which the academics and their managers voiced different views about what was important to the success of the venture. For university managers, their

---

'The ethos of research...recognises interdisciplinarity as the glue, which binds planning and other disciplinary synergies...Research outputs inform academic, professional and wider public audiences set within individually negotiated staff research plans and agendas'.

'The Department's brand is a unique asset...both research and teaching in the Department are characterised by multi- and inter-disciplinary perspectives. It is normal practice, and indeed essential, for staff...to work closely with colleagues in other disciplines'.

'Promote interdisciplinary research within the School, across the University, and externally with other research organisations and with the policy and practice community'.

'The research agenda is a distinctive one, predicated on applying an interdisciplinary and methodologically diverse social science approach to key geographical and environmental questions; much of the research has a strong applied, policy relevant focus'.

'Encourage collaboration within and beyond the School...a reflection of the School's commitment to collaborative, interdisciplinary research. A significant amount of innovative work within the School has emerged across the boundaries of research themes'.

Figure 6.2   The significance of interdisciplinary research

focus is, primarily, the cultivation of image and branding as paramount to success. Thus, part of the collaboration's globalising strategy is product protection by ensuring the brand is enhanced and not harmed by the choice of network partners. The post workshop discussions have centred on how precisely to globalise the research in ways that are coterminous with the brand image of 'world class universities'. The Dean of a Faculty in the host institution said, 'I think there are really outstanding professors in the various campuses, but as institution Z does not appear to be in nearly the league of X or Y, I'd be concerned about our "brands"'. The reproduction of these comments by others involved in the organisation of the programme occurred, with another manager's suggestion that 'we must ensure that the product will be a reflection of the institution'.

These remarks are neither exceptional nor extraordinary, and are indicative of the mentalities of those running higher education in which issues of style and output outweigh those of substance. In contrast, academics, drawn into the initiative discussed above, voiced concern about the substance of the proposed programme. In e-mail exchanges, some noted that it had been concocted as 'an opportunistic marketing opportunity' and 'not a contribution to knowledge'. Others concurred, with further exchanges indicating academics' dissatisfaction with being used to front up a programme that lacks credibility or, as one person suggested, 'passé research that is well out of date'. There is the danger that, in such instances, the rush to 'product package' the academe, as part of market expansion, may well undermine some of the intrinsic qualities and values of good research. Much effort may be wasted, valuable time expended and lost, and, in a worst-case scenario, academics may become part of a research programme that they have little interest in, and no inclination to commit to beyond platitudes.

The emphasis on inter and trans-disciplinary networking, by academic managers, should also be understood as part of a process whereby there is discouragement of individual scholarship that does not have a demonstrable product outcome, and is deemed unlikely to contribute to the broadening of markets. In one example, a Dean of a School of Social Science in a leading British university was asked to outline a strategy to enhance staff income generation. The reply was in keeping with the mantra that is disparaging of the 'lone scholar', with the objective articulated as one of 'flushing out the individual maverick' and getting them to be 'team players', to empathise with the bigger picture and 'to do their bit'. Getting members of the academe to 'do their bit' is, however, a puzzle and a problem for university managers, and is subject, increasingly, to techniques and methods of surveillance and discipline, a theme I now turn to.

Circulating Academic Capital and the Docility of the Academe

A range of writings describes the commercialisation of the academe as leading to the production of docile academics (Dwyer 1995; Goodson and Dowbiggin 1989). The notion of docility is derived from Foucault's writings about surveillance and control, and it is based on the observation that the exercise of power has the potential to reduce the individual into 'a relation of strict subjection' (Foucault 1977, 138). For Foucault (1980, 98), the operations of modern institutions can be defined, in part, by the setting in place of 'net-like organisation', that is, the deployment of instruments, techniques, and procedures to ensure the discipline of specific subject groups, or what Foucault (1980, 98) regards as groups' quiescence and their 'political terms of obedience'. In the context of the academe, the development of the commodity or product base depends, in part, on the exercise by managers of a 'strict regiment of disciplinary acts', and the insertion of forms of governance that will create docility, or an academe that, in Foucault's (1977, 136) terms, may be 'subjected, used, transformed and improved'.

As part of this process, academics are subject to new, and renewed, conditions or contracts of practice and compliance, characterised by the development of a disciplinary infrastructure. This infrastructure, while varying in form and process from one institutional context to another, has a range of familiar, and what appear to be reasonable, features, including research ethics committees, IPR, and knowledge transfer. However, for Bourdieu (1990), these features are neither benign nor neutral but are instruments of control, whereby academics are 'manipulated by the field' and subject to what Zipin and Brennan (2003) call 'dispositional suppression' (see also, Foucault 1980). Such suppression is part of academics' absorption of, and acquiescence to, the new governance structures. This includes the reproduction of the changing, commercial, values of the academe to the extent that they become part of normalised patterns and practices, even if questioned or disliked by individual academics.

Of particular significance is the use of IPR to specify the ownership of research outputs. For some, the situation is akin to a process of alienation in that there is some expectation that academics should 'sign away' the fruits of their labour as part of the contracts entered into with government and commercial contractors (see Drahos 2006; Long 1995; Martin 1998; Palmer 1989 and 1990). Most IPR agreements are constructed to facilitate the private, customer, appropriation of research or, as Drahos (2006, 3) says, 'intellectual property is a form of private sovereignty over a primary good – information'. The problem with IPR is that it vests individual, private, ownership in a product (i.e. 'the knowledge') that is derived from, and is part of, a collective enterprise and a series of social activities. As a number of commentators have suggested, ideas do not stem from one particular source or point of origin but take shape through a complexity of social, political, and institutional processes (Martin 1998; Palmer 1990).

In this respect, the application of IPR raises a number of ethical and moral issues relating to who has legitimate rights to, and use of, knowledge produced under contract to commercial clients. The assertion of rights to intellectual property often means sponsors or customers restricting (rights of) access to knowledge or information that is generated, in part, through the application of the intellectual labour of those in the academe. IPR are characterised by an underlying tension that while 'ideas are public...creators want private returns' (Martin 1998, 6). IPR also has capacity to truncate, or delimit, the processes of knowledge transfer and thus may, paradoxically, undermine the broader objective of the academe to engage in the transfer of knowledge to the fullest extent possible. IPR is no more than the privatisation of knowledge that, in Martin's terms, encourages 'competitiveness over information and ideas' and contributes to undermining the Mertonion ideal of communalism and collegiality (amongst the members of the academe).

Agreements relating to IPR are not only about 'dividing up the spoils of research', but are part of the broader policing of the academe, a process that is to the fore in relation to the specification, even prescription, of the roles, responsibilities, and duties, of the respective participants in the research process. This is the domain of research ethics or a system of/for disciplining members of the academe, to ensure that they do not bring their institutions into disrepute nor upset their corporate clients and customers. Much has been written about the emergence of ethical policing in the academe, and it can be regarded as part of a surveillance system designed to ensure that academic behaviour is coterminous with the corporate objectives of the university. In the UK context, the institutionalisation of research ethics in universities is less to do with asking profound and searching questions about research ideas and practices, and more to do with ensuring the products (of academic activity) will be brought to the market unfettered by controversy or hurt or harm to corporate customers.

The surveillance of research conduct by ethics committees is a recent phenomenon, and has been imposed on British universities by government through the channels of the research councils. In January 2006, the ESRC introduced a research ethics framework, stipulating that funding of research depended on applicants meeting the terms of ethical practice. However, some research shows that the governance of ethics may delay and distort research, and that it errs towards caution and conservatism as part of risk minimisation (to corporate image and reputation) (see Wald 2004; Ward et al. 2004). This contrasts with Merton's (1957, 605) understanding that 'the scientist came to regard himself as independent of society and to consider science as a self regulating enterprise which was in society, but not of it'. While Merton's characterisation is, to some extent, idealised and not wholly representative of the academe at any point in its history, it is clear that the contractual nature of ethical procedure, i.e. signing up to its strictures, is one in which the ideals of 'independent' and 'self regulating' behaviour are unlikely to be fostered and realised.

Delimiting and defining ethical practice and procedure is integral to the capitalisation of knowledge, or producing data in commodifiable forms. The process also depends, in part, on the circulation or movement and mobility of knowledge (see Bourdieu 1990; Gherardi and Nicolini 2003; Hassard and Kelemen 2002). This brings to the fore the significance of knowledge transfer (KT) as integral to the new systems of knowledge accumulation. It is no coincidence that the commercialisation of academic research practices has gone hand in hand with the setting up of infrastructure to facilitate key parts of the process. KT, much like the circulation of capital outlined in Marx's schema of the capitalist system, is vital to facilitating the corporate and commercial ambitions of the universities (see Marx

1976). These ambitions are being realised, in part, through university managers setting up 'KT machinery', or mechanisms designed to encourage academics to capitalise on the knowledge that they are producing.

The process is being pushed by government and the research councils as part of a broader remit, so it is claimed, not only to ensure that academics produce relevant research contributing to society's betterment, but that it reaches out to those who can best make use of it. Thus, the ESRC, and other research councils, have produced extensive guidance about 'how to do' KT, while universities are making significant managerial appointments to ensure that the academe is equipped to deliver the government's KT agenda. Much of this agenda is concerned with style and presentation of the product as part of a brand. For example, the ESRC outlines a KT dissemination process as a series of stages defined by a 'communications toolkit' in which branding and development of corporate identity are critical to ensuring successful outcomes. The KT part of the ESRC's web site also instructs academics how to communicate and write, including appropriate use of grammar and terminology.

This is all well and good but a problem is that much of the KT effort is not necessarily about widening public access to, and consumption of, knowledge. Rather, too much of the KT process seeks, on the one hand, to serve customers and clients that have purchased research data, and, on the other hand, to encourage the publication of papers in esoteric journals that charge expensive subscription rates. In both instances, KT is subject to forms of privatisation or the circulation of data and information characterised by the absence of open access. Thus, contracts with commercial sponsors mean that academics' rights to publish findings will be subject to the terms of contract, with much evidence showing that such rights are often constrained and curtailed. Likewise, KT in the form of academic papers is a major source of corporate publishers' profits that they are unwilling to relinquish. Such papers tend to reside in journals kept in private (university) libraries that charge prohibitive membership fees, so discouraging the public access to, or use of, such sources of knowledge.

If this were not enough, academics are encouraged to view the KT process as part of the production of 'byte-sized' bundles of knowledge to ease the process of dissemination and diffusion. In this respect, much KT activity may be conceived of as the production of finite bodies of knowledge, or what Slaughter and Rhoades (2004, 3) refer to as 'packages of information' that tend to close down the possibilities for further inquiry. Knowledge, in this idealist interpretation, is a commodity, or something with fixity that can be stored, retrieved, accumulated, and converted (see Gherardi and Nicolini 2003). KT, with its emphasis on procedure and process of (product) transfer, seems to miss the point of the university, at least in the Mertonian sense of the word. For Merton (1957), and others, the cultivation of knowledge, as a *raison d'être* of the university, is part of relational and mediated socio-political and institutional relations. Here, knowledge is not static nor finite but infinite in terms of what it might be or become; it is part of contexts of action and interaction (see also, Gherardi and Nicolini 2003). A focus on KT may well undermine this more nuanced understanding of knowledge.

There is also a danger that KT becomes no more than the propagation of the sensational, the headline, and the courting of the media to the point whereby the complexity of data and research findings are subsumed by pressures 'to present a story'. Academics are encouraged to be media savvy and generate news worthy stories. Bourdieu (1998), and others, recognised such trends back in the 1970s (see also, Gouldner 1972). For Bourdieu (1998, 7), too much of intellectual life was complicit with government and business agendas, encouraging 'a social science reduced to journalistic commentary…and uncritical glossing of unscientific opinion polls'. The trivialisation of knowledge was being accompanied by the supplanting of the (critical) intellectual by a new cadre, a process referred to by Bourdieu (1998, 5) as the 'struggle aimed at producing and imposing new intellectuals', that is, those individuals who seek to propagate a non critical approach to the 'self evident' or the 'taken for granted'.

These comments seem appropriate today in a context in which what seems to count is instant knowledge, and a form of knowing that is evidential and based on something that can be presented as fact and 'put to work'. In some respects, university managers argue that they have no option but to encourage a practical and packaged understanding of, and disposition towards, the collation and presentation of knowledge given the highly competitive market that has emerged in relation to the production and selling of ideas. There has been a significant increase in knowledge brokerage through the growth in numbers of think tanks, advocacy organisations, consultancy firms and electronic media, all of which, as Hassan (2008, 1) suggests, are 'suited to the politics of the pro-business, corporate world of the right'. It seems that the universities may well be travelling down that road, aided and abetted by a quiescent academe that, as Rhoades and Slaughter (2004, 55) suggest, are 'turning ourselves into something we are not'.

Conclusions

It is not easy to be certain about the precise direction or scale of changes in the academe, but much evidence suggests that there has been a significant shift towards the commercialisation of research and teaching. This is evident through an increase in universities conducting contract research for corporate organisations, and much more emphasis, by managers, on encouraging academics to produce knowledge with practical applications and marketable potential. The product orientation of the academe has implications for the organisation of the academic labour process, including an increase in the use of casualised contract staff, the creation of inter and trans-disciplinary networks, and much more emphasis on the production of outputs, including academic papers.[3] The prevailing context is

---

3   An important part of the contract culture relates to universities seeking to develop their human and physical infrastructure to enable the new product base to be cultivated and enhanced. To this extent, working for a diverse customer base requires a flexible and

unlikely to encourage intellectual inquiry or free thinking, but, rather, to perpetuate risk averse behaviour, responsive to income and performance targets. For Howie (2005, 8), the situation can be resolved if there is 'freedom from the demands of marketing ideas...[to] release creativity caught up in the madness of an irrational and distended publishing whirl'.

This is unlikely to occur given the demands by both government and research councils to universities to commercialise their activities, and to use the skills and aptitudes of academic staff as part of the process. Academic staff are subject to management directives and controls emanating from a centralisation of activities in universities, or what Slaughter and Rhoades (2004, 49) describe as increasing control by academic managers over 'the intellectual and instructional products of faculty'. The activities of academics are bound into a series of legal and quasi legal contracts relating to the conduct and content of the research process, in which mechanisms of surveillance and control are evident through the context of various institutions, including ethics committees, IPR agreements, and programmes and policies to transfer knowledge. In combination, these institutional mechanisms are part of a process of reputational risk management, and a guarantee, to commercial clients, of the reliability of data generation and delivery by the university sector.

The trend is towards the privatisation of research and its cooption and capture by specialist, partisan, organisations. Despite calls for open access publishing, the generation of data is subject to dissemination to private clients and journals that require subscription. Limits are placed on how data are to be used and by whom, and the KT process is part of a culture that seeks to reduce knowledge to its lowest common denominator. Academics are not unaware of these situations, but are implicated in them gaining ascendancy, often by not speaking out or by ignoring them and seeking to forage their own research in the hope that they will remain unaffected. This complicity in the processes of academic capitalism is part of a broader context in which the moral and ethical basis of the university is less likely to provide the support for what Bourdieu (1998) and others have always held up as its *raison d'être*. That is, standing up to oppressive regimes and for the interests of the powerless, and giving voice to those individuals, groups, and social movements whose views are rarely heard in the dominant literature.

Acknowledgements

My thanks to Sarah Fielder, Marian Hawkesworth and Huw Thomas for comments on an earlier draft of this chapter.

---

adaptable workforce and there is much onus on the hiring of contract research staff. Reay (2004), for instance, notes that after the catering industries, the sector with the highest concentration of contract staff in the UK is the universities.

References

Adorno, T. (1974), *Minima Moralia: Reflections on a Damaged Life* (London: New Left Books).

Adorno, T. (1992), 'Commitment', in Tiedemann, R. (ed.), *Notes to Literature*, Vol. 2, Trans. Shierry Weber Nicholsen (New York: Columbia University Press).

Akerlind, G., Kayrooz, C. and Tight, M. (2007), *Autonomy in Social Science Research: The view from UK and Australian Universities* (New York: Elsevier).

Allen, C. and Imrie, R. (eds) (forthcoming 2010), *The Knowledge Business* (Farnham: Ashgate).

Bourdieu, P. (1990), *Homo Academicus* (Cambridge: Polity).

Bourdieu, P. (1998), *Acts of Resistance: Against the Tyranny of the Market* (New York: New Press).

Brooks, J. (2008), 'Academia and industry have much to gain in partnership', *The Guardian*, Tuesday 18 November.

Clark, B. (1986), *The Higher Education System* (Berkeley: University of California Press).

Clark, B. (1987), *The Academic Life: Small Worlds, Different Worlds* (Princeton: The Carnegie Foundation for the Advancement of Teaching).

Clark, B. (1998), *Creating Entrepreneurial Universities: Organisational Pathways of Transformation* (Guildford: Pergamon).

Clarke, J. and Newman, J. (1997), *The Managerial State* (London: Sage).

Davis, G., Sullivan, B. and Yeatman, A. (1997), *A New Contractualism?* (Melbourne: Macmillan Education).

Deem, R. (2001), 'Globalisation, New Managerialism, Academic Capitalism and Entrepreneurialism in Universities: Is the Local Dimension Still Important?' *Comparative Education* 37:1, 7-20.

Drahos, P. (2006), 'A Defence of the Intellectual Commons', *Consumer Policy Review* 16:3, 2-5.

Dwyer, P. (1995), 'Foucault, Docile Bodies and Post-compulsory Education in Australia', *British Journal of Sociology of Education* 16:4, 467-477.

Economic and Social Research Council (ESRC) (2008), see, http://www.esrcsocietytoday.ac.uk/ESRCInfoCentre/Support/research_award_holders/FAQs2/index1.aspx, site visited on 2 January 2009.

Farkas, N. (1999), 'Dutch Science Shops: Matching Community Needs with University R & D', *Science Studies* 12:2, 33-47.

Feller, I. (1997), 'Technology Transfer from Universities', in Smart, J. (ed.), *Higher Education: Handbook of Theory and Research* (New York: Agathon Press).

Foucault, M. (1977), *Discipline and Punish* (London: Penguin).

Foucault, M. (1980), *Power/Knowledge* (New York: Pantheon).

Gherardi, S. and Nicolini, D. (2003), 'To Transfer Is to Transform: The Circulation of Safety Knowledge', in Nicolini, D., Gherardi, S. and Yanow, D. (eds), *Knowing in Organizations: A Practice-Based Approach* (New York: Sage), 204-224.

Glaser, B. and Bero, L. (2005), 'Attitudes of Academic and Clinical Researchers towards Financial Ties in Research: A Systematic Review', *Science and Engineering Ethics* 11: 4, 553-573.

Goodson, I. and Dowbiggin, I. (1989), 'Docile Bodies: Commonalities in the History of Psychiatry and Schooling', *International Journal of Qualitative Studies in Education* 2:3, 203-220.

Gouldner, A. (1972), *The Coming Crisis of Western Sociology* (London: Heinemann).

Hassan, G. (2008), 'The Limits of the "Think Tank" Revolution', opendemocracy. net, paper available at http://www.opendemocracy.net/article/yes/the-limits-of-the-think-tank-revolution, site visited on 31 December 2008.

Hassard, J. and Kelemen, M. (2002), 'Production and Consumption in Organizational Knowledge: The Case of the Paradigms Debate', *Organization* 9:2, 331-355.

Hessels, L. and van Lente, H. (2008), 'Re-thinking New Knowledge Production: A Literature Review and a Research Agenda', *Research Policy* 37:4, 740-760.

HM Treasury (2006), *Prosperity for All in the Global Economy – World Class Skills. Final Report* (London: HMSO).

Howie, G. (2005), 'Universities in the UK: Drowning by Numbers', *Critical Quarterly* 47:1-2, 1-10.

Imrie, R. (2004), 'Urban Geography, Relevance, and Resistance to the "Policy Turn"', *Urban Geography* 25:8, 697-708.

Imrie, R. and Street, E. (forthcoming 2009), 'Risk, Regulation and the Practices of Architects', *Urban Studies*.

Krimsky, S. (1995), 'Science, Society, and the Expanding Boundaries of Moral Discourse', in Gavroglu, K., Stachel, J. and Wartofsky, M. (eds), *Science, Politics, and Social Practice* (Berlin: Kluwer Academic Press), 113-128.

Lipsett, A. (2008), 'Ministers mull how universities could rescue economy: Government "in market for ideas" on how higher education could respond to rising unemployment and economic decline', *The Guardian*, 7 November, p. 6.

Lo Piccolo, F. and Thomas, H. (2008), 'Research Ethics in Planning: A Framework for Discussion', *Planning Theory* 7:1, 7-23.

Long, R.T. (1995), 'The Libertarian Case against Intellectual Property Rights', *Formulations* 3:1, available at Libertarian Nation Foundation, http://libertariannation.org/a/f31/1.html.

Martin, B. (1998), *Information Liberation. Challenging the Corruptions of Information Power* (London: Freedom Press).

Marx, K. (1976), *Capital: Volume 1* (London: Penguin).

Marx, K. and Engels, F. (2005), *Marx and Engels Collected Works* (New York: Lawrence and Wishart).

May, T. and Perry, B. (eds) (2005), *Universities in the Knowledge Economy: Spaces of Reflection and Places of Expectation* (Maidenhead: Open University Press/Mc Graw-Hill).

Merton, R. (1942), 'The Normative Structure of Science', in Storer, N. (ed.), *The Sociology of Science: Theoretical and Empirical Investigations* (Chicago: The University of Chicago Press), 267-278.

Merton, R. (1957), *Social Theory and Social Structure* (New York: Free Press of Glencoe).

Palmer, T. (1989), 'Intellectual Property: A Non-Posnerian Law and Economics Approach', *Hamline Law Review* 12, 261-304.

Palmer, T. (1990), 'Are Patents and Copyrights Morally Justified? The Philosophy of Property Rights and Ideal Objects', *Harvard Journal of Law and Public Policy* 13:3, 817-865.

Power, M. (2004), *Organised Uncertainty: Designing a World of Risk Management* (Oxford: Oxford University Press).

Prichard, C. and Willmott, H. (1997), 'Just how managed is the McUniversity?', *Organisation Studies* 18:2, 287-316.

Reay, D. (2004), 'Culture Capitalists and Academic Habitus: Classed and Gendered Labour in UK Higher Education', *Women's Studies International Forum* 27:1, 31–39.

Rhoades, G. and Slaughter, S. (2004), 'Academic Capitalism in the New Economy: Challenges and Choices', *American Academic* 1:1, 37-60.

Scott, P. (1997), 'The Changing Role of the University in the Production of New Knowledge', *Tertiary Education and Management* 3:1, 5-14.

Slaughter, S. and Laslie, L. (1997), *Academic Capitalism: Politics, Policies, and the Entrepreneurial University* (Baltimore: John Hopkins University Press).

Slaughter, S. and Rhoades, G. (2004), *Academic Capitalism and the New Economy: Markets, States, and Higher Education* (Baltimore: John Hopkins University Press, Baltimore).

Thomas, H. (2005), 'Pressures, Purpose and Collegiality in UK Planning Education', *Planning Theory and Practice* 6:2, 238-247.

Vavakova, B. (2008), 'The New Social Contract between Governments, Universities and Society: Has the Old One Failed?', *Minerva* 36:3, 209-228.

Wald, D.S. (2004), 'Bureaucracy of Ethics Applications', *British Medical Journal* 329:7460, 282-284.

Ward, H.J.T., Cousens, S.N., Smith-Bathgate, B., Leitch, M., Everington, D., Will, R.G. and Smith, P.G. (2004), 'Obstacles to Conducting Epidemiological Research in the UK General Population', *British Medical Journal* 329:7460, 277-279.

Worthington, F. and Hodgson, J. (2005), 'Academic Labour and the Politics of Quality in Higher Education: A Critical Evaluation of the Conditions and Possibility of Resistance', *Critical Quarterly* 47:1-2, 96-110.

Ylijoki, O. (2003), 'Entangled in Academic Capitalism? A Case-study on Changing Ideals and Practices of University Research', *Higher Education* 45:3, 307-335.

Zipin, L. and Brennan, M. (2003), 'The Suppression of Ethical Dispositions through Managerial Governmentality: A Habitus Crisis in Australian Higher Education', *International Journal of Leadership in Education* 6:4, 351-370.

Chapter 7

Ethical Issues in PhD Research Training

Daniela Mello

This chapter examines the way considerations of ethics may enter the training of PhD students. It does this largely in the context of a discussion of PhD training in planning in Italy. The distinctiveness of the Italian system is explained by contrasting it with approaches to PhD training in the US and the UK. The chapter's primary concerns are: to examine how the institutional context for PhD training may influence its content (with particular reference to formal research training, including ethics); to report on the current provision of training in research ethics in Italian planning PhD programmes and to give a systematic account of the experiences and views of PhD students themselves in relation to research ethics as a component of their PhD studies. This latter element is particularly novel, as there is very little written about the experience of the PhD researcher in planning.

The chapter begins with a discussion of the significance of formal, systematic research training within PhD studies – a feature which remains patchy in Italy, has gained ground in the UK (largely through being obligatory for PhD students funded by the quasi-governmental Economic and Social Research Council) and has long been standard practice in the US. The second substantive section of the chapter examines training for planning PhD students in Italy, including training/ education in relation to ethics. A final substantive section reports on a questionnaire survey on research training and research ethics, with responses from 91 Italian PhD students.

The Significance of the Idea of Systematic Research Training for Planning PhD Students

To introduce the discussion about ethical issues in PhD training we have to focus our attention on the general role that formal training has. To speak about this subject it is necessary to introduce at first a reflection about the different possible meanings that a PhD programme can have and the diverse aims entailed by different conceptions.

Initially, it might appear that the aim of any PhD programme is only to train students to be researchers and that PhD training programmes are usually organised accordingly. But further investigation of the different contexts in which PhDs are undertaken suggests a more complex picture. In particular, we can detect two broad approaches which dominate PhD training in different contexts: the first involves the PhD programmes whose aim is to train entrants to academic life – primarily as researchers; the second one concerns PhD programmes whose aim is to deepen PhD students' knowledge about planning and 'prepare students for a job market' (Djelic 2008, 57). In these, research training – in a general sense – plays a subsidiary role.

If we refer to the Italian context we notice examples of both conceptions. We can find many cases in which a student is guided to learn to be a researcher but we can find also a lot of situations in which the PhD programme is nothing more than a sort of continuation of university studies. In the United Kingdom, on the other hand, the PhD is a research-based degree. Indeed, doctoral programmes with a reduced research component – which, in effect, emphasise a deepening of knowledge of a subject rather than a research training – are entitled 'professional doctorates', and are awarded a 'D.xxx', rather than a PhD (as far as we are aware there are no such professional doctorates available in planning at present). We suggest that these different rationales are related to different possibilities for PhD students after their studies. If there is a real difficulty in securing work in universities for all those who want to be researchers, as in Italy may happen, it is important to give PhD students advanced knowledge about planning that could be useful in many different kinds of jobs and activities. The approach to a PhD as primarily a specialised degree in a particular topic may also arise from the fact that not all the PhD students are really interested in research activities and hence some prefer to have a PhD degree as an entry into certain careers, such as public administration. It is evident, in this case, that the necessity of systematic research training is not so strongly felt.

In Britain, entry to most professions, including planning, has traditionally been possible with an undergraduate university education (though access points for graduate entry – i.e. those holding a masters degree or equivalent – also exist in most professions). A PhD is simply not necessary for a career in planning or other professions, but it has gradually become an essential requirement for a career as an academic in a planning school (Thomas 1981, 1-20). The PhD in the UK essentially follows the model of natural science in emphasising an understanding of the nature of research and an ability to undertake it, as well as contributing (via an original piece of research) to the advancement of knowledge in a given field. Increasingly, it is viewed as a kind of apprenticeship for the academic life. Meanwhile, research skills associated with evaluation and policy review are becoming increasingly salient in public administration to facilitate 'evidence-based policy'. There are many consultancies which compete with universities to provide policy evaluation for public bodies (see Healy, Chapter 10) but their focus is relatively narrow, deploying a limited range of techniques for very specific purposes; a PhD would seem an extravagant way of training for such purposes. The UK approach aims to arm a researcher with a number of tools that will make him first a researcher and second a specialist in a certain area. Employment-wise a doctoral graduate should feel quite comfortable in various institutional settings requiring analytical skills. A similar approach appears to be dominant in the US also.

The different significance of the PhD has implications for the kind of preparation PhD students might be expected to have and also the role that training might have within the programme. Hence in the European context 'most countries have more than one single course/way to acquire a doctoral degree. These courses differ mainly in who provides the money. The more public money is used, the more demands there are made on the doctoral researcher regarding formal training and other tasks. [...] In most cases, the faculty and/or the regional/national graduate school or the national government set the rules and regulations about the training. The content of the training is mostly set at a more local level like the institute, faculty and the university' (Needham 2004a, 117-119). In Italy, students can take part in a PhD programme if they pass a competition about methods and general knowledge on planning but they aren't obliged to follow any course before the starting of a PhD programme. Increasingly in the UK, again apparently following a trajectory of convergence with the US, the expectation is that before embarking on independent research (including in that term a critical review of the current state of knowledge in the field) a PhD student will have taken a programme of taught courses (at a Masters level) in the field of study (planning, public administration, etc.) and in research methods.[1]

Turning now to the formal training contained within a PhD programme, in the case of Italy it is possible to identify two main forms. The first one involves formal training as an unique structure of seminars and lessons linked one to another through a plan of contents organised over the three years of the PhD programme; the second one concerns single seminars and/or lessons, not necessarily linked one to another, that generally tackle the main issues of urban planning. Also speaking of formal training contents we can identifies two different typologies of subjects: the first one concerns the planning subject and so all the issues that are linked to it, the second one concerns methodology with a general meaning, applied to the field of research into urban planning.

The first kind of formal training, dedicated to the subject of planning, is mainly dedicated to planning history and theory and it includes a great variety of topics that change according to the particular curriculum of the PhD programme, from the specific research in which the teaching staff is involved, to the individuation of some matters that are considered fundamental for the PhD's formal training. These courses constitute the base for the knowledge of planning but can't give a direct contribution about the instruments that are useful to do research and to learn to be a researcher.

On the other hand, this is the way that all the courses that are connected to methodology and, specially, those which concern ethics operate. As a result of

---

1 Something like this happens in France too, where a 'postgraduate degree specialised on research training – D.E.A. (Diplôme d'Etudes Approfondies) Urbanisme et Aménagement is a prerequisite of doctoral studies [and in the Netherlands where] a special research school (Netherlands Graduate School of Housing and Urban Research, NETHUR) which offers courses in research methodology and techniques' was founded (Lundahl 1999, 7-9).

these courses all the students are able to undertake their thesis with the correct instruments and are able to deepen the subject in relation to other matters linked to planning.

In Italy, not all the PhD programmes in urban planning have specific methodology courses among the general formal training, as highlighted in Lo Piccolo (2004). A study conducted of the structure of all the Italian PhD programmes (to be discussed in the third section of this chapter) shows that about 50 percent of PhD courses don't have any methodology course. This condition suggests that there isn't any ministerial directive and that the organisation of methodology courses depends on the will and priorities of the specific department and teaching staff.

Those PhD programmes which have methodology courses, organise them in two different ways. From a general point of view, we can say that the attention about methodology aspects is especially focused in the first, or at least at the beginning of the second year of studies because it is considered preparatory[2] to every kind of study, independently of the specific thesis of each PhD student (this has similarities to the UK and US approach).

The first approach, which we can term 'direct', is based on lessons, seminars, workshops organised and performed by teaching staff or by external teachers about 'methods and strategies of social and urban research',[3] or about 'methods and techniques of scientific research'.[4] We can note that they are technical courses whose aim is to speak about the instruments that we can use when doing research. These kind of courses concern both how to write and communicate a PhD thesis (so how to write a bibliography, how to analyse a case of study…) and how to do research, how to analyse questions, what instruments we have to use to find out data, in particular if we want to contend with a sociological analysis.

The second approach, which we can term 'indirect', consists of some seminars, in which the teaching staff or some Italian and/or foreign teachers speak about their own research focusing the attention, especially, on methodological aspects. Another kind of indirect education about methods is seminars organised by students who have recently acquired their PhD for the other PhD students or the possibility to take part in seminars and research activities held by foreign university or research departments.

2　This is the case of the PhD programme in *Territorial and urban planning* of the University of Rome.

3　This is the name of the seminars organised by the PhD programme in *Urban, territorial and environmental planning* of the Polytechnic of Milan.

4　This is the subject of the lessons and workshops organised by the PhD programme in *Territorial and urban planning* of the University of Rome.

Ethics as a Component of Research Training in Italy: How to Build up a Systematic Approach

In Italy, ethics, which until not long ago had not been taken very seriously in the disciplinary debate in planning, has been dealt with during the past few years with a renewed attention and interest both in the academic field and within the professional one through moments of debate analysing its many facets: ethics as an aspect of professional deontology, as a responsibility towards the environmental problem and towards those who are weaker and outcasts.[5]

Faced with such initiatives, the attention given to this matter by the PhD programmes, the cultural activities and formal training which come with them, is rather insignificant. Interviewing the majority of the coordinators of the Italian PhD programmes, it is evident that only a small number of these programmes include attention to ethics. The reason for this is that even if in the Italian academic world there is agreement about the importance of the methodological matters within the PhD training, when it comes to discussing the relationship between ethics and research, no such importance is given to the matter. As a matter of fact, the topic has not been seen as a research training issue, as its facets are multiple and, what's more, it is hard to understand if, how and how much such matter should be dealt with within a defined formal training.

To understand why this might be it is necessary to describe in brief how the PhD programme is generally structured in Italy. The staff responsible for PhD students, in any given department, is composed of a group of teachers from the department. The teaching body aims at organising and managing the training and verifying the researches carried out by all the students during a series of meetings which take place regularly in the course of the three years. The form of the meetings can change from time to time, according to the context in which they take place. They generally take that of a public presentation, during which every student explains the progress of his/her research and is advised about possible developments of their studies. The students will then have to pick a tutor (according to the PhD in question), among the teaching body, whose purpose is to help them throughout the phases of their research, advising them on the choice of the method and the contents of the research.

With this structure, the multiple modalities in which the relationship between the academic institution and those who are 'being trained' is put into practice and the different importance given to the two subjects, according to the cases, result from time to time, in a degree of attention given to ethics, in how the matter is dealt with and what kind of impact it has. The teaching staff can raise the ethical theme among students. It is up to the teaching body to decide whether particular attention will be given to ethical problems connected to the research. In such cases, such a

---

5 The main event was the IV Study day entitled *Urban values between ethics and aesthetics*, organised in Naples by the National Institute of Urban Planning (INU) in March 2008.

topic will be mainly dealt with during specific seminars and/or lectures which will be given by either the teaching body or by invited Italian or foreign teachers.

It can happen that only a certain number of teachers ask their students to examine carefully ethical problems when they are carrying out research that is being supervised by the whole department. In these cases, because the research is bound to a real research commission undertaken by the department, it is clear that the ethical issue must be dealt with attentively because the relationship in question is more professional than simply didactic. Finally, the ethical issue can depend exclusively upon the relationship between the student and the tutor and can be linked to a subjective attention given to such matter by the tutor. It is known, in fact, that within the European tradition doctoral students receive their training mostly in and through the association with a particular professor (tutor). 'This has a number of consequences. First, it obviously generates heterogeneity as each training is likely to be unique and we could be in a situation where there is no common base in the education of doctoral students in a particular field across Europe, within a country or even within a single department or school' (Djelic 2008, 53-54).

Aside from the above-analysed cases, it can happen that the relationship between the teachers and the students is not so close, and so the students are free to decide about their research, and how it will be carried out. In this case, the only people responsible for ethical matters are the students themselves, who will decide when and how to deal with such problems, in accordance with the development of their research. It is quite evident that in such a case, the concern (if any) for research ethics and personal morality go together, having therefore a subjective weight.

Differently from PhD programmes, a greater attention to ethical issues is given during the formal training organised by the PhD schools. The PhD schools, instituted in 2004 constitute a new kind of institution whose aim is to organise and manage the third level of education (PhD training) starting from 'disciplinary ambits, sufficiently vast (as suggested by the European Laws in the matter), and regrouping the many PhD courses which are nowadays taking place in the Universities'[6] aiming at reaching high quality standards within a founding project, which is both cultural and scientific-didactic, integrated and unitary. The main purpose of the PhD schools is to widen the students' training with disciplinary contributions besides these specific ones connected to urban planning, yet not limiting the competences and responsibilities of each PhD programme.

That is why within the School's activities 'there must be (and documented) a common training for all the students, as for instance in the field of Research management and that of the knowledge of European and International Research Methods, thus promoting seminars dealing with disciplinary subjects, common

---

6   Additional note to the ministerial decree law (DM 224/99) on the subject of PhD reform.

courses for all CVs or else integrated courses, organization of Summer Schools and so on' (Djelic 2008, 53-54).

With the institution of PhD schools many changes and integrations were introduced to the traditional Italian training system of each PhD programme. Although such an institution is not always proving to be as expected (some of the problems arise from the lack of effective coordination among the PhD programmes which creates a gap between the competences), it emerges that in certain contexts the training programmes dealing with ethics and methodology are managed well by the PhD schools even though some modules are not necessarily linked with urban planning.

In these contexts ethical issues are tackled in three different forms. The first is the case, for example, of some PhD schools that count among their programmes some general modules about research instruments. These modules are structured as a sequence of lessons performed by high level teachers or seminars organised by the teaching staff. Although they are important, it is evident that the input that these modules can give to the students is limited because they are generally directed at PhD students in architecture, restoration, urban planning and other similar subjects.

The second form is that of the PhD schools that guarantee a certain number of courses dedicated to ethics, even if often associated with a multi-disciplinary formal training (in most cases, the organising of such courses is in the hands of single teachers, who can even come from different disciplinary fields) and so not necessary connected to urban planning. From this point of view the most frequent cases refer to subjects other than planning for which ethics seem to be a more specific and pertinent topic such as environmental ethics. Even though the main topic of these seminars is ethics, they deal mainly with the implications and impact derived from the use and misuse of some technologies on the environment: examine some of the most relevant environmental problems, in the light of the most important scientific and technical matters, draw a general picture on the main topics of the debate on contemporary ethics, evaluate some of the most innovative actions and operative instruments in the institutional, economic, professional and juridical fields and the misuse derived from inadequate environmental knowledge and culture.

The third case, on the other hand, is that of the PhD schools where some modules about epistemology of the scientific and technical research which deal with ethical issues are organised. In this case, differently from the previous ones, the ethical issues are not dealt with as connected to a specific subject, but are more general as they refer to epistemological and methodological topics or they aim to create a common ground of knowledge, which is mainly about juridical contents.

Perceptions of the Need for Training

The voice of students is rarely heard in relation to issues of research ethics. Generally, to ascertain whether ethics is present in a PhD programme and the degree of attention it commands it is preferred to seek information from the teaching council or by analysing the prospectus of the PhD programme. In this study, rather, it is preferred to act by combining the voice of the coordinators with that of the students.

To achieve the objective, a questionnaire was drafted and administered to all Italian PhD students.[7] In this questionnaire the subject of ethics was examined through an all-round vision of the pathway of each PhD student, based not only on analysing the structure of the formal training involved in the PhD programme, but also on his/her personal interests and sensitivity to ethics.

Before administering the questionnaires it was necessary to ascertain how to contact the PhD students, what could be the best way to interview them, obtaining a balance between a swift reply and one with reasonable depth. It was decided to contact PhD students through their e-mail addresses. To do so, it was necessary to find the e-mail addresses of all the students concerned. This stage was far from simple because there is no list of all the Italian PhD students. In some cases some PhD programmes published those of their own students on the Web, but not always are the e-mail addresses given. To get round this, two ways were followed: the first was to contact the secretary's offices of the PhD programmes, the second was to ask the urban planning PhD network, that links a large number of PhD students belonging to different Italian programmes, for the addresses.[8]

Once the mailing list was drawn up, the questionnaires were distributed to all the students of current PhD programmes and to some recent PhDs, the latter chosen for their specific interest in the questions related to PhD studies. The questionnaires were distributed to 379 PhD students belonging to 31 different PhD programmes in 17 Italian cities, that represent the whole Italian PhD programmes in Territorial and Urban Planning. The number of responses received was 91, which is approximately 24 percent of all the questionnaires administered. They covered, even if for each case with a different number of responses, all the PhD programmes examined. Thanks to these responses it was possible to obtain a good picture of the Italian context.

To analyse the responses and reflect on them it is necessary to examine, albeit synthetically, the structure and contents of the questionnaire. It was structured

---

7   Another interesting survey about doctoral research which explores the possibility of structured cooperation between the doctoral courses of all the planning schools in Europe which are members of AESOP was made by the AESOP Working group on doctoral studies (see Needham 2004b, 378-391).

8   The Urban Planning PhD network has been founded by Italian PhD students to promote discussion about urban planning research as tackled in the PhD programmes (see Balducci 1994, 63). It aims, moreover, at increasing the role of PhD students and doctors in the academic and research context.

into three parts: the first part aimed to ascertain whether some modules/seminars concerning research methodology or ethics were organised within the PhD programme. PhD students were asked whether in their PhD programme some formal training was organised, whether this training included some specific modules/seminars on methodology and in particular if there was any module on the subject of research ethics. These questions aim to ascertain, from the student's perspective, whether or not these particular modules are organised in the PhD programme, with no relation to the PhD student's field of interests.

By contrast, the second part of the questionnaire aimed to analyse the field of interest of each student and especially to understand if there is any link between the subject of each thesis and the research activity of the department. The reason for this kind of question lies in the realisation that very often PhD research is independent of that of the university. This situation involves a real risk both for students because it creates a sense of lack of orientation and also for the university because it creates a reduction in productivity for the department. To analyse this matter, the second part of the questionnaire contained some questions about the subject of each PhD student's thesis, the reasons for his/her choice and, especially, some questions to find out whether the thesis was part of a more general research project of the department or it arose from a purely personal interest.

The last part of the questionnaire specifically covered methods and ethics. The first question aimed to find out the methodology that was chosen for the research activity. The other questions concerned ethics: whether the PhD student had ever reflected specifically on ethics, if in his/her thesis there was an overtly ethical approach, how ethics was handled and in what ways ethics could be linked to urban planning research. At the end, to ascertain the state of interest of the institutions in ethics, the students were asked if they knew any institution that was interested in the topic and, lastly, if they would be interested in reflecting further about ethics.

Using the responses to the questionnaires it was possible to assess the ways in which ethics is handled on PhD programmes and, especially, what PhD students think about it, about the role that ethics has with reference to their thesis and about the meaning that it could have in urban planning research. If we analyse the questionnaires in relation to the three sections in which it is structured we note that, for the most part, there is a distance between the ethical contents of the PhD programme and what students think about ethics as a whole and about the importance that it can have in their studies. The responses also show the plurality of meanings assumed by research ethics and the difficulty in teaching it within formal training.

The responses to the first section of the questionnaire show an almost generalised condition of lack of modules on ethics in the formal training of Italian PhD programmes. Among all the PhD programmes that involve formal training, i.e. almost all of them, only 16 percent of students stated that some modules or seminars on this subject were organised. These modules/seminars, as we stated above, are structured very differently from one PhD programme to another, and very often tackle ethics from a really different point of view.

The situation is somewhat different if we refer to modules that deal with research methodology. In this case, the responses to the questionnaire show that about 50 percent of Italian PhD programmes have a specific interest in this matter which is proved by the presence, in formal training, of modules or seminars uniquely devoted to methodology.

What emerges from this analysis is that there is a sharp distinction between the issues connected to methodology and those related to ethics, which results in an imbalance between the two in the number of courses offered. As far as methodology is concerned, there is general attention paid by most Italian PhD programmes especially in the first phase of formal training. As for ethics, on the other hand, there is a certain lack of interest. As previously mentioned, the responses to the questionnaires show that the presence of courses on ethics is fundamentally linked to the interests of the teaching staff from either the PhD programme or the PhD school.

The responses to the first section of the questionnaire are even more interesting in the light of what PhD students said about their own standpoint on ethics and on the ways that they chose to deal with ethics in the context of their research. In response to the question: 'have you ever thought about how to undertake your research in an ethical way?' we note that just one of them referred to the formal training on ethics that they mentioned previously (organised by the university), while all the others responded in a very personal way. This kind of response raises some questions about the roles that specific modules on ethics can have in formal training, especially about the importance that they can have for the PhD student's training, the difficulties connected to teaching this subject, the interest that it can arouse in the students and, finally, the different ways in which such modules can be structured, if they can be effective training courses or just a platform to air some reflections on ethics proposed by some particular tutors.

From the analysis of the various personal meanings with which the PhD students related ethics to their own research and of the different ways that they chose to organise their work to make it ethically sound, it may be observed that ethics is a complex subject and one that people usually tackle from a personal point of view.

The responses can be categorised into four classes, corresponding to a different meaning given to ethics by PhD students. In the first class the meaning is related to integrity about methodology. From this point of view, as some students state in the questionnaire, PhD research can be considered ethically sound if all the research references, whether they are data analysed or bibliographic sources, are handled with truth, great attention and rigour; at the same time, whether the text of the thesis shows, without any possibility of doubt, what was written by a previous author and what is written by the PhD student. Another case in which the meaning of ethics is related to methodology concerns the specific field of specialist studies. In this case, as in sociological analysis, it is really important when dealing with this issue to have a real knowledge of social science methods rather than use inappropriate methods, as it sometimes happens in planning research.

A second class handled the subject of ethics with reference to the type of relationship that could exist between the PhD student and the person or organisation commissioning the research, i.e. the university department where the PhD course is held. Some of the responses to the questionnaire state that it is really important for PhD students to have an ethically sound approach in relation to the teaching staff. This is to say that the students must be free to show their own opinions about the contents of the thesis and must have the courage not to say what the teaching staff wants to hear, but whatever they think is interesting or innovative within the studies that they have done. Obviously, this does not mean lack of attention, on the part of PhD students, to all the suggestions and proposals that can arise from the teaching staff (whose aim is to guide PhD students during their pathway of studies), but that their input must be considered from a personal and critical point of view.

This interpretation of research ethics may be extended to the case in which the PhD research is part of the department's research programme, which is promoted by a public institution or a private company.[9] In this particular case, even if the PhD students have to discuss their thesis with the teaching staff who commissioned the research and ultimately assess it, they must attach even more importance to ethics. This is because the outcome of the study will have not only an academic interest, but will probably be used to highlight some questions and/or promote some projects. To develop an ethically sound approach the department and hence the student will have to pay great attention to the relationship with the research promoter, preventing the latter influencing the research results for its own interests. At the same time great attention will have to be placed on the correctness of data and statements, and on the ways to communicate research results.

The questionnaire responses showed how few cases of Italian PhD research are connected to departmental research. From the analysis it emerges that about 80 percent of PhD theses are totally independent of ordinary research activity. By contrast, the reasons for choosing the subject of the thesis arise, for the most part, from personal interest in this subject or from the wish to continue the type of studies done at university or, in the end, from the intention to steer the thesis towards a future professional activity. As may be noted, these reasons confirm, as we stated above, a general gap between PhD research and its academic setting, as well as, for most PhD programmes, a curious lack of interest in PhD student activities.

The third class that emerges from the analysis of the questionnaires connects the subject of ethics to some specific matters or themes that are part of urban planning. The majority of the students interviewed stated that ethics is strictly connected to land use planning because the aspects of planning and types of actors involved raise questions that must be tackled ethically, because of their public value (see

---

9   Barrie Needham identifies four different possible trajectories for PhD programmes. The second one is 'a traject whereby someone is appointed by the university primarily to carry out doctoral research which is commissioned by and paid by the future user of the research' (Needham 2004a, 117).

Lo Piccolo and Thomas 2008, 7-23). In consideration of this aspect, the responses to the questionnaires underline two possible different types of viewpoints. The first is that of the PhD students who state that the complexity and delicacy of the topics examined in their thesis force them to hold ethics in due regard. The second is expressed by all the students who aim to structure their theses in an ethical way, defining from time to time the best way to do it. Irrespective of these two different positions, it is worth noting that increasing numbers of PhD students are interested in topics that are connected, more than others, with ethics, such as urban policies for a multi-cultural society and areas in crisis, policies related to minorities, participatory planning, all the studies that are connected with the environment such as strategic environmental assessment, sustainable development and new instruments for energy saving.

The last class is probably more complex than the others. It starts from the idea that everything which is connected to the public interests must be ethically sound and links research ethics to personal and moral behaviour. In this case ethics is considered a value that must be followed by everyone regardless of its job or field of studies. Ethics is a personal condition, it is impossible to say or to impose how to be ethically correct. If you are a good person, you will act ethically. Obviously, this becomes much more important when dealing with urban planning which is a subject strictly connected with the public interest. In any case, when tackling this matter, it is important to bear in mind the interests of all the people and not those of a few.

In the light of the above it may be stated that, even if it is only in a few cases in the PhD programme that some formal training on ethics is organised, it attracts great attention and interest from the students of each Italian PhD programme. When asked 'do you think it is useful to reflect on ethics?' and 'would you like to make this kind of reflection?' most students answered both questions positively and, further, they declared an interest in tackling the subject in depth, analysing all the possible meanings and influences that ethics might have in their studies. Nevertheless, sometimes this interest may not be expressed at a conscious level or may not be structured into their research.

Of all the PhD students interviewed, only 25 percent responded negatively to the second question, but the reasons for this kind of response are as interesting as the positive ones: the first type of reply was 'I am not interested because I think that it is already difficult to understand what planning is in our context and in our – already complex – society, that thinking about ethics is only a matter for speculation, that it is not really useful in everyday life';[10] the second was 'I'm not interested because my PhD work is on a subject that is totally different from what might be addressed in the sphere of ethics. I'd like to reflect on ethics only if I have much more time, but now I've just the time to think about my thesis'. The negative responses which, from a certain point of view, might seem commonplace, even trivial, bring into focus a real question which was previously raised in this chapter,

---

10   The same objection is regarded and discussed by Stefano Moroni (1997, 20).

namely the lack of connection that there has so far been between urban planning and ethics. The two subjects are, in fact, considered by some as being far apart, rather than close to each other, to the extent that the ethical problems are thought to be of less relevance than the technical issues derived from urban research. If we refer not only to the academic context and specifically to the PhD context, as the questionnaires can show, just few institutions (apart from university) are interested in ethics or have done studies about ethics. On the contrary, ethics covers the whole field of planning (Thomas 1994, 1-11) and specifically involves different competences, each of which is connected to planning, such as political behaviour, private behaviour, that of the citizens, of professionals and researchers. Just in the last years an increasing interest is coming out, as we can note in relation to the organisation of some seminars, congresses and ministerial research.

Conclusions and Prescriptions

The analysis conducted through the questionnaires gives a clear picture of the Italian context of PhD programmes and shows the degree of attention that each PhD programme gives to the discussed issues and in particular to ethics. Starting from this analysis, some conclusions can be made.

The first is that ethics is tackled in a structured way in only a few PhD programmes. The responses to the questionnaires show that the reasons for this lack of treatment are strictly connected to the Italian condition of PhD programmes and, in a general way, to the condition of Italian urban planning research. The problem can be addressed by considering four main questions:

- What are the true aims of PhD studies in the context of Italian urban planning research?
- What are the contents of formal training and how is it structured in the three years of studies?
- What are the types of relationships that can exist between the teaching council, the tutors and the PhD students?
- What are the methods and instruments through which ethical issues can be tackled?

The first aspect is connected to what we stated in the first section of this chapter, i.e. the role that PhD research has in relation to the research activity of each Italian urban planning department. PhD training is the first and most fundamental component for the training of a researcher. In the examined context, this condition, even if stated in the prospectus of all the PhD programmes and declared by the teachers, is not always applied. The difficulties of working in the research field after the PhD programme, due to the lack of public funds for research, causes, in many cases, a sort of indifference by the teaching council about the path of studies of the PhD students. Their research is not always considered part of an advancement of Italian urban planning research, but as a continuation of university studies, without any relation to the department's research activity, with the only aim to increase students' knowledge of planning.

It is evident that, in this condition, little attention may be placed on methodology and ethics. The general lack of connection between student's and departmental activity, above all if commissioned by an external promoter, in a certain way allows less attention to be placed on ethics and pushes the student to tackle ethical questions from a personal point of view.

The second reason is related to the structure of formal training. As we stated in the previous sections, in Italy there is no single way to organise training courses so that each PhD programme has a different kind of formal training or only seminars and/or modules may be organised. In most PhD programmes formal training is structured in the three years of studies through seminars and modules, usually more frequent in the first year and less in the following, but only in a few cases is there a sound training pathway in methodology and ethics throughout the three years.

The third reason is connected to the first and is related to the relationship between the teaching council and the students. The analysis made through the questionnaires shows that, in a general way, a specific attention to ethics is present in the PhD programmes in which the students are more supervised and guided by the lecturers and tutors. Apart from personal sensitivity to ethics, it is evident that the more interest there is in the student's activity and in their training, the more likely – and necessary – it is to deal with ethics and methodology.

The last reason is related to the concrete difficulty in teaching ethics. The various meanings that ethics may assume as linked to different fields of studies and different points of view make it difficult to have a single common method to teach it and make the task of teaching it much more difficult. The responses to the questionnaire underline this difficulty and hence the reasons for tackling ethics from a personal point of view.

Starting from this reflection, it is important to understand whether ethics is a subject that can be taught or whether it is better to entrust it to the personal interest of each PhD student. In the first case, it is necessary to ascertain what and how must be taught. The complexity of the question and the great number of meanings that are related to it, make it difficult to find a single answer. What we can state, however, is that interest in this subject is growing, not only on the part of institutions but also among PhD students. Most of them stated that they might be interested in exploring ethical issues, especially for some specific reasons that are the following.

The first, that is linked to the current condition of the Italian PhD pathway that we have discussed above, is related to the willingness to assign a new role to Italian PhD students in the academic context. This role will no longer be that of a simple student but that of a potential new researcher. As a result, Italian PhD students will be comparable to other European PhD students whose role as 'young researcher' is widely recognised. In this way it will be possible to address the European aim to make PhD programmes 'intellectual magnets able to mobilize and crystallize the dynamism of more established research communities [and to attract] different kind of external actors playing a role in the diffusion and exploitation of new knowledge' (Djelic 2008, 50).

The second reason is related to the gradual change that is happening in the research field caused by the growing lack of public funds committed to it. From this point of view there is a gradual shift from public to private promoters. This means that even more Italian research is sponsored by companies that have specific interests and that could well steer research to match their interests more closely. In this condition the attention to ethics becomes increasingly important.

The third and last reason is related to the new fields of urban planning research. In particular, the greater focus on ethics seeks to train students to tackle all the questions that are connected to social policies that today underlie urban planning. Also in this case, the link between ethics and planning research is fundamental because of the delicacy of the questions tackled and also the fact that planning researchers have to discuss and interact with citizens and other social actors.[11] The growing number of PhD research programmes in such fields makes ethical issues more important in PhD formal training: PhD students must be given the instruments required to deal with them. Hitherto, little attention was paid to ethics. However, new interest is now emerging which suggests that in the near future greater attention and new reflections will be made.

Acknowledgements

The cooperation of the Italian Urban Planning PhD network has been essential in order to achieve the analysis of this chapter. Grateful thanks are due to all PhD students that have collaborated and in particular to Vincenzo Todaro of the University of Palermo whose help and support were fundamental.

References

Balducci, A. (1994), 'L'Integrazione fra i Dottorati di Pianificazione e Urbanistica', *Critica della Razionalità Urbanistica (CRU)* 2, 63-64.

Cabinet Office (1999), *Modernising Government*. March 1999. Available on-line at: <http://www.archive.official-documents.co.uk/document/cm43/4310/4310.htm>.

Djelic, M.L. (2008), 'PhD Education: Challenges and Opportunities of Europeanization', in Carmelo Mazza et al. (eds).

---

11 It happens, in particular, because urban planning is a 'public activity that has results, in a binding way, on the conditions thanks to which single people or groups of people with different and often opposite interests can reach and preserve scanty resources such as spatial and environmental goods and values' (Moroni 2000, 135).

Fubini, A. (ed.) (2004), *Improving Planning Education in Europe* (Milan: FrancoAngeli).

Lo Piccolo, F. (2004), 'Per la Costruzione di un Comune Percorso Formativo di Dottorato in Europa', *Critica della Razionalità Urbanistica (CRU)* 16, 80-85.

Lo Piccolo, F. and Thomas, H. (2008), 'Research Ethics in Planning: a Framework for Discussion', *Planning Theory* 7:1, 7-23.

Lundahl, I. (1999), 'Strengthening Planning Research: The Continued Work of the Working Group on Planning Research', *AESOP News*, summer, 7-9.

Maciocco, G., Deplano, G. and Marchi, G. (eds) (2000), *Etica e Pianificazione Spaziale. Scritti in Onore di Fernando Clemente* (Milan: Franco Angeli).

Mazza, C., Quattrone, P. and Riccaboni, A. (eds) (2008), *European Universities in Transition. Issues, Models and Cases* (Cheltenham, United Kingdom: Edward Elgar).

Moroni, S. (1997), *Etica e Territorio. Prospettive di Filosofia Politica per la Pianificazione Territoriale* (Milan: Franco Angeli).

Moroni, S. (2000), 'Etica e Piano in una Società Complessa: Riflessioni attorno ad Alcuni Programmi di Ricerca Rilevanti', in Giovanni Maciocco et al. (eds).

Needham, B. (2004a), 'Doctoral Studies', in Alex Fubini (ed.).

Needham, B. (2004b), 'Working Group on Doctoral Studies', in Alex Fubini (ed.).

Thomas, H. (1981), 'Developments within the Education of British Town Planners', in Huw Thomas and W. Keith Thomas (eds).

Thomas, H. (1994), 'Introduction', in Huw Thomas (ed.).

Thomas, H. (ed.) (1994), *Values and Planning* (Aldershot: Ashgate).

Thomas, H. and Thomas, W.K. (eds) (1981) *Plannning Education in The 1970s* (Oxford: Oxford Polytechnic).

Chapter 8

The Responsibility to Ask Questions: The Case of Bias in Travel Demand Forecasting

P. Anthony Brinkman

> However unwillingly a person who has a strong opinion may admit the possibility that his opinion may be false, he ought to be moved by the consideration that however true it may be, if it is not fully, frequently, and fearlessly discussed, it will be held as a dead dogma, not a living truth.
>
> John Stuart Mill

At some point, most planning scholars are likely to come across a notable gap in a particular literature that suggests, at least initially, a workable and interesting research programme. If the topic appeals, it might receive the attention it deserves. Otherwise, the questions are left to others, the answers to which may never come.

The discovery of such ignored inquiries raises important questions related to ethics and planning research. First, what are the questions that planners fail to take up for which they have an ethical responsibility to explore? And, second, what might explain such omissions from planning research agenda? This chapter endeavors to provide answers to the latter by exploring possible reasons for one such gap in the literature – the relative dearth of research into bias in travel demand forecasts. This case is instructive because it suggests that our planning institutions – the academy and the profession – are culpable for much of the un-started and unfinished research that planners have a responsibility to pursue.

The Responsibility to be Comprehensive

As professionals and members of the academy, scholars enjoy, with very few exceptions, the privilege to define and pursue their own research agenda. In the United States, this autonomy, inter alia, is codified in the American Association of University Professors' (AAUP) 'Statement on Professional Ethics' and the American Council on Education's (ACE) 'Statement on Academic Rights and Responsibilities.' These Statements function to petition society for professional autonomy (i.e. academic freedom) in exchange for the willingness of scholars to contribute to social wellbeing and act in a manner consistent with broader societal norms. According to AAUP, the primary obligation of professors '…is to seek and state the truth as they see it.' Left undefined, though, is the subjects of these truths. Certainly, though, society has a reasonable expectation that truth not be selective.

The concept of academic freedom as a right of faculty members, then, implies an attendant intellectual diversity in the academy sufficient to not only ensure the continued sifting and winnowing of ideas, but also to see that all worthy ideas are pursued with equal commitment. Whether or not this assumption of institutionalised contention is misplaced, its unquestioned acceptance obliges researchers to act in good faith to create it or generate its expected outcomes. In sum, scholars not only have a responsibility to answer the important questions, but also to ensure that they are asked.

Bias in Travel Demand Forecasts

The travel demand forecasting methodology widely used throughout the world today was developed in the United States in the mid-20th century. It comprises a system of models commonly referred to as the urban transportation modeling system, or UTMS. Although the intervening years witnessed many refinements to the modeling process, it remains, even now, largely unchanged.

Travel demand forecasts rely on statistical regularities that relate current travel patterns to current land use patterns (e.g. location and intensity of activity and the socio-economic characteristics of the population) and transportation system characteristics (e.g. placement and attributes of the road network and transit system). Transportation planners use these statistical regularities and expectations of future land use to forecast future travel. These forecasts are most commonly used to estimate transit ridership, road service levels and vehicle miles of travel at some future point in time, based on planned improvements to the transportation system in order to understand how any particular alternative might perform.

Almost 35 years ago, John Kain first presented convincing evidence that local officials use biased travel demand forecasts to justify decisions based on unstated considerations. Since that time, Kain and others have demonstrated that travel demand forecasts are systematically optimistic – often wildly so – for reasons that cannot be explained solely by the inherent difficulty of predicting the future. Unfortunately, assessments of the problem seem to generate more questions than they answer. Those searching for solutions find myriad prescriptions in the literature for reforming transportation planning processes. While these represent significant contributions, most writers base remedies on diagnoses that rely more upon conventional wisdom and compelling narrative rather than weighty evidence. For example, a number of very competent researchers have issued calls in the United States for Congress to reduce the federal share of capital funding for mass transit projects as a way to discourage rent seeking behaviour by local officials.

The Responsibility to Ask Questions

Few, if any, however, have collected the empirical data necessary to properly justify their appeals even though the theoretical and practical hurdles for doing so seem not to be particularly formidable.[1]

Understanding the Research Void

Research and anecdotal evidence suggest six issues related to the dearth of research on the extent of bias in travel demand forecasts and the origin of such bias: impropriety, methodology, public perception, misunderstanding, impatience and complacency.

Impropriety

Attempts to avoid embarrassment for the problematic professional conduct (i.e. impropriety) of individuals who model transportation demand may explain the lack of postmortems on travel demand forecasts. Within the transportation planning community, conventional wisdom ascribes biased forecasting to a small number of modelers who deliberately overestimate demand by various means to support funding for projects championed by their clients, agencies or political overlords. This narrative stems, in part, from anecdotal accounts of fudging numbers. A few high-profile cases (e.g. late 20th century light rail transit demand forecasts in Miami and San Jose) received a great deal of attention by not only planning professionals, but the laity as well.

Fullerton and Openshaw (1985) focused on impropriety when they concluded some time ago that 'those who possess the necessary data lack the necessary will to investigate what could turn out to be their own off beam forecasts, while those with the necessary will lack the data that are needed' (193). The implication of stonewalling is clear and seems to correspond with the experience of at least one researcher of forecasting results who found some transit agencies less than helpful (Richmond 1998, 16). Muses an observer, '[these operators] may, indeed, be positively reluctant to supply [forecast and ridership] information, which is understandable given that few systems entirely live up to their expectations' (Walmsley and Pickett 1992, 11). Some might object to this characterisation of the problem by claiming that the data sought by reviewers are not generally available simply because they no longer exist or were never assembled. Even so, the failure to collect and archive such data by those in positions to do so suggests that these planners have little interest in assessing their forecasts – claims of insufficient resources not withstanding.

---

1 A notable exception is Bent Flyvbjerg, who, with his colleagues at Aalborg University, Denmark, published a series of articles on the accuracy of both the cost and demand forecasts of public works projects around the world. See e.g. Flyvbjerg, Holm and Buhl 2002 and 2005.

Also premised on presumption of questionable activity, the US government too conceivably plays a role in effectively suppressing research related to assessing travel demand forecasts. Curiously, more travel demand estimates have undergone scrutiny in Great Britain than in the United States. This appears attributable, at least in part, to recognition by the United Kingdom National Audit Office (UKNAO) and – in England particularly – by the Secretary of State's Standing Advisory Committee on Trunk Road Assessment and its predecessor that ex-post analyses are valuable (Brooks and Trevelyan 1979, 251; UKNAO 1988, 12). In contrast, after the US Urban Mass Transportation Administration published unflattering research about forecasting, the US Department of Transportation (USDOT) no longer seems eager to fund similar forays nor does the agency appear to have implemented any of the report's recommendations. It is perhaps not responsible to speculate on the motivations of USDOT except to note that it has the enormously difficult task of balancing the competing demands of Congress, transit advocates and the highway lobby.

Transportation scholars that compete for the research dollars that USDOT controls have considerably less influence with the agency. If the ostensible reticence of USDOT to fund further studies on forecast accuracy is real, it behooves academics interested in future support to steer clear of the topic – and providers subsidised or contracted by USDOT to steer clear of the academics – even if the wherewithal for such a study is available from other sources. This dynamic may help explain why some researchers avoid tough questions when it comes to documenting forecasting bias. While instances of such are by nature subtle, Johnston et al. are forthright in at least one account when noting that they are 'unwilling to determine if the local elected officials directed the...staff to fudge the [operating and maintenance] assumptions' (1988, 467). This dynamic leads directly to questions about the responsibility of scholars and underscores the inherent difficulty of maintaining an independent voice within the academy amid pressure to satisfy colleagues and win the support of funders. In this light, Lave's admonishment is unsurprising. '[There] is evidence of bias. We have a professional duty to examine and improve predictions' (1991, 10).

Methodology

Methodological difficulties can also dissuade investigators from pursuing questions of forecast accuracy. Chief among these is the inability to employ a strict experimental or quasi-experimental design to explain forecasting error. Rarely are forecasting assumptions and methodology transparent and even more rarely are vintage models preserved in working order. As Kain, Pickrell and others have demonstrated (US Department of Transportation 1990), though, this does not preclude the production of useful and authoritative studies that not only document error, but also provide defensible conclusions concerning its origin. Perhaps more precisely, those with the qualitative research skills to address questions of ethics likely do not have the quantitative competencies to interpret numerical modeling and the quantitative scientists who gravitate to (i.e. self-select) technical fields like transportation planning probably lack the qualitative skills and interest to examine their work more holistically.

In any case, the methodological demur of planning researchers often seems disingenuous and politically motivated. For example, an Institute of Transportation Engineers (ITE) committee claims methodological problems prevented it from examining the accuracy of forecast travel demand on major transportation facilities and, similarly, the Department of Transport in England questions forecast comparisons that employ less than ideal methods. The simplistic arguments that both present, however, seem merely justifications for abandoning efforts that might have produced findings unflattering to fellow professionals (Institute of Transportation Engineers 1980, 25; UKNAO 1988, 16).

Public Perception

Unlike in traditional fields in the academy, planning research is largely prescriptive and often supported by agencies that look to planning scholars to solve immediate problems identified by expressions of public disapproval. For example, how do we control low-density growth at the periphery of our urban areas? How do we ease congestion on urban freeways? How do we provide water to fast-growing cities in arid regions? Sometimes even fanciful problems find currency with the public because of their intuitively plausible character. Coupled with crisis forecasts created of simplistic techniques, these promise to also generate research funding. Ultimately, the difference between funded and unfunded research rests on the collective experience of proposal reviewers and comments on grant proposals to study bias in forecasting have commonly reflected skepticism that the problem is real or widespread. This is perhaps best explained by the incredulity expressed by citizen watchdog groups when confronted with bias in forecasting. If the public takes little notice, so likely will the funders. Why, then, has inaccurate travel demand forecasting yet to attract grassroots attention? Presumably because construction of transportation infrastructure takes a long time and memories of the original demand estimates are short lived.

Commonly, public agencies revise downward their demand forecasts as construction on transportation improvements nears completion. Such was the case for Denver International Airport (Goetz and Szyliowicz 1997, 263), BART (Hamer 1976, 70) and light rail in the Banfield corridor of Portland (Pickrell 1990, 4-5) to name three. Typically, this allows local officials to declare early success when initial demand exceeds the revised forecast. The Channel Tunnel for which later demand forecasts reflect greater optimism is the notable exception. Because of the project's unique financing, the optimism served 'to preserve the confidence of the shareholders and banks when cost overruns became apparent...' (Flyvbjerg, Bruzelius and Rothengatter 2003). Even if unrealised promises produce a negative backlash, the elected officials who made them are usually no longer in office when construction is completed since project lead-times are long. Alternatively, others explain the public's lack of attention in economic terms, contending that, at least for rail transit,

> [v]oters remain rationally ignorant because they can afford to...having better things to do than investigate the opportunistic assumptions underlying agency forecasts or undertake the calculations necessary to annualize the opportunity and replacement costs of the capital tied up by existing or proposed rail systems (Moore II 1994, 50, 52).

In the case of toll roads, forecasting failures may have drawn little attention simply because none have yet resulted in a monetary default (Muller 1996, 20).

Misunderstanding

The research void may, more than anything, stem from the implicit assumption of transportation planning and engineering scholars that they understand the forecasting bias problem. Conference proceedings, trade publications and journal articles usually treat bias and inaccuracy as one and ascribe it to flawed methods. This conclusion provides the answer to any potentially interesting questions and, as such, obviates the need for systematic study to identify the cause of bias. Likewise, it may help explain why the transportation planning research agenda tilts disproportionately towards improving and expanding demand estimation techniques. Progress, the narrative suggests, will ultimately make discussions of estimation bias moot.

Although the intuitive nature of this narrative could explain its prevalence, reducing the problem of biased forecasting to rudimentary methodology most likely reflects a Kuhnian attempt by some scholars to suppress a fundamental novelty (i.e. bias), because it threatens the basic commitments on which modelers' methods rest. It implies a change in the rules governing the prior practice of model building and would require those who develop travel demand forecasting processes to reframe the problem as one of judgment rather than of method, which travel demand forecast modelers are at constant work to improve.

The literature is littered with examples of censoring or otherwise ignoring evidence of slanted forecasting presumably because it subverts an understanding of bias as simply inadequate techniques. 'It is especially important to suggest improvements to the technical procedures needed to produce credible forecasts' (Dunphy 1995, 113). This conclusion is typical of those found in studies that focus on optimistic travel estimates. Other articles are conspicuous by their failure to acknowledge the systematic nature of the error they present (e.g. see Brooks and Trevelyan 1979; Mackett and Edwards 1998; Muller 1996; Walmsley and Pickett 1992).

Impatience

Some scholars speculate that participants in the debate have concluded that they will never agree on the dimensions of the forecasting problem and therefore have focused their energies elsewhere. If this is correct, it could help explain other sizable gaps in planning knowledge. Rittel and Webber (1973) long ago reminded planners that their problems differ significantly from those of the natural sciences. Their wicked problems have no stopping rule, and the research scholar must ultimately abandon the problem for lack of time, money or patience.

> The process of solving the problem is identical with the process of understanding its nature, because there are no criteria for sufficient understanding and because there are no ends to the causal chains that link interacting open systems, the would be planner can always try to do better (162).

Complacency

A final reason research on bias in travel demand forecasting is lacking may be connected to a misplaced assumption that travel demand forecasting has no influence on policymaking. If researchers truly believe their work has no impact on the lives of others, then the ethical questions for them – from a teleological perspective, anyway – go away and biased forecasts are of no concern. Although it did not include transportation planning researchers, a relatively recent study of thirty travel demand forecasters (Brinkman 2003) found that the subjects distinguished themselves by perceptions of their professional influence and by the degree to which these self-assessments correspond with job satisfaction. Nearly one third fell into the group where job satisfaction was rated high and professional influence low. For these modelers, the technical challenge of forecasting is their primary source of satisfaction. It seems reasonable, therefore, to conclude that researchers may harbor similar attitudes, which allow them to work contentedly with no concern for bias in their work or that of others.

Bunker Mentality

When viewed through a broader lens, these six issues seem to reveal the picture of an embattled profession preoccupied with projecting a public image that is at once cohesive, highly functional and relevant. Most likely, such is a response to a perceived crisis of autonomy and, by extension, professional identity. Autonomy, of course, has been the Holy Grail of the, so far unsuccessful, quest to identify a unifying paradigm for planning. It is, after all, their methods that most clearly define the traditional professions of medicine, law, divinity and military, as well as such allied fields of planning as engineering and architecture. Lacking such, planning has had to rely on its common purpose to provide its identity.

According the American Institute of Certified Planners' (AICP) Code of Ethics and Professional Conduct, that common purpose is service to the public interest – an idea far too nebulous at this point to provide an identity.

The challenge, as it were, was to provide a face for the public interest by, in essence, identifying the ends of planning, i.e. the outcomes that serve a singular definition of the public interest. Today's planning orthodoxy most definitely reflects a level of success in this enterprise. Transit, land trusts, high-density development, centralisation, mixed land use and quantitative data are, without question, now paragons of good planning. Professional publications and the content of planning conferences all vouch for this contention. Rarely do these provide any critical analysis of the goodness of these venerated ends.

More telling, however, is the multiplicity of ways the profession has closed ranks to maintain its orthodoxy. For example, Planning published an article by its Executive Editor, Ruth Eckdish Knack (2000), which freely used the term 'contrarian' to refer to planners who do not hold to planning orthodoxy. Regardless of whether the reader interprets the term in context as a pejorative, it's worth reflecting on the reason for its use to describe fellow professionals. Professions – voluntary groupings of likeminded experts – are notable for their commonalities.

More directly related to the case study presented here, the American Planning Association (APA) felt it necessary to distance itself from an article published in the Journal of the American Planning Association on the accuracy of cost forecasts for public works projects (Flyvbjerg, Holm and Buhl 2002). In an unsigned letter posted on its website, the APA took the unprecedented step of essentially rebutting the conclusions of the authors that were published in their own journal, that systemic pessimism in cost forecast is symptomatic of 'strategic misrepresentation,' i.e. lying, by planning professionals. With the proverbial heat from members of the APA being unbearable, the profession chose to get out of the kitchen. In this case, the intolerance for alternative conclusions, even well researched ones, rests not only with the professional organisation, but its individual members as well.

The relatively small size of the planning academy compared to that of related fields such as geography, engineering, and architecture, coupled with a tremendous diversity of sub-disciplines, may tend to create small homogenous groups comprised of planning scholars where individuality is often sacrificed for the sake of group cohesiveness. How could group-think pervade the academy where scholars chant the mantra of independent critical thinking reflexively? The incentives to conform in small, and often inward-looking, intellectual communities, as found in the planning academy, are ostensibly much stronger than those to challenge convention. In these academic communities, a smaller number, so as to make double-blind peer reviews problematic, especially when new ideas are the focus, defines career success. Simply put, the fear of isolation is stronger than the more distant possibility of fame in other quarters.

Challenge for Planning

In *On Liberty*, John Stuart Mill argues that it is the duty of both individuals and governments to form the truest opinions that they can and to 'fully, frequently and fearlessly discuss them' (2002, 29). By not doing so, '[i]f the opinion is right, they are deprived of the opportunity of exchanging error for truth: if wrong, they lose what is almost as great a benefit, the clearer perception and livelier impression of truth, produced by its collision with error' (14). Yet, as the full opening quotation of this chapter makes very clear, more pernicious is the risk that the truths that flow from planning research lead to dead dogma, where the grounds of the opinions are forgotten.[2]

If the lack of research on bias in travel demand forecasts is attributable to some or all of the suggested causes presented here and can be generalised to other neglected planning related questions, dead dogma may pose a greater threat to the professional autonomy of planners than the lack of a unifying paradigm. Planners' propensity to chafe at new ideas and feel threatened by the questioning of long held beliefs are signs of an inward looking profession more interested in preserving what little autonomy it has rather than building on it with practice and research. A sustained public, professional and academic discourse among planners that remains above politics may do just this by providing a forum where the public interest is thoroughly debated based on comprehensive research agenda that inform. This, however, will, likely require a sea change. Planning professionals must climb out of their bunkers and embrace their duty to question. Doing so would likely unify the profession in society's mind as a bastion of constructive and comprehensive deliberation over the definition of the public interest.

Turning the tide, i.e. changing the behaviour of planning researchers, can perhaps, best be accomplished by moving to implement three broad strategies. First, the profession and planning schools must adopt and teach Mills' ideas of the liberty of thoughts and discussion. If this cannot be accomplished informally, the American Institute of Certified Planners should enshrine them in their Code of Ethics and Professional Conduct and the Planning Accreditation Board should move to include them in its curriculum guidelines. Duty to question and the danger of dead dogma should be as familiar to planners and planning students as the concept of the public interest. A unique interest and skill to question conventional wisdom could, perhaps, ultimately be paradigmatic for the profession. In any case, placing Mill in an honoured place would go far to provide the needed ethical awareness of the importance of comprehensiveness in research.

---

2 Anecdotal evidence abounds, at least among those who dare challenge planning orthodoxy, of students, professionals and scholars who bristle at 'audacious' suggestions, such as transit cannot deliver on the promises of its advocates or farmland preservation for agriculture is needless, yet have trouble fashioning a reasonable argument for their accepted view.

Second, admission committees for planning programmes should rethink how they select students, especially doctoral candidates. Regardless of motivation, be it self interest or an unreflective adoption of academy norms, selecting students who, inter alia, match the research interests of faculty is a fundamentally flawed approach. A criterion to replace such should work to select students who can challenge faculty and fill important gaps in the knowledge of planning.

Third, and finally, the profession and the academy need to drastically change the incentive system for those working on planning research. Too often, it seems, research is recognised for its familiarity and ability to advance the work of entrenched faculty or the amount of public buzz it generates. Planning researchers need to publicly value those they have up to now referred to as contrarians in a pejorative sense.

Recognition and careful consideration of the dearth of research into demonstrated bias in travel demand forecasting raises important new questions for planning researchers. Foremost among these is whether there exist other sizable gaps in the planning literature that need addressing. Failure to recognise these and take action not only violates the duty to question, it also puts the professional autonomy of planners at risk by losing faith with the public they purport to serve. (Behaviour that is contrary to the expectation of society violates the trust from which professional privilege flows.) Yet, recognising ignored inquiries is probably not enough to impel researchers to take them up. It requires understanding how our planning institutions, especially the profession and academy, play a role in the problem. Paradoxically, this may be the biggest gap of all in our knowledge.

References

Brinkman, P.A. (2003), *The Ethical Challenges and Professional Responses of Travel Demand Forecasters*, PhD diss. 106 (Berkeley: University of California Transportation Center).

Brooks, J.A. and Trevelyan, P.J. (1979), 'Before and After Studies for Inter-urban Road Schemes', in Planning and Transport Research and Computation Co. Ltd.

Button, K.J. and Pitfield, D.E. (eds) (1985), *International Railway Economics: Studies in Management and Efficiency* (Aldershot, UK: Gower Publishing Company Ltd.).

Dunphy, R.T. (1995), 'Review of Recent American Light Rail Experiences', in Transportation Research Board.

Flyvbjerg, B., Bruzelius, N. and Rothengatter, W. (2003), *Megaprojects and Risk: An Anatomy of Ambition* (Cambridge: Cambridge University Press).

Flyvbjerg, B., Holm, M.K.S. and Buhl, S.L. (2002), 'Underestimating Costs in Public Works Projects: Error or Lie?', *Journal of the American Planning Association* 68:3, 279-95.

Flyvbjerg, B., Holm, M.K.S. and Buhl, S.L. (2005), 'How (In)accurate are Demand Forecasts in Public Works Projects?', *Journal of the American Planning Association* 71:1, 131-46.

Fullerton, B. and Openshaw, S. (1985), 'An Evaluation of the Tyneside Metro', in Kenneth J. Button and David E. Pitfield (eds).

Goetz, A.R. and Szyliowicz, J.S. (1997), 'Revisiting Transportation Planning and Decision Making Theory: The Case of Denver International Airport', *Transportation Research Part A: Policy and Practice* 31:4, 263-80.

Hamer, A.M. (1976), *The Selling of Rail Rapid Transit: A Critical Look at Urban Transportation Planning* (Lexington, Mass.: D.C. Heath and Company).

Institute of Transportation Engineers (1980), 'Evaluation of the Accuracy of Past Urban Transportation Forecasts: An ITE Informational Report', *ITE Journal* 50:2, 24-34.

Johnston, R.A., Sperling, D., DeLuchi, M.A. and Tracy, S. (1988), 'Politics and Technical Uncertainty in Transportation Investment Analysis', *Transportation Research Part A: General* 21 A:6, 459-75.

Knack, R.E. (2000), 'Contrarians: To Most of US Sprawl is an Anathema. For Some, It's the American Dream', *Planning* 66:12, 20-23.

Lave, C.A. (1991), 'Playing the Rail Transit Forecasting Game', *TR News*, 156, 10-12.

Mackett, R.L. and Edwards, M. (1998), 'The Impact of New Urban Public Transport Systems: Will the Expectations be Met?', *Transportation Research Part A: Policy and Practice* 32:4, 231-45.

Mill, J.S. (2002), *On Liberty* (Mineola, N.Y.: Dover Publications, Inc.).

Moore II, J.E. (1994), 'Commentary on "The Recent Popularity of Light Rail Transit in North America"', *Journal of Planning Education and Research* 13:1, 50-52.

Muller, R.H. (1996), 'Examining Toll Road Feasibility Studies', *Public Works Financing* June, 16-20.

National Audit Office, United Kingdom (1988), *Department of Transport, Scottish Department and Welsh Office: Road Planning* (London: Her Majesty's Stationery Office).

Pickrell, D.H. (1990), see US Department of Transportation.

Planning and Transport Research and Computation Co. Ltd. (1979), *Highway Planning and Design: Proceedings of Seminar N Held at the PTRC Summer Annual Meeting, University of Warwick, England from 9-12 July 1979* (London: PTRC Education and Research Services Ltd.).

Richmond, J.E.D. (1998), *New Rail Investments – A Review* (Cambridge: A. Alfred Taubman Center for State and Local Government, John F. Kennedy School of Government, Harvard University).

Rittel, H.W.J. and Webber, M.M. (1973), 'Dilemmas in a General Theory of Planning', *Policy Sciences* 4:2, 155-69.

Transportation Research Board (1995), *Seventh National Conference on Light Rail Transit: Proceedings of the Conference at Baltimore, Maryland, November 12-15, 1995* (Washington, D.C.: National Academy Press).

UKNAO (1988), see National Audit Office, United Kingdom.

United Kingdom, Department of Transport, Transport Research Laboratory (1992), *The Costs and Patronage of Rapid Transit Systems Compared with Forecasts: Research Report 352* (Crowthorne, Berkshire: Transport Demand Division, Traffic Group, Transport Research Laboratory).

US Department of Transportation, Urban Mass Transportation Administration, Office of Grants Management (1990), *Urban Rail Transit Projects: Forecast Versus Actual Ridership Costs* (Washington, D.C.: US Department of Transportation Technology Sharing Program).

Walmsley, D.A. and Pickett, M.W. (1992), see United Kingdom, Department of Transport.

Chapter 9

Environmental Planning Research: Ethical Perspectives in Institutional and Value-Driven Approaches

Filippo Schilleci

The Review was planning an environmental ethics issue the following year and Isabel had been soliciting papers. Perhaps somebody would write about the ethics of litter. Not that there was much to say about that: litter was unquestionably bad and surely nobody would make a case in its favour. And yet why was it wrong to drop litter? Was it purely an aesthetic objection, based on the notion that the superficial pollution of the environment was unattractive? Or was the aesthetic impact linked to some notion of the distress which others felt in the face of the litter?

Alexander McAll Smith, (2004), *The Sunday Philosophy Club*,
Pantheon Books, New York

Introduction

Dialogue between the principles and practice of spatial planning and environmental planning has always been difficult, even conflicting. Or, indeed, non-existent. The research I am presenting here focuses on Italy, where domestic legislation has always treated the two subjects as being distinct and has persisted in its determination to keep laws governing the territory separate from those designed to protect the environment. The few attempts, starting in the mid-1980s, to bring the two subjects together under common rules do not seem likely to be further examined and developed and thus become established practice. However, while they may appear to be distinct disciplines, it seems contradictory to persist with this separation, since problems concerning the environment will necessarily have real consequences on the territory. As the situation not just of Italy but of the entire planet amply demonstrates.

The reflections set out here are part of a wider, and still on-going, research programme that I embarked on some years ago into this relationship, from both a theoretical and practical perspective. I have been monitoring what happens in certain areas of Sicily of high natural worth but which, thanks to the action of man, must now be considered at risk (see Schilleci 2003). This type of research is limited almost exclusively to the academic world and I have been able to take it forward thanks to funding from the Ministry for the Universities and Scientific Research.

The aim of the investigation is to gather data to use as possible indicators to manage protected areas properly, not just from the policy but also from the ethical point of view. It uses questionnaires that were designed after clearly identifying the 'principles' and which analyse how the various managing agencies relate to local communities and identities.

In conducting the research I started from principles developed and corroborated through wide reading and the reflections arising from that reading. This led to a determination to conduct a study based not just on discovering the facts, but on certain convictions that would guide the investigation in an ethical manner. The investigation encompassed a number of spheres, given that environmental research is conducted not just by the academic community but also, and sometimes in different forms, by the institutions and associations which, although private or NGOs, collaborate with the public sector in managing protected natural areas. In some respects the research also served to verify a pre-structured methodological approach to these principles, which will be described below.

The following thought expresses fairly clearly the value-driven starting point, and therefore method, that I adopted to formulate the research designed to analyse environmental planning policies in Sicily.

> Man respects nature when, in acting on it to adapt it to our needs, he neither opposes it nor considers it as a mere object to exploit and plunder, but adapts to its 'laws' and protects its beauty. A rule of conduct that technological man seems to have forgotten. That is why ethics are called upon today to play a decisive role. To establish duties in this highly important sphere of human activity ethics must enter into a field from which it has previously – always, perhaps – been excluded: the field of *techniques*. Ethics must intervene in this sphere not to indicate *how* to do a certain thing or take a certain action, but *whether* and *why* to do so (Quarta 2006, 14).

The chapter is composed, essentially, of three parts: The first, introductory part, which is more theoretical in nature, probes the assumptions on which the study was based and the way we intended to use them in speaking of a value-driven approach to research in the environmental planning field, which is grounded in environmental ethics. The second starts from the ethical principles taken as the basis for the research. It provides a framework to the research and is intended to invite a reflection on the relationship between protection and development/exploitation, looking to protected area policies in Italy and more specifically in Sicily. Lastly, the third part analyses some experiences in the management of protected areas – as areas of possible conflict between institutions and local communities. It first asks which type of research is conducted to manage such areas in an ethical manner. It then highlights that development can be produced without necessarily disregarding the ethical principles intrinsic to conservation or sustainable use projects designed not just to promote economic development.

The Place Studied in the Research

My analyses were guided, as specified in this chapter, by the considerations made in constructing a method that might also provide an answer to the ethical dilemmas enunciated above, through a value-driven research practice. At the same time, I wanted to verify whether prescriptive rules might have repercussions, in the research and in practice, on the actual management of protected areas in Sicily.[1]

The place studied: the Region of Sicily. This choice was based on a number of factors, underpinning which is a vision of the regional context as part of the national context. The first of these factors is linked to the very central role this issue has come to play in Italy over the last 20 years or so, and the wide-ranging debate that has developed and continues to engage both the academic and institutional communities. A second factor is the focus traditionally placed in Italy on cultural values in general and, since the early 20th century, on the landscape and areas of natural value in particular. And a third factor is that Sicily anticipated what was happening at the national level. Sicily's regional law establishing protected areas dates from nearly 30 years ago, which means that we can now start evaluating the results of the policies adopted in this field.

My research focused on two spheres of study: the different approaches to research, which underlie the practice, by the institutions and associations engaged in planning and managing protected natural areas.

The future of these delicate areas, which are constantly at risk and where ethical conflicts can arise at any time, is a constant gamble – a gamble in which Jonas (see Jonas 1984) said that identity and human existence cannot be put into play. Changing the environment most certainly means changing man's living conditions. It is an inevitable step, of course, but on the basis of which criteria and values? The question is not one of choosing between *good* and *evil*, but of establishing a hierarchy of values.

(My) Value Driven Approach

To this end I monitored the management of some of these areas, focusing on two aspects in particular. The first is more closely linked to institutional, therefore more general, research, which in many cases seems to be conducted almost as a duty, as I will show later. The second refers to all those actions, in research as in practice, that the managing body has introduced as complementary but important policies to achieve more suitable development and better use of the area.

In conducting my research as described in this chapter, I use a grid of principles to examine the relationships between the issue of moral conscience and policies of

---

1 I feel that until reflections and theories – which are, after all, of fundamental importance in the evolution of policy – become accepted practice, it will be difficult to understand their true value or indeed shortcomings.

122 *Ethics and Planning Research*

development, protection and place. As a useful reference in constructing the grid I took one of the first documents[2] to lay down some fixed points on the question at the international level: the 1992 Declaration of Rio de Janeiro.[3]

The Rio Declaration

Reading the text of the Declaration and examining the 27 principles on which it is based, I find frequent references to environmental *morality* and *ethics*. The need to 'equitably meet developmental and environmental needs of present and future generations' and 'decrease the *disparities* in standards of living' (principles 3 and 5) is declared. The Declaration clearly states that 'environmental issues are best handled with *participation* of all concerned citizens' and that the role of women, as of the youth of the world and *local communities* must have 'a vital role in environmental management and development [...] because of their knowledge and traditional practices' (principles 20 and 22). It also states that 'environmental protection shall constitute an integral part of the *development* process and cannot be considered in isolation from it' (principle 4).

The Rio Declaration can be considered one of the first documents expressing a clear will to plan development using ethical principles. My research, on the other hand, aims to investigate the contribution that the institutions and many environmental associations have made to the national and international debate through their basic research to formulate policies for action. My goal was to tackle not just the difficult task of constructing a common pathway based on the above themes, but also, and above all, the arduous attempt to identify a way to apply this to reality through a management model that still addresses development.

My considerations follow on from this last statement to explore two questions. First, to examine man's general attitude to nature, i.e. by re-interpreting the man–nature relationship from the ethical and moral perspective, bearing in mind their mutual responsibilities (see Jonas 1984). And second, the various approaches to managing the environment, again with respect to the ethical principles taken as an initial assumption.

It is clear from the above that the action of man and the preservation of environmental values are closely connected. Researchers of this relationship rightly

---

2 I certainly do not wish to imply that this is the only document to address the subject; however, the first to address it in an almost systematic manner, including from the relational point of view, is the Declaration of Rio.

3 The Declaration, the outcome of the United Nations Conference in Rio de Janeiro in June 1992, established a 'new global partnership' through the creation of new levels of cooperation among States, key sectors of societies and people, working towards international agreements which respect the interests of all and protect the integrity of the global environmental and developmental system. It contains 27 principles, approved by the United Nations conference on the Environment and Development and confirmed by the UN General Assembly in December of the same year (see United Nations 1992).

state the need for ethical rules that inform human behaviour, and consequently the present and future effects of its actions (see Pearce and Turner 1990), while also constructing methods and policies that promote development.

Local Development

In defining the ethical principles that guided my research on policies on protected areas, another question I felt to be of great importance, as mentioned in paragraph 1, was that of 'local development' (see Magnaghi 2000). The reasons underlying this very real re-focusing of the scientific and political debate are numerous. Particularly worthy of mention is the attempt to launch policies promoting territorially defined socio-economic development. Development based on local systems and which accentuates the dimension of 'economic-social-cultural enhancement' and also aims to provide a dynamic and proactive response to anti-conservationist dissent.

Many other questions may also be connected to the issue of local development: economic, social, cultural and political. Key to the issue is the central role that place is seen to hold within development dynamics. Giancarlo Paba states that the

> local dimension is a *chance*, an opening, an opportunity: not a symbol of resistance to modernisation, but a normal, and therefore at all times modern, form of establishing in a given place a sense of community life, the judicious exploitation of resources and opportunities, and a way of using a specific form of territory (Paba 1998, 106).

This leads to the consideration that another factor must be added to the framework used to construct new protection actions: the role of local communities. This role must, more than anything else, be recovered by reappropriating the communities' place in 'land project' initiatives.

Local communities can adopt the standpoint of people who

> with their capacity to bring affective values back into play and produce virtuous rules that reaffirm new co-development relationships between culture and nature and between settlement and environment, could create a possibility of survival for this delicate, fragile and highly complex organism. However, if within this great family the focus is once again placed on the role played by the actors by virtue of their planning and programming capacity, all this is done by assuming ways of reappropriating and reconstructing the 'community' that refer to models of belonging and relating with places profoundly and irremediably detached from the process introduced by modernity (Decandia 2000, 30).

Environmental Crisis

The aim is to overcome the *environmental crisis* already identified in the relationship between man and environment through an ecological awareness that man needs to rediscover. That is, he needs to recover the ability to recognise the environment as the space in which he himself exists, and not as some extraneous factor. Something with which he is in a direct relationship, recognising that man and nature are mutually intertwined (see Disch 1970; Rolston 1988).

Once again we see reiterated the need to work towards an operational approach that no longer considers the territory as a 'container of economic activity' but as a place rich in 'values' that must strongly influence the rules of the transformation. An approach which, as Patrick Savidan suggests, should seek to establish truth and valid principles while also drawing up a framework that any citizen may use to decide if an action is moral (see Larmore and Renaut 2004).

Development

When reflecting on the relationship between protecting *resources* and exploiting these resources to trigger *development*, I sought from the outset to describe development using the adjective *ecological*, the aim being, as Morin suggests, to view each phenomenon in its relationship with the environment (see Morin 1980). In this type of relationship, the two principal actors are always man and place, man and environment; a relationship that today seems to have become problematic. A problem that has arisen, has grown and has sometimes been tackled, but has still not been resolved. We find long periods in the past during which man established a relationship with places, seeking their true meaning and finding his place, with the utmost respect, in the natural system. But then comes a time when this relationship of 'mutual respect' becomes distorted, because man begins to 'impose himself on places'. The *relationship* becomes a *conflict* (see Hösle 1991).

In this case too, my research was based on finding out the reasons for this conflict. For reasons arising from new economic models, man began to change his settlement patterns. Since then, setting aside any ethical approach, viewing the environment as an object devoid of value and letting himself be guided by personal interest, his relationships with places seem to be based mainly on factors evaluated in purely monetary terms and not *also* in multiple non-monetary terms. The old quest for place as signifying a relationship of belonging and the outcome of a complex 'constructive and interactive process that occurs over time between society and the environment' (Decandia 2000, 28), becomes more of a quest for place as the best environment for a one-way exploitation of its potential. Man seeks places that he can consume without thinking about their future, and therefore about the future of mankind itself.

Man has lost sight of the principle whereby the land is a place in which to live while respecting its rules and trying to find the best way to experience its resources and to exploit them without transforming and transfiguring them. The mistaken idea of nature as a container of inexhaustible or at any rate renewable reserves has been reinforced by an attitude that sought to maximise economic advantage from it.[4] So, for example, progress relegates a wood, a lake or an animal's life to the background (see Blackstone 1980), giving rise to theories that define man as the 'cancer' of the planet (see Lovelock 1988).

Of the various themes that emerged both during my research on the principles and later, during the investigation stage, the interests that are placed in discussion played a key role, depending on the initial standpoint. Starting from an environmental standpoint, the values deemed to be important are, for example, the enrichment of environmental variety and complexity. A viewpoint that focuses on the *use* of the territory, after the advent of the technological age, may be conditioned by economic factors that see it as having another type of value as an inexhaustible mine from which to draw without limits (see Meadows et al. 1972).

Ethics and Environmental Policies

The principles I took as my starting point, drawn from the Rio Declaration, refer to an ethics of the environment.

My aim here, however, is not to propose an essay on ethics. It is, rather, to present some reflections on the methodology I used to construct my own ethics to follow as a researcher. Most notably concerning the origins of ethics and their development up to the formation of environmental ethics, and looking to the most recent literature in environmental research (see Hargrove 1989).

Ethics is an ancient and, of course, much debated topic. Plato, in *The Republic*, and Aristotle, in his *Nicomachean Ethics*, pose the question of how to define it; of how to apply it in the art of governing; and of its role, through knowledge, in action.

Aristotle observes that wisdom, in its more general sense, is

> the most finished of the forms of knowledge. It follows that the wise man must not only know what follows from the first principles, but must also possess truth about the first principles. Therefore wisdom must be intuitive reason combined with scientific knowledge – scientific knowledge of the highest objects which has received, as it were, its proper completion.[5]

Plato discusses politics and the 'just city', and poses the question of who should be entrusted with the task of governing the city, educating it and pursuing the common good through unity, of making the city the theatre in which the individual can pursue

---

4   Criticism of these theories led to the concept of sustainable development and the Meadows Report, which questioned the myth of relentless development and underscored the difficult relationship between economic development and the protection of the environment.

5   Cf. Aristotle, *Nicomachean Ethics*, VI, 7, 1141 a 16-20.

self-improvement and along with others build a good life for all (see Vegetti 2005). He speaks of ethics and politics as factors in understanding the common good.

This subject is treated in philosophy, though not, until Plato, as an independent subject, since it is cited in discussions of 'wisdom'. We probably only find it being treated on its own merits with the advent of Hellenistic philosophy (see Vegetti 2006). But by its very content it is clearly an issue that does or should influence all the decision-making that might have repercussions on the life of the community. It should therefore be considered, by right, an integral part of many other disciplines.

It is probably for this reason that we find many attempts to delineate and define the exact meaning of ethics, and how to apply them. Some commentators view ethics as resting on an indisputable base and others maintain that, in view of their very essence and rationale, ethics cannot be absolute, since to be absolute they would have to have been formulated ethically at the outset (see Larmore and Renaut 2004).

Ethics of the Environment

The subject of the environment, unlike that of ethics, can be viewed as a contemporary issue, which probably originated more as a 'problem' and only later became a discipline *a posteriori*.

Research in this field has been firmly established for some years now. And many scholars have stated that the environmental crisis has many causes: cultural, economic, political and technical, which

> can be traced back to a single, fundamental cause, i.e. the profound change in values that came with modernity and is commonly called a *moral crisis*. The environmental crisis is therefore primarily an *ethical crisis*. And it is highly significant that the *primacy of ethics* in addressing ecological problems is acknowledged not just by moral philosophers or religious authorities, but also by scientists, with one of them going so far as to state that in today's world 'ethics is all'[6] (Quarta 2006, 133).

The need for an ethical approach, long denied by modernity, must instead be acknowledged. Because without an ethical approach 'freedom self-destructs, man is reduced from an end to a means and nature, transformed into a cheap commodity, is debilitated and annihilated' (Quarta 2006, 133).

These sources have also played a part in constructing an ethical structure for my research on environmental planning, by triggering new thoughts and considerations.

---

6   As declared by Edward Osborne Wilson, an American biologist, who in his studies on the environment stated the importance of the ethical approach (see Wilson 1998).

Ethics and environmental problems, therefore, are related. Leopold first proclaimed the need for a *Land Ethic* in 1949, as a new moral concept that views man's duties as including respect for his fellows and for all living creatures – and for the entire planet. And then in the 1970s it did indeed become clear that the causes of environmental disruption have their roots in ethics (see Passmore 1980; Jonas 1984; Apel 1987).

This has led to the construction of an ethics of the environment,[7] which began to take shape in the 1970s as an autonomous school of thought looking at the environmental crisis and its problems from a philosophical standpoint rather than seeking to resolve them through technology (see Leopold 1949; Cobb 1972). Today, however, it has developed as a discipline that poses the question of why and how man must care for the environment, in all its complexity.

Indeed, since they are interrelated, the problems of the environment should not be treated on a sectoral basis. Species preservation, for example, or even the increasingly topical problem of pollution and waste disposal, overlap with other questions concerning values, ethics, equality and rights. The term 'value' is highly important: it can be represented, in this context, by the relationship between value expressed through individual and collective preferences and the physical functions of the ecosystem (Pearce and Turner 1990).

Just how weak is the idea that nature is stable, unassailable, capable in all circumstances of regenerating and promptly healing any wounds inflicted by man and his activities, has become increasingly clear. Probably inspired by the 'god of the market', this idea was driven by the principle of *doing* without *knowing*: maximum capacity comes up against minimum knowledge of purpose (see Jonas 1984).

All of which has led to the environmental crisis. And consequently, the need to intervene with principles and ethical rules to lead man back from his delirium of omnipotence and help him once again recognise his limits, which are those of a being whose intelligence is, after all, finite and limited.

Man must recover his sense of responsibility so that, according to the principle of accountability (Jonas 1984), when he is about to make a decision he feels the need to obey the moral obligation of *thinking*. This follows on from his realisation that the consequences of his actions could affect not just his immediate surroundings and future, but also people who are far away (in space and time).

---

7   Generally, environmental ethics is defined as that part of environmental philosophy which considers the ethical relationship between human beings and the natural environment. It exerts influence on a large range of disciplines including law, sociology, theology, economics, ecology and geography. Environmental ethics is properly a sub-section of environmental philosophy, which includes environmental aesthetics, environmental theology and all the other branches of philosophical investigation (e.g. epistemology, metaphysics, philosophy of science, etc.).

The Research

I will highlight different ethical approaches in conducting research in the field of environmental planning. My ethical value-driven approach (compare section 2) is shared with other planning academics and it is mainly confined to academic research. There are, undoubtedly, other ethical approaches in the field of environmental planning research.

Nevertheless, the principles described in the previous sections structured my research project. The aim was to foster an understanding of the relationships between the following three factors while also seeking to identify any repercussions and possible policy developments for protected areas. In other words, understanding what relationships there are – and if there are no such relationships, why not? – between:

- *local communities*, which find themselves coexisting with a system of constraints regulating protected areas, and which often do not see these areas as reflecting their own identity, rights and needs;
- *local development*, which accentuates economic-social-cultural enhancement, including as a dynamic and pro-active response to anti-conservationist dissent;
- *protection*, in light of a new conservation philosophy that moves from passive, defensive positions to active positions with respect to natural resources and also directly involves individuals in active participation (see Giacomini and Romani 1992).

As stated above, the object of my analysis is the approach to research as adopted by the institutions engaged in the planning of protected natural areas and by the public and private bodies whose job is to manage them.

Institutional Approach

In Italy, the institutional approach to environmental planning research is grounded on 'normative ethics', in the sense that research must follow a normative theory established by actual laws and institutionalised practices (i.e. 'rules' of conduct deriving from European directives).

Environmental planning laws are only partially shaped by principles of environmental ethics. The procedures envisaged by the various laws limit the scope of the research to an analysis of the territory. And what is more, these analyses are often entrusted to individual specialists who conduct them according to their own ethical principles. Until some years ago what was missing was an ethics that could guide the analysis in a unified fashion, since the only 'rules' were the relevant legislative provisions.[8]

---

8   For an example that clarifies the concept, we can analyse the process of drawing up a territorial plan for a park. The analyses conducted have often been limited to those listed by the law, thus producing research that is almost 'institutional' in nature.

Luckily, it seems that something has changed in the last 20 years. And even if we cannot say that the practice of *using* the land has changed in its principles – we would probably need to cancel out too many years of malign policies – the way of *thinking* about it, and especially about the environment, has to a large extent altered, thanks in part, clearly, to individuals and organisations. By consciously thinking about the environment and placing its values firmly back in the foreground, along with its history and identity, they have initiated policies designed to *protect* it in order to pursue a better model for living. We have finally realised that land is not a renewable asset, and that environmental problems must interrelate ever more closely with the disciplines involved in governing the land. We have realised that planning processes that focus solely on built spaces without giving the proper consideration to natural spaces have produced nothing but a poorer qualify of life. We have realised that we need to change our approach, an approach that must be guided by ethical principles, if we are to avoid repeating the same errors.

Today we know that the interests of states and governments are focused on identifying

> social and collective actions that take the form of re-actions. Actions, that is, that rehabilitate nature because, especially in advanced societies, it is under threat. It is being constantly eroded in its very essence and is sending out messages about its lost integrity. This means that today's forms of mimesis, which we find in mass communications – from bio-architecture to advertising, from eco-tourism to natural products – all speak of society's attention to ecosystems while carrying within them the implicit connotation of loss, consumption, a decline in 'naturalness' which is always a historic-social loss (Beato 1999, 39).

And all this is channelled through a quest, by the disciplines working in planning, for a unified concept that encompasses both environmental problems and local development problems.[9]

Indeed, recent years have seen a degree of contamination between the two spheres. We do not mean here that ethical principles have become firmly established as policy tools; merely that attempts have been made in this direction.

Italian laws   In Italy a number of laws touching on this sector have been issued, thus paving the way for designing a structure that focuses more closely on the needs of the environment.[10] Laws issued in 1985, on the protection of areas of

---

9   These changes can be found not just at the national but also at the European level. Many EU programmes have given rise to new ways of understanding territorial development initiatives, at both the theoretical and the operational and practical levels.

10   The difficulty of *contamination* also arises from the different paths followed by town planning and environmental protection (the 'historic' reference is clearly to laws 1497 and 1089 of 1939, which govern the protection of the artistic heritage and landscape, and to Law 1150/1942, which is still today the national town planning law). It was only with

special environmental interest,[11] and in 1991, establishing protected areas,[12] arrived somewhat late with respect to the 'environment question' that emerged in the late 1960s and became even more apparent in the 1970s, when the 'limits of development' and the irreparable harm done to the environment by the excessive and indiscriminate development of the post-war decades became evident.

This is not the place to put either the intentions or the actors on trial. However, the results show us a country where protected areas today account for 10 percent of the territory and, in the light of the current cultural debate, would actually be better described as *crystallised* rather than protected. This quality of 'crystallisation' has led to a 'debate on the protected areas', a debate that until a few years ago was also defined, restrictively no doubt, as a 'debate on parks and reserves'. This new name, which uses the term 'area', introduces an important concept: these places are no longer considered as single objects, but as parts of a wider system, i.e. the territory of the region, without rigid limits and boundaries.

Speaking of a *system of areas*, we can rightly refer to the practice of 'reading' and planning the land from an environmental continuity perspective, a basic principle in the idea of the ecological network. Over the last 20 years this subject has become increasingly well-established through research and practice. These are based on the initial idea that an ecological network can be understood either as a set of natural (or semi-natural) areas interconnected through *linear infrastructure* or, in a somewhat detached and abstract manner, as relations and connections between actors. These may be independent of the location of the linkages, and tend to cancel out any tendency to confine natural areas to numerous little islands each ignoring the other (see Nowicki et al. 1996; Bennett and Mulongoy 2006).

The introduction of protection without boundaries has altered the narrow concepts of protection that for years had mainly been subject to quantitative criteria. These were linked to local decisions that did not take the ecological principles that have always governed nature into account. This shift has opened up the debate to

---

Law 431/1985 that these paths begin to converge, by giving environmental protection a full planning, territorial and socio-economic relevance. The very culture of planning has shifted its focus to include environmental problems, while consideration of the territory is increasingly integrated with that of the city and a vision tending increasingly to include an ecological perspective is gaining ground. Since 1985, a number of planning instruments have been added to the perhaps overly wide repertoire of such instruments. Established by very specific laws, they seek to respond to the pressures triggered by the environmental question. Briefly, and without going into their merits, we might mention the 'Landscape-Environmental Plans' and 'Ecologically Oriented Town or Land Planning Provisions' under Law 431/1985; the 'Catchment Basin Plans' established by Law 183/1989; and the 'Parks Plans' envisaged by Law 394/1991. None of these instruments, however – when and if applied – contemplate a 'relational vision'.

11   Law 431/1985. 'It is only with this law (…) that we can speak of an "environmental turning point" in Italian planning: a turning point, to be sure, that was announced, hoped for or feared far more that it was actually achieved' (see Gambino 1996, 23).

12   Law 394/1991.

policies based on systems of areas rather than individual communities. A system that is guided, at least in principle, by ecological standards that once again place man on a par with the environment. While previously it was man who depended on nature, now it is the opposite (see Kieffer 1979). Man, as a member of local communities, therefore assumes the task of looking after the environment, since his actions become decisive to its very future.

In Italy, on the subject of local communities, and bearing in mind the points made earlier about local development, institutional research seems to have forgotten this issue, or partly ignored it until now.

Such an approach does not yet seem to play a key role in national planning and management policies either of protected areas or of areas of high environmental worth. This is true notwithstanding the attempts made to foster such a development, as mentioned earlier when discussing contamination between the environmental and town planning spheres. Only in some regional legislative frameworks have such attempts produced noteworthy and interesting developments. The regions that are lagging behind in cultural and legislative terms most certainly include Sicily. Here, policies – often malign – have sought to undermine the health of the territory. And they have often succeeded, with the result that today the territory is very fragmented from both the physical and the legislative points of view.

A last note is needed on the instruments/policies that, on the question of planning for protected areas, and unlike the system of ecological networks, are a legal obligation. These are essentially three in number: the Land Plan for the Park; a Reserve Zone Plan for the reserves; and a Plan of Use for protection or pre-reserve zones. These normative instruments, as mentioned above, require a standardised set of research/knowledge.

What cannot yet be verified, however, is how the ethical approach in research activities can be transmitted throughout the three planning instruments that regulate the life of the reserves. A notable delay by municipal bodies and environmental associations in drawing up the planning instruments, raises doubts as to the feasibility of the transition between theory and practice we mentioned at the start of this section. The fault certainly does not all lie with the managing body. Much of the responsibility lies with the policies followed by Regione Sicilia, which often seems to have forgotten Plato's lesson on ethical and political factors and understanding the common good.

In all three instruments, indeed, any consideration of the central issues of environmental philosophy in addressing the project is at present left to the researchers.

Territorial planning in Sicily   In Sicily, my research revealed a very fragmented regional territorial structure. To better understand the rules that have led to the construction of such a territory, a brief overview of some of the legislative references might be helpful.

The territorial planning processes of the island's regional government, Regione Sicilia, are still today regulated by a law dating from 1978.[13] This law identifies two planning levels: regional and municipal, and entrusts to the latter, through General Regulatory Plans, the entire 'superstructure' of the Region's town planning regulation.[14] References to environmental issues are notable mainly by their absence.

In purely environmental matters, however, the path followed by Regione Sicilia to safeguard and protect the natural heritage has developed since the 1980s with the establishment of protected natural areas – Reserves and Parks.[15] The aim here is to safeguard habitats and maintain biodiversity in areas of high environmental value, while also promoting development linked to the sustainable use of land resources and traditional activities.[16]

The systemic view led my research towards the ecological network system. But in the regional context, there are objective difficulties in translating the concept of ecological network into a working tool to be used alongside other regional planning instruments. At present, it has neither a specific characterisation nor an operational strategy that translates into procedural or administrative actions.

In this regional legislative framework, however, the only initiative addressing the subject of ecological networks in Sicily that is worthy of mention concerns

---

13   Law 71/1978, considered *provisional*, has been added to repeatedly over the years to bring it into line with changes in the national framework and to fill gaps and remedy weaknesses.

14   To remedy the lack of an intermediate planning level for strategic decisions and opportunities regarding the land, a Province-based level was established in 1986. This, especially within sustainable land development and nature conservation policies, has come to play a fundamental role in the implementation of regional strategies, by referring in turn to the municipal level. It might be possible in this context to identify new environmental duties and responsibilities by viewing it as a place of contact between the two spheres, territorial and environmental.

15   Through the relevant law, which pre-dates the national legislation by ten years, Sicily's system of protected areas now consists of four Regional Parks (Etna, Madonie, Nebrodi and Fluviale dell'Alcantara) and 89 Nature Reserves covering a total of 279,000 ha., or just over 10 percent of the regional territory. This is a highly significant system in terms of the number and extent of the protected areas of high environmental, as well as social and economic, value. In addition, in implementation of the European Community's Oiseaux (79/409) and Habitat (92/43) Directives, 233 Sites of Community Importance (Italian acronym SIC) and Special Protection Zones (Italian acronym ZPS) have been identified for Sicily.

16   This system of protected natural areas, however, has turned out to be mired in contradictions. Not only has no systematic environmental protection policy ever been introduced, but a high percentage of protected areas, even relatively small ones, are located close to towns and cities with a strong presence of settled areas, either in or near the towns themselves.

the 'Sicilian Ecological Network Integrated Regional Project'.[17] The Project is a Regione Sicilia tool for the implementation of nature and biodiversity conservation and sustainable development policy in areas of high natural worth, in accordance with the policy lines contained in the Regional Resolution of 21 May 2001.[18]

My research analysed the project. It seems that the moral approach to the research on which the institutions are basing the regional project has been put to one side. 'Environmental policy' does not seem to have played any role in constructing the research methodology used to design the project. It almost seems, if we analyse the proposal, that the institutional approach to research is once again being driven purely by economic concerns, although an attempt is being made to mediate with the needs of nature.

The 'Sicilian Ecological Network', considering the prevalent role of utilitarianism ethics, has the strategic objective of constructing new models of land management designed to conserve by enhancing the resources of the endogenous heritage, and by ensuring that the various components of the Network become privileged environments in which new forms of intervention can be tested. At the same time, however, it presents problems in view of the total absence of any reference to a relationship with land and town planning instruments. It also, and above all, seems that the only question posed was *how* to do things, and not *whether* or *why* to do them.[19] Which brings us back to the key issue: institutional research methodology that seems to ignore research in this field.

Environmental Associations' Approach

My study of the research conducted by the institutions did not reveal any positive or encouraging results, demonstrating once again the gaps in the institutional research on this subject. The situation was slightly different for research conducted by associations. Associations that have produced papers calling for a shift of focus from a scale of 'principles' in the research to one of 'applications', and which were equally useful to the construction of the grid, most definitely include the World Wildlife Fund.

---

17   Approved with D.G. 376 in 2004 as part of the 'Regional Operational Plan for Sicily 2000/2006', an institutional and financial instrument, and Sicily Region's Programming Supplement – Measure 1.11.

18   Sicily Region's Regional Operational Plan for Sicily 2000/2006 'Implementation of the ecological network in Sicily'. To establish the Network, the Region drew up a targeted programming strategy and equipped itself with specific tools that involved Structural Fund programming, within which specific measures and instruments for integrated territorial and strategic planning were drawn up.

19   In addition, the absence of a planning structure defining the strategies and relationships between the various initiatives could produce an abstract representation of 'ecological network' that is difficult to localise in territorial terms. Above all, in the presence of a primarily financial tool such as the PIR, it could create a high risk of initiatives that are not consistent with the basic principles of the ecological network.

In recent years the WWF has produced an interesting dossier[20] intended as guidance for anyone tackling the difficult task of drawing up a plan for a protected area while fostering the maintenance and growth of social capital in ethical terms, as well as community cohesion and cultural life and factors such as education, health and training.

Divided into five parts,[21] the dossier aims to define the criteria and methodologies for the optimal planning of protected areas that are the fruit, on the one hand, of experience and professionalism, and on the other of environmental ethics.

For a better understanding of the methodology recommended to devise the Plan, it is advisable to read the whole paper; here, we restrict ourselves to quoting the key points, later used to construct the grid. At the same time we stress the need to find a bridge joining planning, on the one side, and the wishes and knowledge of local communities, on the other – indicated as 'the construction of consent' – for the management of a protected area. This goes beyond the traditional boundaries of 'administrative actions' and passive protection and more closely approaches 'development', whose importance and need we have previously underlined. The WWF lists five sectors[22] within which actions should be undertaken:

1) Participation   in other words, the search for a relationship between population (local communities) and protected area through participation, compromise or co-planning, advisory or control activities. This is quite an important step, especially if considered 'from the point of view of easy interpretation and clear information with the desire to gain social consensus for the creation of Parks'. All the actors involved in the decision-making process have a legitimate desire to believe that their own suggestions might have had some kind of effect. 'All those decisions that are not a direct result of a participative process including all actors are generally not likely to be put into practice, since they are seen by those who have been left out as a sign of abuse of power'. This paper suggests the need for an approach based on clear methods, that is to say, a policy that makes citizens aware that they can take an active part in formulating the plan. With precise rules, obviously, inspired by environmental ethics that suggest that the decision of how, whether and why to make certain choices and decisions should not be delegated to one single body.

---

20   Drawn up in November 1998 and entitled *WWF Guidelines for the Park Plan*. Two years later, in 2000, a second dossier supplementing the first was written. Its title was *The Environment, from Constraint to Opportunity: Establishing and Supporting Local Park Communities*.

21   The five sections are: Context and goals of the dossier; Objectives, principles and criteria for the Plan; Consensus-building; Operational structure for the Plan; and Implementation of the Plan.

22   To these five points should be added another, concerning the Local Agenda 21 and Environmental Action Plans that 'might be a useful element for discussion and encourage the definition of the different stages of the Plan, and more specifically the participative element'. Given their intrinsic quality of 'involving' all the social partners, these instruments pursue lasting and self-fuelling development.

2) Consensus This is usually seen as the last step towards the approval of a plan. 'Effectiveness and efficaciousness of decisions are closely connected to intensity of interest (will to act) and consensus (which could be defined as shared interest) shown with regard to the value of each decision and the decision-making method used'. It is thus clear that, in the drafting of a plan, interest plays a role that should not be overlooked:

> The notion of interest is generally associated with the idea of a profit, of an economic benefit; as a matter of fact, this interest is backed by well-constructed and profound psychological and social reasons. Beside the so-called primary needs, there are also needs of safety, security and stability, of belonging to a group and territory, of self-esteem, cognitive and aesthetic needs and needs of self-fulfilment. One more element that is usually underrated, or better, seen as a source of danger instead of as a possible motivational drive, is the relationship between man and his territory, based on protection and interaction. We need to understand what motivates the local communities to create and protect a splendid natural park if the credit for any possible success is then completely ascribed to external managing agencies.

3) Effectiveness[23] It is essential to consider all the interests acting on the territory, including self-fulfilment and jurisdiction over the individual's own territory; this could be done through an informal, flexible, all-embracing procedure, within which no-one would feel excluded beforehand but which could determine both positive and negative clashes of interests. 'In many cases it is possible to find solutions that can minimise the problems caused by the presence of potentially clashing interests provided that this happens in an explicit way and before decisions reach a point of no return. These are the so-called Win-Win solutions, that is, solutions that maximise the mutual satisfaction of the parties concerned in the matter, rather than favouring compromise. At present, especially in Anglo-Saxon countries, very diverse techniques to promote consensus and participation in the management of the territory are adopted within local communities'.[24]

---

23 This 'point' of the guidelines is introduced, with others, as something that must be re-considered and reviewed on each and every planning occasion.

24 It continues: 'We mean Community visioning and Community-based Environmental Protection, to name just two procedures centred on psychological and social motivations. Even though they may seem difficult to put into effect, one could begin with collective *brainstorming* procedures regarding general objectives. This procedure should try and involve all present subjects; regional and local agencies' representatives, associations, universities, schools and interested citizens. The results of such a survey could be useful to draft a final paper containing a list of provisional directives contributing to the strengthening of the identity and specificity of each park and its inhabitants'. Both procedures, therefore, play the card of psychological and social motivation by initiating a collective brainstorming procedure that must seek to involve all the actors present: representatives of regional and local institutions, associations, universities, schools, interested citizens, and disadvantaged or vulnerable associations and social categories.

4) Training For a winning strategy, it might be useful to devise introductory training and information courses with special reference to a given protected area, making the local community feel an integral part of the planning procedure, thus 'improving dialogue and participation of local populations'. By Capacity Building we mean:

- creating plans that not are alien to the local reality and identity and at risk of being refused/boycotted by the community itself;
- starting involvement and participation from the lowest level upwards, including all present/possible actors;
- starting a specific process to get acquainted with and understand the environmental issue;
- starting local compatible development programmes and processes;
- creating tighter connections between the environment and economic and social activities;
- favouring new life-styles for local communities.

5) Education This is seen as a very important issue. Natural protected areas should play a new role and 'become a real training ground where each citizen's environmental awareness and sensitivity could be developed and improved'. This role could be played on different levels. The protected area can become a laboratory for the achievement of sustainable development 'where schools and visitors could take part in or get to know a real process moving towards sustainable development'. Consequently, the protected area could not only offer traditional tracks showing the cultural and landscape peculiarities of the territory, but also the social and economic reality that 'testifies to the possible and desirable future prospects of the territory'. The protected area could even become a place where schools, communities and local agencies could interact, thus making the school 'a cultural driving force and full member of the local community'.

This five-point framework leads us to imagine precise intentions of initiating more articulated, innovative and complex planning processes in Italy. It also suggests a more open management – and living – policy for the protected area that also looks to the local development of the territory and the rediscovery of a moral approach to nature, through a co-penetration between man and his world, and nature itself (see Venturi Ferriolo 2003).

But the research I conducted also leads to other considerations. The reality, especially viewed through the grid designed taking into account all those principles highlighted in the research through a reading of the documents mentioned above, appeared very different.

A case study   The case study presented here concerns the experiment which Legambiente,[25] one of the bodies selected by Regione Sicilia to manage nature reserves on the island, has been conducting for some years to develop protected areas in a more modern manner. Legambiente's clear aim has been to respond to real needs identified by research, especially academic research, in the environmental field. To achieve this, it has modelled its activity, of research first and action later, on an innovative ideology and from a perspective of economic-social-cultural exploitation and enhancement that is codified in a new *environmental philosophy*[26] (see Des Jardins 2006).

Legambiente manages six reserves in Sicily Region, namely *Grotta di Carburangeli* (Palermo), *Lago Sfondato* (Caltanissetta), *Grotta di Santa Ninfa* (Trapani), *Isola di Lampedusa* (Agrigento), *Grotta di Sant'Angelo Muxaro* (Agrigento) and *Maccalube di Aragona* (Agrigento). It has been managing these reserves for about ten years on average, a fairly limited period to see definitive results, but sufficient to examine the goals set and above all the management approach and some of its initial outcomes.

From Legambiente's reports and the initial results of the monitoring it emerges that the activities carried out thus far also include – in addition naturally to planning and research, habitat and species conservation, and environmental recovery and improvement – environmental education, the dissemination of knowledge, and social and economic promotion and development at the local level. It also seems clear that the underlying intention has always been to launch initiatives designed to involve ever wider social categories. Legambiente's aim here has been to prevent decisions taken to regulate the life of and in the reserves from seeming to be imposed from above, as would be the case if it took upon itself the critical decisions of *how*, *whether* and *why*. Its motivation is not just to seek consensus, but also to consider as many needs as possible in order to construct a system of rules and regulations that determine how to resolve any possible or probable conflicts of values (see Næss 1986).

One of Legambiente's strong points in environmental education for the general public has been the introduction of awareness-raising initiatives in schools with

---

25   Legambiente, we read in the National Statute approved in Florence in December 1999, 'is a countrywide association of citizens that operates to protect and enhance nature and the environment, natural resources, the health of the community and of animal and plant species, the historic, artistic and cultural heritage, and the territorial and landscape heritage. In favour of life, production and consumption styles and for education and training inspired by eco-development and consumer protection, a balanced and respectful relationship between human beings, other living creatures and nature'.

26   *Environmental philosophy* came into being as a discipline that can respond to questions concerning the relationships between man and the environment. It is considered a branch of contemporary moral philosophy that is intended to question the plausibility of extending the scope of morality beyond the confines of human inter-relations and to define a system of moral rules to follow if and when our behaviour affects the life and condition of non-human entities not produced by man.

a view to extending young people's education to include the man/environment relationship. They also define as obsolete the habit of interpreting this relationship through opposing categories, such as useful and harmful or costs and benefits, which thus far have overshadowed other values connected with the profitable use of the environment. One product of this policy was an educational booklet published in 1998.[27]

In these and other cases, the production of educational and study material and the enthusiasm of both schools and the population in general have shown how *participatory* actions are much more productive, for the protected area itself, than *imposed* actions. Considerations that are confirmed in the 'guiding principles'.

As mentioned earlier, my research extended to the entire region and, therefore, to all the protected areas. For the issues discussed in this chapter it seems appropriate to mention other management bodies' experience to gain an understanding of how the efforts to establish day-to-day management procedures are flanked by others inspired by environmental ethics. A system of ethics which, in addition to safeguarding the environment in a new relationship between man and his natural surroundings, is based on equal dignity and equal rights for human beings.

These include, in the field of community involvement and promotion, two fairly recent experiments promoted by Regione Sicilia's Azienda Foreste Demaniali (Forestry Agency)[28] in two nature reserves, in collaboration with other institutional bodies.

The first testifies to a clear intention to conduct the traditional planning and management of protected areas taking an approach inspired by research guided by ethical principles. In October 2007 the first nature guide in Braille, designed to remove barriers to the enjoyment of these areas,[29] was presented at Sughereta di Niscemi, one of the reserves managed by the Agency. At the same time, a 600-metre path was opened in the Reserve, lined at intervals by specially made information panels in Braille explaining the fauna and flora to be found in the reserve.

---

27   Cf. Riserva Naturale Integrale Grotta di Carburangeli, *La grotta e l'uomo*, 1998, p. 3. The introduction states that 'the idea of producing an educational booklet for primary and junior middle-school pupils arose from the experience gained through our activity in local schools in these early years of managing the Grotta di Carburangeli nature reserve'. Actions and products that look to, and are mindful of, local culture. Or we could take the experience of the *Laboratori Ambiente* (Environment Workshops) in the Grotta di Santa Ninfa nature reserves, which produced a number of educational leaflets drawing on the work of school pupils.

28   The Forestry Agency is another body identified by Sicily Region for the management of protected areas.

29   The guide was produced by the Provincial Office of Caltanissetta in collaboration with the Regional Braille Printers of the Italian Union of the Blind and Visually Impaired. It represents added value for a body that has made the protection of biodiversity and development of the territory its strong point since nature protection, viewed as an asset, is a resource for the community's economic and cultural growth.

The second project, which in some respects is linked to the first, saw the managing body of the Monte Cammarata Reserve stage Italy's first Nature Paralympics in May 2008, in a splendid natural setting.[30] The aim in involving such a wide range of regional organisations, from schools to municipal councils, from sports clubs to associations for the disabled, was to bring sport and nature together under the banner of 'participation without barriers'.[31]

These and other initiatives give grounds for hope that the ethical principles of environmental philosophy are gradually being included in the instruments used in an analysis designed to construct projects to develop the new man–nature relationship. Unfortunately, however, we must also note several episodes that suggest there is still a long way to go in educating the community on the merits of an ethical relationship with the environment and with others from the same community. While the creation of the path for blind people suggests a real integration process, the subsequent theft of the rope marking the pathway, and the damage done to the explanatory panels in Braille, mean that this process has taken one step forward and many steps back. Just as the fires started by arsonists, which often lay waste to large swathes of the protected areas, destroy not just the vegetation but also some works carried out from the perspective of the above-mentioned integration process.

In conclusion, it is true to say that initiatives undertaken by the associations are not directly related to research as they take a more practice-oriented approach.

Once again, therefore, the principles guiding the research point to results suggesting that the transition from theory to practice clearly still has many obstacles to overcome.

---

30 The event was organised in collaboration with the Sicilian Paralympic Committee and with the patronage of the Regional Schools Office, the Regional Education Department, the Sicilian branch of the Italian National Olympic Committee (CONI), Federparchi and ENEL CUORE Onlus (a non-profit social organisation).

31 The choice of the Monte Cammarata Reserve to stage the event was by no means random. For some time now, the Reserve has been accessible both to disabled people and to visually impaired and blind people, as the management body had created a 700-metre path that can be covered by wheelchair, along with a specially equipped area that is free from barriers and fitted with suitable toilet facilities. Some of the participants at the Nature Paralympics had physical disabilities but were able to walk, while others were wheelchair-users or had psychological or physical impairments. The games amply demonstrated how sport can be a great opportunity for socio-cultural integration for disabled people. The presence of members of the Paralympic team from the Beijing 2008 Paralympic Games was hugely significant to the integration of and between differently able and non-disabled people.

Verifying the Principles

Considering the nature and limits of the institutional and environmental associations' approaches, as illustrated in Chapters 3 and 4, my 'academic' research moved towards analysing this relationship in the context of managing protected areas, to verify whether or not ethical behaviour exists in Sicily. This type of research is limited almost exclusively to the academic world and I have been able to take it forward thanks to funding from the Ministry for the Universities and Scientific Research. It focuses on ways of combining *active environmental protection, local development* and the *identity of local communities and places* with the question of *protected areas* (Parks, Reserves, SICs and ZPSs) – on which those engaged in land planning have already being focusing their attention for some time now. At the same time, it has involved an effort to define a number of rules, designed not to create restrictive categories but primarily as rules of conduct, for all those actions which the bodies responsible for managing the Region's protected areas must initiate for their land protection operations.

In conducting this research, the normative ethics of the institutional approach was very limited. A major difficulty we encountered in analysing the management of Protected Areas in Sicily was the lack of agreed rules. This was aggravated by the complex planning system, particularly for nature reserves. Under the law regulating the establishment of protected areas in Sicily, the management of reserves can be entrusted to various types of body.[32] And, as mentioned earlier, we also have the problem of two different instruments, drawn up by two different bodies, to manage a single area.

The law, like the individual founding decrees, lays down a number of principles; but these fall well short of including 'rules of social conduct'. A protected area should also be considered as a social space; the problem needs to be viewed more as an interaction between society and nature, taking a more complex approach than one that is purely sociological. This approach, a basis for developing a sociology of the environment, views the human race and its organisational forms on a par with other living species. It therefore gives priority to an analysis of material interactions between environment and society (see Catton and Dunlap 1978; Dunlap and Catton 1979).

According to my value driven-approach, as stated in Chapter 2, I found that environmental ethics influence the field of environmental sociology. As a very young discipline, its true meaning and significance are still being debated. A definition that we feel is appropriate and useful to our study is Bell's (see Bell 1998). Closely reflecting Dunlap and Catton's comments of 20 years earlier (see Dunlap and Catton 1979), Bell states that environmental sociology concerns the study of

---

32 Articles 9 (for parks) and 20 (for reserves) of Sicily's Regional Law 98/1981 list possible management bodies for the protected areas. In the case of parks, this is the park agency established *ad hoc* for each; in the case of reserves, it may be a province, the regional agency for publicly owned forests, nature associations, or universities.

the community in the widest possible sense. Included in that community are human beings, plants and inanimate nature, and the discipline studies the interconnections between the members of this community and any related conflicts.

The Future of the Research

Considering the road travelled thus far in my research, the theories examined, thoughts expressed, and experiences reported, it seems natural to look back and comment on some of the initial principles.

I used the principles established by WWF as a framework of reference to:

- structure my research coherently with environmental ethics;
- build up some indicators to be used in my research in order to monitor institutional and associational policies.

The institutional approach is unsatisfactory from the environmental ethics perspective. And the associations' main interest is more in action than research, with my research project revealing a sort of overlapping/ambiguity between research and action. It appears, in short, that associations are more interested in education and practice than in research.

The aim of the research was to question the relationships between man and the natural environment from the perspective of philosophical ethics. But not by asking ourselves *what is the meaning of* good or duty, just or unjust. The question that my research addressed, rather, was intended to establish *what it is* good or evil, just or unjust, *to do or abstain from doing* in our relationship with the environment. These questions led to my interest in environmental philosophy and prompted me to construct the investigation grid used in the study. A study that is constantly being up-dated, thus enabling me to conduct the research in a way that remains consistent with the questions posed from the outset.

Some of the results show that in Italy, and in Sicily in particular, the principles and questions of environmental philosophy are coming to be an integral part of the cultural equipment of the people and bodies responsible for governing protected areas, areas that we need have no hesitation in defining as 'at risk' and subject to conflict. Is the demand to conduct research perhaps increasing? Has the idea of the need for interdisciplinary research to counteract a certain weakness in planning and environmental research finally reached a decisive stage? Maybe so, although it seems that some obstacles still remain to be addressed.

The Loneliness of the Researcher

The value-driven approach of academic research, notwithstanding its limits, can benefit from the associations' approach to grow and develop its skills and try to influence the institutional approach.

All of this brings us back to the need to establish rules of behaviour that can serve as a guide to help us achieve universal consensus. Some commentators assert that these rules need to be channelled through an ethics of good administration; others merely say that all we need to do is limit individual greed, a hypothesis expressed by *Sistema Gaia* (see Lovelock 1988; Watson 1991). All actions that are designed to establish a more general *Land Ethic* (see Leopold 1949; Norton 1990) that leads us, if we are to defend nature, to re-evaluate man's dominance over it.

Once again the role of research, formulated through ethical principles, appears decisive. In spite of this important role, however, the researcher appears to stand alone and isolated from what I have defined as 'institutional research'.

Through cultural evolution, promoted by the researcher and producing active participation by the entire community, we shall have to re-establish the primary role of research work designed to produce knowledge to operate in the territory and to modify the normative theory which informs the institutional approach.

It is only after this stage in the research that the people who engage on the day-to-day governance and management of areas of high natural worth will be able to move on from battling each day in their routine management and administration tasks to introduce and implement ethical policies that combine protection, development and conservation in a newly harmonious man/environment relationship.

References

Apel, K.O. (1987), 'The Problem of a Macroethic of Responsibility to the Future in the Crisis of Technological Civilization: An Attempt to Come to Terms with Hans Jonas's Principle of Responsibility', *Man and World* 20:1, 3-40.

Beato, F. (1999), *Parchi e Società, Turismo Sostenibile e Sistemi Locali* (Naples: Liguori Editore).

Bell, M.M. (1998), *An Invitation to Environmental Sociology* (Pine Forge: Thousand Oaks).

Bennett, G. and Mulongoy, K.J. (2006), 'Review of Experience with Ecological Network, Corridors and Buffer Zones', *CBD Technical Series* 23, 1-102.

Blackstone, W.T. (1980), 'The Search for an Environmental Ethics', in Tom Regan (ed.).

Catton, W. and Dunlap, R. (1978), 'Environmental Sociology: A New Paradigm', *American Sociologist* 13:1, 41-49.

Cobb Jr, J.B. (1972), *Is It Too Late? A Theology of Ecology* (Denton: Environmental Ethics Books).

Decandia, L. (2000), *Dell'Identità. Saggio sui Luoghi per una Critica della Razionalità Urbanistica* (Catanzaro: Rubettino).

Des Jardins, J.R. (2006), *Environmental Ethics: An Introduction to Environmental Philosophy* (Belmont: Wadsworth Publishing Co.).

Disch, R. (1970), *The Ecological Conscience: Values for Survival* (Englewood Cliffs, NJ: Prentice-Hall).

Dunlap, R. and Catton, W. (1979), 'Environmental Sociology: A Framework for Analysis', in Timothy O'Riordan and Ralph C. d'Arge (eds).

Gambino, R. (1996), *Progetti per l'Ambiente* (Milan: FrancoAngeli).

Giacomini, V. and Romani, V. (1992), *Uomini e Parchi* (Milan: FrancoAngeli).

Hargrove, E.C. (1989), *Foundations of Environmental Ethics* (Denton: Environmental Ethics Books).

Hösle, V. (1991), *Philosophie der Ökologischen Krise* (Munich: C.H. Beck'sche Verlagsbuchhandlung).

Jonas, H. (1984), *The Imperative of Responsibility* (Chicago: University of Chicago Press).

Kieffer, G.H. (1979), *Bioethics: A Textbook of Issues* (Menlo Park-London-Amsterdam: Addison Wesley Publications Company Reading).

Larmore, C. and Renaut, A. (2004), *Débat sur l'Éthique. Idéalisme ou réalisme* (Paris: Éditions Grasset and Fasquelle).

Leopold, A. (1949), *Sand County Almanac* (Oxford: Oxford University Press).

Lo Piccolo, F. and Schilleci, F. (eds) (2003), *A Sud di Brobdingnag. L'Identità dei Luoghi: per uno Sviluppo Locale Autosostenibile nella Sicilia Occidentale* (Milan: FrancoAngeli).

Lovelock, J. (1988), *The Ages of Gaia: A Biography of Our Living Earth* (Oxford: Oxford University Press).

Maclean, D. and Brown, P. (eds) (1983), *Energy and the Future* (Totowa, NJ: Rowman and Littlefield).

Magnaghi, A. (2000), *Il Progetto Locale* (Turin: Bollati Boringhieri).

Meadows, D.H. et al. (eds) (1972), *The Limits to Growth* (New York: Universe Books).

Morin, E. (1980), *L'Écologie Généralisée* (Paris: Éditions du Seuil).

Næss, A. (1986), 'The Deep Ecology Movement: Some Philosophical Aspects', *Philosophical Inquiry* 5, 10-31.

Norton, B.G. (1990), 'Context and Hierarchy in Aldo Leopold's Theory of Environmental Management', *Ecological Economics* 2:2, 119-127.

Nowicki, P. et al. (eds) (1996), *Perspectives on Ecological Networks* (Arnhem: ECNC).

O'Riordan, T. and d'Arge, R.C. (1979), *Progress in Resource Management and Environmental Planning* (Chichester: Wiley).

Paba, G. (1998), *Luoghi Comuni. La Città come Laboratorio di Progetti Collettivi* (Milan: FrancoAngeli).

Page, T. (1983), 'Intergenerational Justice as Opportunity', in David Maclean and Paul Brown (eds).

Passmore, J. (1980), *Man's Responsibility for Nature* (London: Duckworth and Co.).

Pearce, D.W. and Turner, K.R. (eds) (1990), *Economics of Natural Resources and the Environment* (London: Harvester-Wheatsheaf).

Platone (2005), *La Repubblica* (trad. it. di F. Sartori) (Rome-Bari: Editori Laterza).

Quarta, C. (ed.) (2006), *Una Nuova Etica per l'Ambiente* (Bari: Edizioni Dedalo).

Regan, T. (1980), *Matters of Life and Death. New Introductory Essays in Moral Philosophy* (New York: Random House).

Rolston III, H. (1988), *Environmental Ethics: Duties to and Values in The Natural World* (Philadelphia: Temple University Press).

Schilleci, F. (2003), 'La Trasformazione dei *Luoghi*. Lettura, in Chiave Ecologica, delle Relazioni tra Dinamiche Ambientali e Attività Umane nel *Sistema Naturale* in Sicilia', in Francesco Lo Piccolo and Filippo Schilleci (eds).

United Nations (1992), *Rio Declaration on Environment and Development*, Rio de Janeiro, A/CONF.151/26, 1.

Vegetti, M. (2005), 'Introduzione', in Platone.

Vegetti, M. (2006), *L'Etica degli Antichi* (Rome-Bari: Editori Laterza).

Venturi Ferriolo, M. (2003), *Etiche del Paesaggio. Il Progetto del Mondo Umano* (Rome: Editori Riuniti).

Watson, A. (1991), 'Gaia', *New Scientist* 1776, 1-2.

Wilson, E.O. (1998), *Consilience: The Unity of Knowledge* (New York: Knopf).

Chapter 10
Ethics and Consultancy

Adrian Healy[1]

Introduction

We've all heard the jokes. You know, like the one where if you ask the consultant the time he, or she, will borrow your watch; look at it; tell you what the time is, then charge you £500 for having done so. There are plenty of others. Consultancy, it seems, is a profession for those with a different ethical code to academics, or others in society. The very fact that a consultant's perspective is included in this book reflects a lingering suspicion that this is the case. Yet in an age when many consultancy firms now have a published ethical code does this remain true? Indeed, was it ever true?

In the following chapter I seek to explore the ethical dilemmas facing consultants and consider whether these are unique to that wide-ranging profession. It is by necessity a personal reflection based around more than a decade of working in the world of public-policy consultancy. Naturally, my own background and predilections, my own moral, or ethical, code influences the approach that I take here. I have not drawn on particular texts in writing this piece, but I have undoubtedly been influenced by the writings and thoughts of many over the years. My thanks go to them along with my apologies to those that feel that references and further reading are required in a text, for I include neither here. In exploring this area I draw heavily on the approach adopted in ECORYS, the company for which I work, in terms of core principles. However, the wider practical issues arise from personal experience or experiences that I have been made aware of by others. They do not necessarily relate to ECORYS itself.

ECORYS is an international consultancy company which operates in around 48 countries, but mainly in the EU. It was formed in 2001 through the merger of the UK company, ECOTEC Research and Consulting, and the Dutch company NEI. ECORYS undertakes assignments primarily for public sector clients, from local authorities through to the European Commission, working in a wide range of policy spheres at all points of the policy cycle, from basic research and feasibility studies, through to implementation, monitoring and evaluation.

So what do I understand by the term ethics? Generally speaking it refers to the explicit or implicit values of a person or a group. In doing so it addresses concepts such as right and wrong, and good and evil. It is these values that are

---

1   All views are those of the author only and do not reflect the view of ECORYS.

often set out in a code of ethics. But ethical behaviour is also a dynamic concept, in that held values influence, consciously or unconsciously, the nature of decisions taken. Many considerations of ethics in this context necessarily deal with what are acceptable normative standards of behaviour. Importantly, they also address the notion of responsibility. To what extent is it acceptable to argue that 'I didn't know' or, more classically, 'I was only following orders/doing what I was told'?

A second branch of ethics is more descriptive in character, analysing what people actually do in practice and seeking to understand ethical values from this perspective. This branch tends to be more applied in its approach. This accepts that different groups in society may hold different values and act in different ways. This is particularly so when we consider the private business sector and has led to the opening of an important branch of ethics over recent years dealing with the specific area of business ethics. This is a form of applied ethics that examines ethical rules and principles within a commercial context and the various moral or ethical problems that can arise in a business setting. The interesting question that this raises is whether the consultant is then subject to different values and ethical considerations than the academic researcher who does not work in a business setting? This leads me to consider whether there is a degree of moral relativism at work here. Do, or should, consultants face similar value systems to those working in other professions, particularly those working in similar fields of activity such as academic researchers? Does either party act differently? If they do, then does either party act wrongly?

There is, of course, no natural division between academics and consultants, many academics undertake consultancy assignments and many consultants engage in academic research. This blurred boundary of consultancy and academia provides fruitful future territory for exploring notions of relative ethics. In considering the ethical dimension in the world of consultancy I focus on public-policy research consultancy, not the many other forms of consultancy, for it is here that there are, perhaps, the greatest overlaps with the world of academic research. In what follows I also focus primarily on the notion of corporate ethics and of the ethics of consultancy *per se* rather than the ethics of undertaking research. I do so partly to provide a slightly different perspective from the other chapters of this book but mainly because I feel that this is the area that defines the ethical dilemmas of consultancy.

A Code of Ethics

Many consultancy companies now have a code of ethical behaviour of some form or another. In some cases it is an explicit statement of what is acceptable behaviour, of the principles that underpin the business, in others it is a more general statement of the values of the Company. Figure 10.1 provides an example of such a code. It is not unique in its content and serves to highlight a number of key points.

ECORYS enjoys a reputation for conducting its business with integrity and with respect for the interests of those our activities can affect. This reputation is an asset, just as real as our people and brands.

Our first priority is to be a profitable business and that means investing for growth and balancing short term and long term interests. It also means caring about our customers, employees, shareholders and suppliers, and the communities in which we conduct our operations. In the course of meeting our business objectives, we consider it essential that all employees understand and comply with our values and therefore share the ECORYS way of doing things.

It is very easy in the realm of business ethics to make high sounding statements of little practical value. The general principles contained in this Code are the bedrock; more detailed guidance tailored to the needs of different countries and companies already exists and will be further developed.

This Code of Business Principles is a core ECORYS statement and we commend it to all our stakeholders.

Standard of Conduct

ECORYS conducts its business with honesty and integrity and with respect for the interests of those with whom it has relationships.

Obeying the Law

ECORYS companies are required to comply with the laws and regulations of the countries in which they operate.

Employees

ECORYS companies are required to recruit, employ and promote employees on the sole basis of the qualifications and abilities needed for the work to be performed. ECORYS is committed to providing safe and healthy working conditions for its employees worldwide. ECORYS believes it is essential to maintain good communications with employees, normally through company based information and consultation procedures.

Conflicts of Interest

ECORYS expects its employees to avoid personal activities and financial interests which could conflict with their jobs. Steps are taken to ensure that employees receive appropriate guidance in areas where such conflicts can arise.

Figure 10.1   The ECORYS Code of Business Ethics

Public Activities

ECORYS neither supports political parties nor contributes to the funds of groups whose activities are calculated to promote party interests. ECORYS companies are encouraged to promote and defend their legitimate business interests. In so doing they may either directly, or through bodies such as trade associations, raise questions and discuss particular government actions or decisions. Where their experience can be useful, they are encouraged to cooperate with governments, individuals, agencies and other organisations in the development of proposed legislation and other regulations which may affect such legitimate interests. ECORYS companies are also encouraged to respond to requests from governments and other agencies for information, observations or opinion on issues relevant to business and the community in which we operate.

Product Assurance

ECORYS is committed to providing products which consistently offer value in terms of price and quality.

Environmental Issues

ECORYS is committed to running its business in an environmentally sound and sustainable manner. Accordingly its aim is to ensure that its processes and products have the minimum adverse environmental impact commensurate with the legitimate needs of the business.

Competition

ECORYS believes in vigorous yet fair competition and supports the development of appropriate competition laws. Employees receive guidance to ensure that they understand such laws and do not transgress them.

Reliability of Financial Reporting

ECORYS accounting records and supporting documents must accurately describe and reflect the nature of the underlying transactions. No undisclosed or unrecorded account, fund or asset will be established or maintained.

Bribery

ECORYS does not give or receive bribes in order to retain or bestow business or financial advantages. ECORYS employees are directed that any demand for or offer of such bribe must be immediately rejected.

Figure 10.1 continued   The ECORYS Code of Business Ethics

Application

This Code applies to ECORYS companies throughout the world. Where ECORYS companies participate in joint ventures the application of these principles will be actively upheld; this will significantly influence the decision to enter into or to continue in any joint venture.

Compliance

It is the responsibility of the Board of ECORYS to ensure that the principles embodied in this Code are communicated to, understood and observed by all employees. An independent Internal Audit function supports the Board in monitoring compliance with the Code. The Board of ECORYS will not criticise management for any loss of business resulting from adherence to these principles. Equally, the Board of ECORYS undertakes that no employee will suffer as a consequence of bringing to their attention, or that of senior management, a breach or suspected breach of these principles.

Figure 10.1 continued   The ECORYS Code of Business Ethics

Source: www.ecorys.com/code-of-business-ethics/index.php.

Firstly, there is the motivation behind the code. As with many Companies, ECORYS has a certain reputation and its Code of ethical behaviour is designed to safeguard that reputation. As such the Code can be seen as both a statement to potential clients of ECORYS's values as well as a set of 'rules' for its employees. In both cases one of the purposes of the Code is to maintain the reputation of the Company. Reputation is important as it is one way of building the trust of clients and so assist in securing future work. In this respect ethical considerations can both enhance a reputational asset but also protect that asset against erosion.

The Code itself is presented as a statement of 'bedrock' principles. These are the foundations on which all other ethical considerations should be based. More detailed guidance can also be developed. This is not surprising given that to develop a detailed code covering multiple potential considerations could necessitate many pages of guidance undermining the benefits of a readily accessible short statement of core values. What is, perhaps, more surprising is the statement that different countries may require differential guidance reflecting a recognition that standards of behaviour can vary between countries. This reinforces the notion that ethical standards can be relative as well as absolute.

In terms of the bedrock principles themselves these are broadly uncontroversial. A requirement on staff and the Company to obey the law; to avoid discriminatory behaviour, and to not engage in bribery will raise few eyebrows. The requirement to avoid conflicts of interest and public activities which may give the perception of a conflict of interest is reasonable in terms of protecting the company's reputation as an independent body able to offer impartial advice, although the nuances of this can be more complex and are discussed further later.

The code also includes consideration of wider issues. These are essentially statements on the values of the Company. One covers environmental concerns whereby the Company seeks to set out its environmental values and, broadly, how it seeks to abide by these. Such a statement is not unusual at a time when many companies are seeking to highlight their wider environmental and social responsibilities. A second is the statement regarding competition law – a clear value judgement by the company based on the belief that it will prosper most strongly in markets where conditions of free and open competition prevail. In this respect this is not just a response to wider ethical beliefs of society as a whole but a statement of its own beliefs and values. Thus an ethical code provides an opportunity to nail ones own colours to the mast; to provide a statement of the values of the Company as a whole.

The final dimension of the Code that merits highlighting here comes under the heading of Compliance. Here ECORYS sets out where responsibility for compliance with the Code rests. Implicit is the assumption that responsibility rests with the relevant employee although provision is made for staff to bring matters of concern to the attention of senior managers. What is made explicit is the responsibility of the Board (the senior management level) to make staff aware of the ethical foundations of the company and to monitor compliance. Most importantly, the Code makes clear that 'no employee will suffer as a consequence of bring to (The Board's) attention, or that of senior management, a breach or suspected breach of these principles'. In doing so, the Company seeks to remove the pressure that may be felt by an employee not to raise awkward issues, even where this may result in a loss of business for the firm.

Ethics in Practice

As many writers have pointed out, when confronting ethical dilemmas one needs more than just a code of ethics for guidance. Experience and personal values play an important role in applying corporate guidance regarding such 'goods' as integrity (adherence to moral principles), honesty and respect for the interests of those one has relationships with (transparency and openness) in practice. Indeed it is in the grey world of everyday practice that most ethical dilemmas truly emerge. These are rarely strong concepts where there is arguably a 'correct' response but more often weaker versions where the ethical response is open to debate. In the following section I outline a number of areas of consultancy where ethical debates can commonly be found.

Impartiality

One of the most damning phrases for the receipt of any report is 'they would say that, wouldn't they'. This slightly world-weary term suggests that perhaps the published report is partial in its presentation of its subject matter and the conclusions that it draws. There is a grain of truth in this. Many consultants and firms are known to have a particular take on an issue – for example those with strong environmental credentials. This is not just a reflection of their personal values but also of the reputation of a firm in a particular market area. Firms are often hired on the basis of their sympathy with the client's own set of values. This is particularly true when working with clients in both the private sector and in the voluntary and charitable sectors. Consultant's then view the evidence from a particular perspective and interpret the findings in that light. Whether this is unethical behaviour is a challenging question.

This brings us to a second reason that consultant's reports can be seen as partial. Consultants are commissioned to answer a particular question, rather than to provide an impartial assessment of a whole topic. Depending on how the question, or objectives of the research, are phrased this can lead to what appears to be a partial approach. For example, much consultancy work will take the form of identifying how best to implement a particular policy, rather than a questioning of the value of the policy itself. In so doing it might be seen as supporting the particular policy perspective as well. In practice most consultants do seek to be objective, their long-term success depends on being seen to be professional and trustworthy. However, objectivity may not, in itself, be value-free.

Naturally one can ask at what stage does it become unethical to sit back and advise on the implementation of a policy that might in itself be considered unethical? This is a much stronger question and one that runs to the heart of normative ethics. Most consultants do have strong moral standpoints which guide the types of work that they take, in some cases this may lead them to turn down pieces of work, but, more often, it influences what they are willing to 'bid' for. It is worth remembering that consultants make choices as to what pieces of work they submit tenders for and the influences over these choices are many, and potentially include ethical considerations. However, these considerations can be very personal, as well as corporate, and there is not necessarily any universal value that these encompass, hence the interest in applied ethics.

In seeking to demonstrate objectivity and impartiality there is a strong push for demonstrating the evidence-base on which conclusions and findings rest. Yet, this in itself raises potential ethical questions. Firstly there is the question as to what interpretation should be placed upon the information and the facts that have been generated. As we know, there is rarely one truth, one correct answer; rather there are different interpretations that can be placed on the information available. This can range from the weight to be attached to individual responses – are all equal or do some carry more significance than others? – through to the conclusions to be drawn from the assemblage of the information as a whole. The desire to escape from this dilemma can lead to a tendency to simply report all of the information available, but consultants are, on the whole, being paid to draw relevant conclusions from the available data; they, in effect, are being paid for their opinions.

Linked to this is the question of what is left out. Little research can ever be fully comprehensive, the options are limited by the available budget, the expertise of those involved and the framing of the original research questions. Compromises have to be made. The question is whether those compromises are made explicit and to what extent these compromise the findings drawn, either knowingly or unknowingly. There is an important role for methodology here, one that is too often overlooked in consultancy reports which concentrate primarily on the key messages. It is the methodology that is adopted that provides the litmus as to whether the results presented are likely to be robust or may, perhaps, be open to a different – perhaps more selective – interpretation. Yet, on the whole, clients are looking for short, sharp reports that provide clear answers and are not hedged around by caveats. We return to this point when I consider transparency and openness.

Is the Client always Right?

The role of the client in influencing the structure, style and content of the final report cannot be understated. In some cases the influence is marginal but very valuable; providing context, suggesting a slightly different form of words, offering a final check on how certain passages are understood by others. In other cases the influence can be more significant. This can be positive, improving the overall look and content of the report through utilising particular skills, knowledge and expertise of the client. In these cases the research and the report can be seen as more of a partnership approach than a typical client-contractor relationship. In other cases the client may seek changes to the report which the consultant does not feel are merited by the research findings. There is always pressure to come up with headline figures, the number of jobs created by a certain project being evaluated for example, but equally there can be pressure to drop certain criticisms, to include certain policy commitments and so forth. The examples do not particularly matter, the question is how the consultant deals with the pressure and, in the current context, what the ethical dimension to this is.

In short the question is whether the client is always right, or at what point does one walk away? This is where ethical considerations come to the fore. Essentially the consultant is seen to be endorsing a particular perspective. Does there come a point where the consultant decides that they are no longer willing to be associated with that perspective, or where the pressure to deliver certain results is regarded to be no longer tolerable? Clearly the answer is yes. The question then becomes one of degree. At what point is this invisible threshold crossed? This will probably differ for all individuals and companies. However, given that contractual obligations will have been entered into it is not as straightforward as simply deciding to terminate an agreement. There will be penalties involved, depending on the extent to which one or other party is seen to be acting unreasonably. This is where it is crucial that the Company is willing to stand behind whatever decision is taken.

Where the consultant has been commissioned to provide the evidence in support of, or against, a particular perspective then clearly there is a prior acceptance of the questions to be asked. How that material is used is then a matter for the client to decide. However, where disputes about interpretation and presentation emerge during the contract that cannot be resolved, consultants will typically consider what it will cost them, in terms of time and money; their wider reputation as a trusted deliverer of services, and their future relationship with that client and other potential clients, to stand by their values. Against this they may balance the longer-term impacts on their reputation for undertaking good quality work of acquiescing in reporting material in a way in which they are uncomfortable. These are not decisions which are taken lightly.

Honesty and Integrity

Honesty features strongly in most value statements and it would seem axiomatic that any consultant should be honest. In that they should be trustworthy, fair and not set out to mislead. Where are the ethical considerations here? Well, one of the most significant is that the consultant should also be fair as to what is in the client's best interests. This can lead to some difficult conversations, and may mean turning down an approach for work. To give an example: a local authority approaches a consultancy to assist them in developing a bid to a competitive funding programme for regeneration. The authority has little experience in this area and is not well-prepared. The consultant is pessimistic about the chances for success in such circumstances. Should the consultant assist the authority in developing such a bid or be honest, refuse the commission and appraise the authority of their probable chances of success?

In practice, this is not a strong dilemma, although turning down work is always difficult! In the long-run it is not in the consultant's interest to be associated with poor bids, or to gain a reputation for poor advice. In contrast it is in their interest to gain a reputation as an honest and fair party. In the short-term this approach may also pay dividends. In the above example for instance the authority may, and in a particular case did, take the consultant's advice, postponed their intent to bid and retained the consultancy for a year in order to bring their practices and procedures up to the required level, leading to a successful application for funding some 18 months later. However, there are other examples where consultants are perceived to have exploited the naïvety of clients, to have indulged in what many might regard as 'sharp' practices. These are the stories that gain consultants a particular reputation. There is doubtless truth in many of these stories. So, are these consultants acting unethically? This is a moot point and must lie at the heart of any debate on ethical behaviour.

One area where there is perhaps less debate is around the issue of bribery and corruption. Most would agree that it is unethical to offer or to receive bribes in order to transact services. Yet even here lie significant grey areas. Many consultancies will offer corporate hospitality, hosting events, inviting clients to join them at sporting occasions, concerts or simply taking clients (and potential clients) to lunch. At what point does this cross the line and become unethical behaviour?

Transparency and Openness

How open and transparent should a piece of research or consultancy be? How much of a report should be made public? Where the research is funded using public money this becomes a significant question. In practice the ethical dimension of this is rarely considered at the level of the consultant. It tends to be the decision of the client whether to publish a report or not. However, that decision can itself influence the conduct of the research. In particular a decision to publish a report or not may influence the level of critical comment included in the report, which then turns back to the ethical questions regarding truth raised earlier. On the whole it is probably fair to surmise that publications that are drawn up for publication are less 'hard-hitting' than those for an internal audience. The question facing the consultant is the extent to which this is acceptable?

In some cases the consultant can argue that it is the process that is more important than the final report, that the trenchant criticisms have been made in internal versions of the report, or reported verbally to the client. The message has been passed to those that 'matter', who have the power to act and make the necessary changes. In these circumstances it might be felt that no further good will be achieved by making those criticisms public. In other cases the consultant may feel that this is not so. At this stage the ethical dilemma really raises its head, as to what action can, and should the individual or the organisation take. There may be legal constraints on the scope for action, for example many contracts will include clauses restricting the information that can be made public, or passed to the media. Equally the consultant may fear that to 'go public' will restrict their ability to gain work in the future. However, the costs of inaction can also be high, particularly if a firm loses its reputation for trustworthiness, honesty and integrity.

One additional consideration under the heading of openness and transparency is the extent to which report findings respect the anonymity of those interviewed and the confidentiality of the material provided. On principle, wishes for confidentiality should always be respected. It is for the consultant, as researcher, to assess whether this provides a more robust report or whether inaccurate assertions are being made behind the mask of anonymity. Even so, where the confidentiality of sources is respected this can make external scrutiny of the veracity of a report more difficult. This, in turn, places a premium on the reputation of the consultancy as a trustworthy and objective reporter of material.

Intellectual Ownership

In the case of much consultancy research, ownership of the intellectual property produced rests with the client. Yet much consultancy work rests on a synthesis of the ideas of others. Whilst in the academic literature the identification of those whose ideas are being drawn upon are fully referenced, this may not always be so in consultancy reports. Is this an example of an area where there is a certain degree of relativism in the standards applied? Certainly a consultancy report will credit key sources, will attribute quotations and will respect all identified intellectual property rights. Equally, plagiarism is as wrong in the case of consultancy work as it is in the academic sphere. However, it is also true that consultancy reports tend to contain many fewer citations and references than academic research papers. There is a valid question to ask as to whether consultancy reports do adequately reflect the origin of some of the concepts on which they build. Or whether they simply build their arguments on a lesser number of core texts. Equally though, are there occasions when ideas first expressed in what many call 'grey literature', that is consultancy reports, fail to be fully credited by the academic literature?

The matter of how 'grey' literature is handled is an interesting one as the question is occasionally asked as to whether consultants have an obligation to contribute to the development of knowledge through their work, whether this is in the field of economics, sociology, planning or other academic discipline. Many consultants would argue that they do so already although this is not always reported at academic conferences or published in academic journals; rather it is contained in published consultancy reports. Others would argue that where they are not developing new knowledge themselves they are certainly contributing to its wider dissemination around the policy community and its application in practice. In this respect consultants do intervene in contemporary debates and it would be wrong to consider consultants as disinterested observers. As with many academic researchers, many consultants have strongly formed values and a desire to improve public policy responses to contemporary concerns through strengthening levels of knowledge and understanding of the issue at hand.

Conflicts of Interest

This is perhaps the area where there is the greatest scope for what might be termed 'simple' ethical dilemmas. The question is often not whether there is a conflict of interest in practice; many consultants will argue that they are professionals and so can draw the necessary lines to make sure that this does not occur, but whether there might be any perception of a conflict of interest. It is worthwhile noting that this forms one of the key principles of the Code of Ethics published by ECORYS in Figure 10.1: 'ECORYS expects its employees to avoid personal activities and financial interests which could conflict with their jobs'. This does not preclude staff from engaging in, for example, political activity, but does lead to an expectation that they will be open about these activities, and declare any potential conflicts of interest that might arise.

At a corporate level there is also the potential for conflicts, or perceptions of conflicts, of interest to occur. These can take many forms and I merely highlight some of the more common below.

Are you able to work for two clients on the same topic at the same time? Arguably this all depends upon the circumstances. If you are helping two clients to develop local regeneration strategies then there should be no conflict of interest. Indeed there may be mutual gains from the transfer of knowledge that may occur as a consequence of this. However, it would generally be felt to be inappropriate to assist two clients to develop competing bids for support from the same competitive regeneration fund. The grey areas for this would be where the consultant is able to field two entirely separate teams and to demonstrate that adequate 'chinese walls' were in place to limit the flow of sensitive information. In this instance it might be appropriate, but only where each client was fully aware of the situation and was comfortable to proceed on that basis.

One area where it is clear that a conflict of interest does exist is where the organisation is administering a programme on behalf of a client. In those circumstances it would be entirely inappropriate to advise a different client on how to bid for funding from that particular programme or scheme. There would be a perception of a potential conflict of interest in any future assessment of such an application. Equally, where a consultancy has supported the development or implementation of one of more projects for clients under a particular programme it could be construed that you had an interest in that programme, making it inappropriate to seek to evaluate the programme as a whole at a later date. This can become a practical issue for clients, for, occasionally, so many consultancies have been involved in developing different aspects of a major national programme, the field of potential evaluators can become very limited. It can also have practical implications for large consultancies with multiple offices. In these circumstances it is important for the consultant to be aware of what projects have been undertaken over time across the company as a whole; and whether these might constitute a potential conflict of interest for work that he, or she, is in the process of bidding for.

Finally there is the question of accessing privileged information. This is not only an area where there is potential for conflicts of interest to arise but can be seen as an ethical issue in its own right. Privileged information can come in many forms, some is accessed as a consequence of other work that the consultant has undertaken, some is acquired through meetings and discussions, other can be accessed through hiring those that have been party to particular discussions. The common denominator is that you have it and others do not. The ethical question is how you got it and, what you do with it. One of the reasons that clients hire consultants is that they know things the client does not, that they have access to a wider set of sources of information. This is fine. However, any consultant must be clear that material provided in confidence for a particular study or purpose remains confidential and is not used as the basis for future sales pitches to other clients. Again it comes back to the notion of trust and reputation as the basis for a sustainable business model over time.

In hiring staff consultants will seek out those with the most up to date knowledge of a particular policy area, and future proposals for change. Naturally, this can lead to potential conflicts of interest and access to privileged information; or perceptions that this is the case. One of the means adopted by the UK Government to restrict the transfer of such privileged information is to enforce a period of extended leave between senior officials leaving the civil service and beginning work in a commercial capacity. The belief is that the knowledge possessed by that individual will have lost some of its currency after a period of time has passed.

In a business that is predicated upon the knowledge of the individuals involved, the transfer of knowledge through changes in employment status will always be something of a dilemma.

Research Methods

I have chosen not to focus on the question of research ethics in this piece as in many cases I feel that the ethical considerations facing consultants as researchers and academic researchers do not significantly differ. Certainly consultants base their approach on their prior experience, often informed by their training in a particular discipline, and their ontological beliefs. However, consultants are also likely to choose different methodological approaches depending upon the task at hand, buying in expertise where they may not have access to appropriate skills themselves. The choice of the theoretical framework to be adopted clearly has ethical implications and this is not always fully considered by the consultant seeking to respond to a particular invitation to tender, rather the consultant considers which approach is most likely to provide a robust framework for meeting the criteria set out in the tender documents. In doing so, they will also consider the perceived interest of the client and will seek to tailor their approach in a way that maximises its chances of acceptance by the client.

It is worth highlighting here, once again, that the consultant is not acting alone in this situation. They are responding to a competitive tender where they may be in competition with several, or even dozens, of other companies and individuals to provide the consultancy services requested. This can act as a spur to be innovative, but can also lead to complex choices about the balance of what is likely to be acceptable to the client, affordable by the client and deliverable.

Do Consultants Face a Different Code of Ethics to Academics?

In most instances the ethical considerations that a consultant faces are similar to those of any other researcher. Considerations of truth, balance, honesty and integrity in research are universal and apply equally to academic researchers and consultants. In this respect the ethics of research are not a relative concept. However, there are areas where the academic and consultancy worlds diverge and here different considerations may apply. Where it is considered that it is the role of academic research to promote new understanding and to generate new 'knowledge', then the weight attached to transparency and the integrity of the research process is likely to be that much stronger. In contrast, consultants, who are applying recognised concepts to practical situations on behalf of a particular client, are likely to focus more strongly on the implications of their work in a particular context. Similarly where consultants work to meet the specified demands of these clients then the reported results may be more partial than might necessarily be the case under objective academic research.

As with all things, it is hard to generalise here, exceptions can always be identified. However, at the risk of simplicity, I would suggest that the key is to recognise the different purposes of work undertaken under the aegis of client-commissioned consultancy advice against that undertaken for purely academic purposes. Where there is a blurring of these boundaries, with academics undertaking consultancy commissions, and consultants engaging in academic research then there is a risk that confusion may occur as to what is acceptable behaviour; if not in the eyes of those undertaking the research then in the eyes of third parties. In practice, slightly different standards do apply and, although the differences may not be significant, they can add up.

Interestingly, although Cardiff University has a very strong set of guidelines on research ethics, it does not have a wider code relating to corporate practices or to the values of the institution; as ECORYS and other companies do. Whether this is a common feature of the academic institutions I do not know, but it does seem to suggest different perceptions as to the role and purpose of ethical codes and of how the ethical dimension is perceived.

Conclusion

In practice consultants do face a range of ethical dilemmas and engage in ethical decision-taking on an almost daily basis. This is not only in the nature of the research that they undertake but also how this is reported and how it is procured. In most cases these decisions are made without reference to ethical codes of conduct and ethical considerations are rarely consciously examined. That is not to say that they are not present though, merely that the values are embedded in behaviour.

I have highlighted a number of the areas where ethical considerations are present, but have resisted the temptation to provide answers to some of the questions posed, as I believe that there are no absolute answers here. Consultancy, like academia, covers a broad church and arriving at such common principles takes time and awareness. As a community we develop our own standards of appropriate behaviour. This community is made up of different members with different expectations and power relations. In the case of the consultant, the role of the client in determining the nature of the research undertaken and how the information is used can be understated and deserves more attention in the literature. In an ideal world there should be a shared commitment to common ethical principles.

The focus on ethics and business behaviour in the world of consultancy is to be welcomed. There is an increasing acceptance of what is acceptable behaviour in terms of the research process itself, shared by researchers in academia and consultancy alike, and the extension of this to how such results are used, and procured, can only be to the benefit of the policy community as a whole. In this respect we may find that it is the consultancy firms, who deal with these issues on a daily basis, which are in the vanguard of this debate.

Finally, it is worth noting that ethical behaviour is self-reinforcing. Acting in an ethically sound manner is in one's own self-interest. Over the longer-term it can actually lead to the procurement of more work for the so-called shadow of the future hangs over us all and the policy research community is a small one. Reputation is crucial in securing consultancy assignments and those that are regarded as engaged in 'unethical' practices are unlikely to prosper.

Chapter 11
Researching Planning Practice[1]

Patsy Healey

This chapter first identifies four types of research relationship with planning practice, and then presents, in the form of personal biography, a number of examples of practice-related research. It then moved on to discuss in detail a particular example of research on the implementation of development plans undertaken for the Department of the Environment. This is used to illustrate the complexity of the potential influence of research on practice and the ethical issues it is necessary for researchers to confront. The chapter concludes with some reflections on the approach to and the need for research related to planning practice.

As planning academics, why do we do research? Why do we research the topics that we do? And what kinds of research should we do? In the past twenty years in Britain, as social science has permeated the planning domain and planning academics have been required to meet University performance criteria (publications, citations, research grants), planning academics have been pressured to 'do research'. The Royal Town Planning Institute's Research Board has struggled to define an appropriate agenda for such research. Planning students are taught how to do research. But what kind of research falls within the planning domain, and what sort of research could and should planning academics do?

There are many dimensions to answering this question. One helpful way is to identify types of relationship between planning practice and research. Four are discussed below: research which is an integral part of practising planning; evaluation research; social scientific research 'on' planning practice; and research with practitioners to help them improve their practice.

There are many areas of planning work which demand the exercise of research skills. Evaluation, project appraisal, transport modelling, market analysis, and preference surveys might fall under these headings. Breheny notes how such practical tasks, once performed by planners in the public sector, are now vigorously undertaken by academics and ex-academics for the commercial and consultancy sector, reflecting the privatisation of expertise in the planning field.[2] In this case, items of knowledge are being produced as direct inputs to particular planning tasks. The primary focus is on substantive issues, or 'what' questions.

---

1 This chapter is derived from a paper presented at the Anglo-Italian Planning Colloquium in Reggio Calabria, 23-25 March 1990.

2 Breheny, M., 'Chalkface to Coalface: A Review of the Academic-Practice Interface'. *Environment and Planning* B: *Planning and Design*, 16, 1989, pp. 451-68.

162   *Ethics and Planning Research*

Evaluation research arises when planners and their clients want to know if plans, policies and actions would work or have worked. As the public sector in Britain has come under increasing pressure to justify its actions and the efficiency with which it performs them, so there has been an increasing amount of such research. This could be done in-house by agencies. However, there is increasing pressure for independent evaluation, either for a client, or as an independent contribution to debates on policy and methodology. Such research is focused on 'how' questions as much as 'what' questions. How are policy effects produced? How could national or local policy-makers act differently to produce more appropriate effects? Both kinds of evaluation may then feed into subsequent planning work, at the level of policy instruments, particular policy review or project development exercises or at the level of individual practice. However, the flow of knowledge generated from such research into practical action is neither certain nor straightforward to identify.[3] The history of British urban policy provides a fascinating case of the complex interrelations of research and practice.[4]

Both of the above types of practice-related research are part of the general task of developing 'knowledge for action in the public domain', to use Friedmann's definition of planning.[5] But there is another kind of research, in which social scientists have traditionally been encouraged to engage, namely the analysis of human affairs to discover 'what is going on' and to develop interpretative frameworks for such a descriptive and analytical task. While most academics who engage in such work would identify some useful purpose which research of this kind serves, it is not necessarily linked to any specific practical purpose. There is usually a key methodological difference between this kind of research and the previous two categories.

In the first two, a critical task is to define the practical context of the research. What does the client want? Whose policies are we evaluating? With and for whom? In the third, the critical task is to define the research question, the context within which it is relevant to ask such a question and the terms in which it can be addressed. It produces research 'on' planning practice rather than research 'for' planning practice. Research 'on' practice may often conclude with proposals 'for' practice, but the link between the production of such conclusions and an influence on practice may be very indirect, if not impossible to detect.[6] A major problem for such academic social scientists is to reach the 'policy community' which

---

3   Smith, R., 'Implementing the Results of Evaluation Studies' in Barrett, S. and Fudge, C. (eds), *Policy and Action*, London, Methuen, 1981, pp. 225-45.

4   See, for example, Edwards, J. and Batley, R., *The Politics of Positive Discrimination*, London, Tavistock, 1978.

5   Friedmann, J., *Planning in the Public Domain*, Princeton, Princeton University Press, 1987.

6   For example, the work of Simmie, J. (*Power, Property and Corporatism*, London, Macmillan, 1981) and Elkin, S. (*Politics and Land Use Planning: The London Experience*, London, Cambridge University Press, 1974) has reached the planning community primarily through the use of these texts in planning courses.

frames and carries out policy. Certain people, such as Peter Hall, play a key role in identifying significant social science research findings and communicating these to policy and planning communities.

The fourth area of research is similarly 'on practice'. It may take the form of a management appraisal study which reviews how people perform their tasks. This has a strong normative agenda (to improve performance) and may result in the production of principles for better work performance. Such research may then feed directly into management practices. If produced interactively as part of the development of self-management capabilities, it may take the form of self-monitoring action research, or it may be more exploratory, seeking to identify the way planners accomplish their work, in order to formulate methodological and behavioural principles for better practice strategies. The work of Forester, Hock and others in the US-based 'Planning Practice Research Network' is of this nature, linked to the ideal of developing more progressive and democratic forms of planning practice.[7] Such research is centrally concerned with how things are done at the level of individuals.

There can be little doubt that planning activity benefits from all the above kinds of research, and that it is legitimate for planning academics to be involved in such work. It is also clear that other academics are in a position to make a significant contribution in all these four areas. Is there anything particularly useful which academics who are specifically 'within' planning can offer? Many other disciplinary traditions may produce more rigorous research findings and methodologies. While planning practitioners and planning academics should be encouraged to search widely for research findings of relevance to their problems and purposes, there is nevertheless a particular research responsibility which academics who are part of the 'planning community' should take on. This is the task of focusing research findings specifically to 'translating knowledge into action' in particular situations. This involves interrelating 'what' and 'how' issues, substance and process, and situating specific problems in wider contexts. Those researchers working from within our planning culture are accustomed to interrelate 'what' and 'how' issues, substance and process. It is normal for us to link context and specific instance.

A Career in 'Researching Planning Practice'

The rest of this chapter is more personal biography than systematic review. It aims to describe some examples of research work, to draw out questions about the extent to which the research contributed to 'knowledge' and to providing knowledge 'for action', and to comment on the ethical questions which 'researching planning practice' may raise.

---

7 See Forester, J., *Planning in the Face of Power*, Berkeley, University of California Press, 1989, and Hoch, C., 'Conflict at Large: A National Survey of Planners and Political Conflict', *Journal of Planning Education and Research*, 8 (1) 1988, pp. 25-34.

I have done very little of the first kind of research, primarily because my personal interests have been in process questions, and the interrelation between substance, process and context. I have done some evaluation work. The most significant client-directed exercise of this kind was that on the implementation of planning policy, commissioned by the Department of the Environment in 1981/1983,[8] which will be discussed later.

From 1989 to the present, I have been engaged in 'independent', university-funded research on urban regeneration and the development industry. This in part involves developing the bases for an evaluation of British urban policy in the 1980s from the point of view of its impact on real estate development activity and, indirectly, on local economic development. I have also done a number of pieces of 'anthropological', or ethnographic research on planning activity and the development process, in which I have been concerned to discover, interpret and explain the nature of planning activity undertaken, the form and dynamics of physical development processes and the relationship between the two.[9]

As I will explain, in our work on the implementation of planning policy, we tried in parallel to pursue the Department of the Environment's agenda of evaluation and impact research, and our own more social scientific connections.[10] In this research, I have used my membership of the planning community not only to gain entry to social situations and the explanations offered by those involved in these situations, and to gain access to documentary material, but to help me to identify and interpret what I discovered. This potential for empathy and trust, however, carried with it certain ethical and methodological obligations. It also led to some interesting side effects in the form of exchange of knowledge and debate about alternative practices among the planners upon whom I was conducting the research. In this way, the research could sometimes come to assume the attributes of the fourth type of research identified above.

Nevertheless, in this research, I have acted primarily as an 'anthropological observer', a 'voyeur' as a Newcastle colleague has shrewdly noted, rather than as a deliberate facilitator of interactive learning. This is most clearly reflected in my *Local Plans* book,[11] which is not about how to produce and use a local plan (although this could be learned from the book), but about how people have produced and used local plans and what this might tell us about the nature of

---

8 Healey, P., Davis, J., Wood, W. and Elson, M.J., *The Implementation of Development Plans*, 1982, and Healey, P., McNamara, P.F., Doak. J. and Elson, M.J., *The Implementation of Planning Policy and the Role of Development Plans*, 1985 (both reports to the Department of the Environment).

9 Healey, P., *Local Plans in British Land Use Planning*, Oxford, Pergamon, 1983; Gilbert, A. and Healey, P., *The Political Economy of Land: Urban Development in an Oil Economy*, Aldershot, Gower, 1985.

10 See Healey, P., McNamara, P.F., Elson, M.J. and Doak, A.J., *Land Use Planning and the Mediation of Urban Change*, Cambridge, Cambridge University Press, 1988.

11 See Healey, P., op. cit., N9.

planning activity. I have taken a similar position in a line of research I have been engaged in over the past twenty years, namely my concern with the way planners contribute their expertise in practice.

This interest grew out of my PhD research, where I sought to establish the different meanings being given to planning in certain Latin American contexts, and how this was being interpreted by planners in different planning offices. This made me curious about what ideas planners in Britain were using as guides to their practice, and resulted in my study with Jacky Underwood and others on *Planners' Use of Theory in Practice* in the London Boroughs during the 1970s.[12] A critical ingredient of the success of this research was that both Jacky and I had previously been London Borough Planning Officers and so were accepted by those about whom we were conducting research. Once again, I was essentially an 'anthropological observer', though for Jacky the exercise was more for clarification in relation to certain value commitments.[13] Yet both this and my PhD work[14] were critical in helping me relate broad debates in planning theory to what it meant to be a planning practitioner. In retrospect, my research interests were focused by a similar tension to Jacky's: how to resolve the dysfunction between my experience as a planner in London in the 1960s and my idealistic wish that, through involvement with planning, I could somehow help to make the world a better place.

Such personal factors are important for two reasons. Firstly, much apparently objective research is implicitly guided by researchers' value orientations and dilemmas, and it helps in communicating and understanding what a piece of research has to offer to make these explicit. Secondly, these value orientations now provide a purposeful direction to my most recent work – firstly, that on the way planners in their daily practice address issues to do with their values, skills and the nature of the knowledge they use, i.e. their expertise;[15] and secondly, my current involvement in monitoring and evaluating new urban policy initiatives aimed at tackling one of the most difficult of contemporary issues, that of creating more opportunities in the mainstream economy and society for residents of

---

12   Healey, P. and Underwood, J., *The Organisation and Work of London Borough Planning Departments*, London, Centre for Environmental Studies CP18, 1977; Healey, P. and Underwood, J., 'Professional Ideals and Planning Practice', *Progress in Planning*, 9 (2) 1978; Underwood, J., *Town Planners in Search of a Role*, Bristol, School for Advanced Urban Studies, University of Bristol, 1980.

13   See Underwood, J., 'What is Really Material: Rising Above Interest Group Politics' in Thomas, H. and Healey, P. (eds), *Dilemmas of Planning Practice*, Aldershot, Avebury, 1991, pp. 147-55.

14   Healey, P., *Urban Planning under Conditions of Rapid Urban Growth* (unpublished PhD thesis), London, University of London, 1973.

15   Healey, P. and Gilroy, R., 'Towards a People-sensitive Planning', *Planning Practice and Research*, 5 (2) 1990, pp. 21-29; Healey, P., 'A Day's Work', *Journal of the American Planning Association*, 58 (1), pp. 9-20; Thomas, H. and Healey, P., op. cit., N13.

areas of concentrated disadvantage.[16] In the former work, I have been strongly influenced by John Forester's work on planning as a communicative process, and his commitment to processes which inform open debate rather than mystify and reinforce established power relations.[17]

The research on how planners accomplish their work is to an extent an example of the fourth type of research identified above. Forester's texts certainly have some attributes of a 'how to do it' management manual. But I have arrived at this concern through a long journey arising from my research on the implementation of development plans, on local plans, and from my grounding in planning theory. This has given me a secure foundation of understanding of the economic, social and political-institutional dimensions of planning activity, within which to locate, observe, interpret and advise on the fine-grain of how to carry out planning work. This contextual understanding has also provided the basis for attempting a wider contribution to debates on policy directions.[18] I made this point to stress that if the connection between my own research work and what I propose to policy-makers and practitioners is so complex, it is hardly surprising if the flow of ideas and understanding between 'research' communities and 'practice' communities is diffuse and unpredictable. This does not mean that connections are not made. It means merely that we cannot tell in advance if, when and how they will be made.

Researching the Implementation of Development Plans

This section of the chapter describes an example of a research project undertaken 'for' practice, in this case a central government client.[19] I will briefly describe the research context, strategy and findings. I will then comment on what impacts the research has had, what kind of contribution it represents, and the ethical dilemmas which undertaking research of this kind presented.

The research was commissioned in two stages by the Department of the Environment (DoE). The system of structure and local plans had been in place since 1968. By 1981, most local authorities in England had submitted structure plans, over 200 local plans had been placed 'on deposit' and over 80 had been

---

16   This is the stated objective of the Government's 1991 'City Challenge' initiative.

17   Forester, op. cit., N7.

18   See Healey, P., 'Directions for Change in the British Planning System', *Town Planning Review*, 60 (3) 1989, pp. 123-49; and Healey, P., 'Places, People and Policies: Plan-making in the 1990s', *Local Government Policy-Making*, 17 (2) 1990, pp. 29-39.

19   For a more detailed account of this work, see Healey et al. op. cit., N9, especially the appendix; and Healey, P., 'The Role of Development Plans in the British Planning System', *Urban Law and Policy*, 8, 1986, pp. 1-32.

adopted. Already, the system was being criticised for delay.[20] Since 1979, with a radical reforming Conservative administration in power in central government, questions were being raised about the value of the planning system and especially the apparently cumbersome plan preparation system. This seemed to produce policy frameworks which were out of date, at least for a government seeking to reduce the constraints on land and property markets. In this context, the Department saw merit in commissioning research to assess how the system was actually working. Our brief was to investigate how far development plans were being implemented. The resources available for this work were considerable, allowing the employment of two full-time researchers for three person years (net) in total, in addition to the input of myself and my colleague Martin Elson.[21]

We were aware of some dimensions of our client's political context. Those commissioning the research wanted to know if and how the system of structure and local plans was working. They also wanted to learn about what implementing plans might really involve. So they welcomed, as we did, an active involvement in the development of the work. We nevertheless had to negotiate a number of principles with respect to research strategy. There was a tendency for the client to see the relationship between plan and implementation in a one-dimensional way. In their view a plan indicated what was to be developed, where and on what terms. We were to find out if such development had happened, and if not, why not. In other words, they adopted a 'conformance' approach.[22]

We renegotiated the question to encompass the implementation of planning policies and the role of development plans in policy implementation. We did this for two reasons. Firstly, we insisted that it was wrong to equate policy intentions with what was in plans. Policies were evolving phenomena which may periodically be recorded in plans. So we had to devise a research strategy to discover whether the policies recorded in plans were exercising a guiding influence on development, or whether other sources of policies were more important. Secondly, the relationship between development plans and development control in Britain is a flexible one.[23] Nor are structure and local plans in Britain necessarily expressed in the form of a specific land use map. In many instances, policies are expressed as performance criteria to be brought to bear upon a particular project and proposal. We therefore emphasised the need for a research strategy which allowed us to identify how the performance criteria proposed in plans were brought to bear on projects. It made an entirely quantitative approach inappropriate.

---

20   House of Commons Expenditure Committee, *Eighth Report: Planning Procedures*, Vol. 1, London, HMSO, 1977.

21   The researchers were initially Julian Davis and Margaret Wood, followed by Paul McNamara and Joe Doak.

22   Barrett, S.M. and Fudge, C., 'Examining the Policy-Action Relationship' in Barrett, S.M. and Fudge, C. (eds), *Policy and Action*, London, Methuen, 1981, pp. 3-32.

23   See Davis, H.W.E., Edwards, D., Hooper, A.J. and Punter, J.V., *Planning Control in Western Europe*, London, HMSO, 1989.

Table 11.1　Implementation matrix for South Staffordshire housing

Housing policy guidance for:	Planned outcomes	Agents	Powers and resources	'New' organisational devices/modes of operation
Rural development hierarchy – directing limited development to key villages	Development to take place in named villages and not elsewhere	District Council County Council (DoE) and Private Developers	Development control	None
Residential land provision/ allocation – allocate enough land for existing and future needs	Development to take place on allocated sites/villages	County Council District Council (DoE) and Private Developers	Local plan Development control	Land Availability Study 1979 with HBF
Local needs – provision will be made (as a priority) – land release to be phased	Houses to be built and occupied by 'locals' Phased release of sites Local authority housing provision	District Council (Housing) District Council (Planning) County Council (DoE) and Developers	Local authority housing (DC) Agricultural occupancy conditions (Local Plan) Phasing Development Briefs	
Phasing development with infrastructure provision – coordinated development of housing with related services	Development of housing to proceed with or after service provision	District Council County Council Developers STWA Highways (CC) Gas/Electricity Health/Social services	Development Control Local Plans Development Briefs Negotiation Programme of Community Development	Programme of Community Development Transport Planning for South Staffordshire
Type of housing – to offer as wide a choice as possible	A variety of house types, sizes and tenure to be built/ encouraged	District Council (Housing) Private Developers District Council (Planning)	Local Authority Investment (new and conversions) Private sector negotiations inc. Development Briefs	None
Use of Section 52 agreements – may be required for provision of off-site infrastructure	Receive financial payment from developers for off-site infrastructure work	District Council Private Developer (Public Utilities and Highways)	1971 Town and Country Planning Act Section 52	Negotiation through Development Briefs

Source: Healey, P., 'The Role of Development Plans in the British Planning System', *Urban Law and Policy*, 8, 1986, p. 9.

Table 11.2 The extent to which the strategic themes have been implemented

Urban regeneration themes	Containment/conservation themes
Redirection to the urban core (GMC) Substantial efforts expended on regenerating the urban core but undermined by structural decentralising forces and the interest of peripheral districts in investment attraction.	*Urban concentration* (GMC) Some compromises have been struck with regard to strategic (economic) and local (housing) priorities, but there is evidence of effective implementation overall.
Maintenance of the regional centre (GMC) Regeneration initiatives in the regional centre have recently begun to have effect, but competitive district centres have continued to expand.	*Conservation of resources and amenity (GMC)* Resource conservation given high priority in allocation process. Varied pattern of amenity (open land) conservation where fringe allocations have been proposed.
Urban regeneration (WMCC) Despite considerable effort expended on regeneration, theme seriously hindered by structural economic factors and resource uncertainty. Also undermined by switch in priorities to economic regeneration of the conurbation as a whole.	*Resource conservation and efficiency (WMC/Staffs)* Mineral reserves and good quality agricultural land have been conserved despite attempts to compromise this theme. Infrastructure provision has proved problematic in South Staffordshire.
Economic regeneration (WMC/Staffs) Slow take-off of peripheral industrial estates reflects national recession and its severe local impact. Recent attempts to release prime land at Marston Green/ Bickenhill.	*Environmental protection and enhancement (WMC/Staffs)* Protection of open land compromised by recent policy shift toward economic regeneration through peripheral development. Evidence that environmental enhancement being progressed more widely in recent years, despite uncertainties over financing.
Housing improvement (WMC) The evidence suggests that housing improvement is progressing, but that deterioration in existing stock is nullifying the work of improvement teams.	*Growth accommodation and management (Staffs)* Growth allocated without too many difficulties but subsequent development has been hindered by some infrastructure problems.

Source: Healey, P., McNamara, P.F., Doak, J. and Elson, M.J., *The Implementation of Planning Policy and the Role of Development Plans* (report to the Department of the Environment), 1985.

This led to a further methodological debate with our clients. They would have preferred an approach which sampled from different situations across the country. We argued that an essential element of the research would be a sensitive understanding of the context within which plans were produced and used. This suggested that we concentrate on a few locations. In the end we worked in three research situations, the Western Outer South East, the West Midlands and Greater Manchester.

The research strategy we developed was similar to what is sometimes now called a 'cascade' approach, moving from a broad overview, through to case studies at various levels of detail. We reviewed policy development in each area, and how this produced the content of structure and local plans. We then analysed the plans separated into their broad themes or policy directions, specific policy sectors and detailed proposals, and sought to identify performance indicators for these (see Table 11.1). At this stage we focused upon selected areas which were the subject of particular policy attention in order to make our task manageable. Using secondary data and documentary material, we then assembled information with which to assess each performance indicator. This gave us substantive conclusions as to how far policies were implemented.

Table 11.2 summarises our main findings with respect to progress in achieving the broad structure plan directions. To assess how far plans had been significant in producing these findings, we then undertook 13 intensive case studies of particular projects, using interviews and documents in our search to identify the specific role of plans in producing the outcomes identified. It became clear to us that the answer to the question 'how far have plans been significant in implementing planning policies?' depended upon the type of situation involved and the type of task being undertaken. We concluded that the plans had been much more important in shaping development in city centres and the urban fringe than in inner city areas and in areas of open land beyond the fringe.

We explained this in terms of different kinds of tasks involved in policy implementation. Where policy implementation depended upon the coordination of public sector activity and investment, plans had little effect. This was partly because of the increasing lack of resources available to the public sector, but also reflected the limited power of the plan and of planning considerations in the decision making of government agencies generally. Where implementation required the regulation of private investment in conditions of relative land and property market buoyancy, and if all levels of government were prepared to back the policies, then structure and local plans played an effective and significant role in guiding development. We concluded that structure and local plans had a useful role to play in guiding development. By resolving conflicts in advance at the plan-preparation stage, greater certainty was provided to developers, decision making was speeded up and coordination encouraged. Where plans were less effective, the reasons lay in conflict over policies, in the failure to imagine appropriate policies, and in the lack of power of the plan with respect to the project of other public sector agents. We concluded:

> Our evidence confirms that while peripheral restraint has been effectively achieved, urban and economic regeneration has not. The often substantial efforts of local authorities in support of regeneration policies have merely resulted in cushioning local communities from the full consequences of economic recession and regional decentralisation.

Planning policies have thus acted selectively on processes of land use change and development. Where policies involve moderating and organising current trends in development investment, or where conflicts of interest have to be resolved to arrive at a decision on land allocation, the planning system largely provides the necessary powers to implement policy, through the machinery of plan-making, the framework provided by agreed planning policies in plans, and the powers of development control.

But the limited range of powers and resources which can be manipulated through policies in structure and local plans have had a marginal impact on the processes by which investment has been withdrawn from large areas of the older parts of the conurbations. Nor are they serving to attract significant mobile investment. Consequently, urban regeneration is not taking place. It is difficult to avoid the conclusion that for the latter to succeed, a larger, more coordinated and consistent programme of public action is required.

The fact that planning policies aimed at urban regeneration are having little impact does not imply that the only role for the planning system lies in regulating existing market demand. Our case studies provide much evidence, if on a small scale, that where consistency of purpose and coordinated action can be achieved, the tools of the planning system offer a useful way of articulating a framework for change which can help to maximise the investments of all concerned. But under current conditions, such consistency and coordination is very difficult to achieve. In other words, it is the political-administrative context as much as economic conditions which make urban regeneration so difficult to achieve. Nevertheless, the current strong pressures for decentralisation suggest that the general policy of conserving the existing spatial structure of our conurbations will have to be fundamentally reviewed (pp. 21-24).

We then went on to say:

The 1968 development plan system thus remains a robust approach to managing land use change in an effective and legitimate way (p. 92).

We noted that the system was criticised because of the complexity of plan preparation, the failure to deliver agreed policies (which we had shown to be only partially true), and because of their policy content. Our final sentence stated:

We should not blame plans for the political inability to face up to policy choices and their financial and institutional implications (p. 93).[24]

---

24 All quotations are from Healey et al. 1985, op. cit., N8.

What has been the impact of this research? A simple conclusion could be: none at all! The report was presented in 1985. A year later the Department produced a discussion paper on *The Future of Development Plans*,[25] which proposed the abolition of structure plans. Our report was thus received by the Department at a time of considerable internal debate on future directions for the planning system. We were required to present our findings to a seminar for senior civil servants and DoE planning staff from different regional offices. The discussion of our report was wide ranging, and focused on the internal discussion over the future of structure plans. We knew that the regional office staff felt our conclusions were valid. At the end of the discussion, we were asked to reconsider our conclusions in the light of the debate. This we declined to do. Did we thereby sacrifice potential influence at the shrine of intellectual integrity?

However, it is possible to tell another story, though perhaps it is up to others than myself to do so. Firstly, the conduct of the research itself generated considerable learning, by ourselves, by the DoE officials who commissioned the research, by the various actors in the public and private sectors with whom we conducted the research, and by participants at seminar discussions on the research. Ideas infused across what were tending to become difficult boundaries, between central and local government, and between the public and private sectors. We in turn were able to provide helpful encouragement to innovative ideas. Also, more generally, in these discussions, the idea of planning as an effective mechanism for the mediation of conflicting interests in the management of environmental change was progressively 'talked up'. By the mid-1980s, it was quite normal for civil servants and local government planners to think of planning in this way. Our research did not of course invent this approach, but it helped to consolidate an emerging interpretation of the reality of planning practice.

Secondly, our work provided ammunition for those, including ourselves, who felt it necessary to criticise the DoE's proposals for abolishing structure plans. Ultimately, there was a very substantial consensus of criticism on this point, as property interests found they agreed with conservation interests over the need for strategic plans as a basis for effective conflict mediation.

Thirdly, officials in the Department did not forget our report. I am aware of its use as briefing material. I would certainly be interested to know if it has been used at all in the current 'refurbishment' of planning with a change of Minister. A revised consultation paper which retained the proposal to abolish structure plans was issued in 1989. However, by 1990, the role of plans was being strongly reaffirmed in government policy, and structure plans have been retained in the 1991 Planning and Compensation Act.

Fourthly, the research has contributed to the knowledge base of planning. We partly sought to achieve this by the publication of our report, and a few articles on

---

25   Department of the Environment, *The Future of Development Plans*, London, HMSO, 1986.

the work (which have been used extensively in undergraduate texts).[26] We have also used the research as the basis for a more social scientific account of the nature of the planning system as a mechanism for the mediation of conflicting interests in the management of environmental change.[27]

Thus it would probably be fair to say that while this research was formally a piece of client-directed 'policy evaluation' research, it has developed into a social scientific analysis. It has also involved a not unimportant element of 'active learning' by all who became involved in the research process.

What challenges does conducting such research present? There are of course considerable intellectual, methodological and management challenges which a project of this nature presents. Specifically, we were taking a lot of risks by attempting to develop our own analytical ideas as we carried out the work. But more specifically, we had to play our research role very carefully. It was essential that we were trusted by the various parties involved even if they were critical of each other. We also became party to knowledge from one quarter which could be very useful to someone else. We therefore had to develop a sensitivity to what was confidential and what was exchangeable information. We in effect produced our own 'confidentiality contract' with those we approached for access to information and documentary material. We in particular avoided being overly critical of any of the participants.

We also checked all our written material with those closely involved in the research. This was partly to correct errors of fact and potential breaches of confidence. It also usually led to extensive and often critical comments on our interpretation. This was very useful to us, though it required time. All comments had to be respectfully treated and acknowledged, and time had to be made available for recipients to read reports. We could easily have been seen as either creatures of central government or trouble-shooters for the local government lobby. Instead, I think we were considered to have a reasonable understanding of everyone's situation, independent but sensitive. It is up to others to assess whether this has compromised the contribution our research has made. Despite such potential compromises, the socially responsible researcher must act morally when researching planning practice in the way we have done.[28]

Conclusions

Three generalisations may be drawn from this personal experience of researching planning practice. Firstly, researching planning practice in the ways I have done is a

---

26 See, for example, Bruton, M.J. and Nicholson, D., *Local Planning in Practice*, London, Hutchinson, 1987.

27 Healey et al., op. cit., N10.

28 The Society for Social Research has a useful code of ethics to provide guidance on how to achieve this.

much messier business than, for example, quantitative studies of market behaviour for a property company, or independent social scientific inquiries into aspects of planning. The researcher and the researched are involved in more complex political, institutional and professional relationships, which is why ethical issues are so important. Research activity thus tends to have a collaborative quality.

Secondly, it is not difficult to propose a few proverbs for the conduct of researching planning practice, although these are merely restatements of general principles for the conduct of effective research:

- Think carefully about what kind of research you are undertaking. If more than one type is being carried out in parallel, be clear what each involves and about the way you will move between the two;
- Be rigorous about research strategy and method, essential anyway if qualitative, intensive research is involved;
- Be very conscious of the institutional context of the research. Expect your client to shift position during a project, and to have complex relations with those you need to work with on the research;
- Build up relationships of trust and respect with all those you will need to work with;
- Give back something to all those whose cooperation is necessary for the research;
- Deliver to your client's brief, but do not compromise your integrity (which means you need to know your own 'sticking points');
- Do not expect to exercise too much influence. Research is only one input in the flow of knowledge, ideas and information which influences planning policy and practices;
- You can stay hopeful by noting that the impact of research about planning practice upon that practice may be more long-term and more diffuse then you realise.

Finally, we could do with a great deal more research of this kind. In Britain, the institutional context of planning has changed quite dramatically since the early 1980s when we conducted our work. Specifically, much more planning work is now being undertaken in consultancies. Meanwhile, after nearly a decade of a more liberal regime, plan making and plan-based action are now in fashion again. This time, the private sector will clearly be the primary development initiator.

I am personally interested in two kinds of question. Firstly, what relations between plan and action are likely to develop? Will the planning system prove a sufficiently effective regulatory framework for the development dimensions of local economic and community development strategies, environmentally sustainable policies and for negotiating with the private sector for contributions to infrastructure, community development and environmental quality? Secondly, can we learn more about the nature of democratic forms of communicative practice in the planning field, and ways we can make this more 'comprehensible, sincere, legitimate and truthful', to quote Forester?[29] This brings me to one last purpose for researching planning practice, namely to provide insights and to test possibilities to assist in the development of planning theory for practice.

Acknowledgements

I would like to acknowledge the thoughtful comments on this chapter made by one of those involved in the research episode described in the text. The views reported here are, of course, entirely my own rather than those of any other of the researchers and research clients involved in the work discussed.

Editorial Note

This chapter first appeared as a paper in *Town Planning Review* 62:4, 447-59, 1991. It is reproduced by permission of the author and Liverpool University Press.

---

29   Forester, op. cit., N7.

PART III
Ethics in the Practice
of Planning Research

Chapter 12

Toward a Naturalistic Research Ethic: Or how Mediators must Act Well to Learn, if They are to Practice Effectively

John Forester and David Laws

Let's face it: we hurt each other all the time. We hurt the people we love the most: we act blindly, jump to conclusions, can't see when we need to, can't hear what we should, help too much or too little. This is where ethics begins: how we treat one another for better or worse, how we act, and how our acting produces consequences that shape human flourishing and welfare.

In the context of research, ethical practice involves protecting or harming research subjects, endangering or safeguarding the well being of those researchers might study. How might a research project manipulate subjects more or less, intrude upon their privacy more or less (or not at all), provide them opportunities for informed consent to participate or fail to provide those opportunities? These are questions that are central to the domain of 'research ethics', a domain which does not usually extend to thinking about the ways that research might influence emerging relationships among these actors and contribute to, or detract from, their subsequent flourishing and development.

This chapter will explore 'research ethics' in a practical, even 'naturalistic', way. We will learn about ethical considerations as performed in the practice of the mediators of public disputes. When mediators work with conflicting parties, they conduct practical research. They interview parties and bring these parties together if they are willing and interested. They help the parties explore the issues in dispute, they foster a creative process of exploring and proposing new options for joint action, they empower parties to create their own agreements, and more. As a matter of their 'natural' practice, mediators must learn and must help the parties learn; in order to learn, they must face a series of ethical challenges.

So by referring to 'a naturalistic ethics of research', or a naturalistic research ethics, we refer to the situated, practical, already occurring ethical analysis – ethical questioning and inquiry – taking place in the flows of applied research practice that typify certain broad types of planning. Naturalistic ethics leads us not to ask so much what planners in any given setting might typically do, or what they should refrain from doing, but, instead, to ask what kinds of research-related ethical questions might characteristically confront planners (who might then answer those questions in many different ways). In community planning, for example, planners might well ask about ways of researching community welfare, or about studying and assessing the desired kinds of relationships that could be developed or protected or encouraged (or not) with various community members.

We can learn about such applied research ethics from the practice of public dispute mediators, because as they must learn on the job and help others to learn, they face challenges that can teach us about parallel challenges facing planners: to help adversarial negotiators with little trust and less expectation of fruitful collaboration to learn and, through their learning, to develop practical options that they may all come to prefer. Thus mediators' work helps disputing parties to do better (in the parties own terms) than they would if they had to negotiate with each other on their own.

How is this possible? If disputing parties, left to their own devices, each act to protect themselves by hiding information and strategically mis-representing what they care about and what they can do, we should hardly be surprised that their resulting agreements suffer from the foundations of deceit, fabrication, exaggeration, and flimsy information that they rest upon. We have little reason to think that such a foundation would lead to stable, well-informed, fair, and productive agreements. Because mediators' goals are not only to learn themselves, but to extend the learning they initiate to the parties involved, they also face the traditional questions about research ethics from a practical perspective that is revealing.

A homely example might help. Chris and Max want to find a nice place to go for a business lunch. They've just met and both want to position themselves favourably with regard to a pending project. Both want to look good; neither wishes to appear pushy, stubborn, or picky. Most of all, neither wants to feel that the other has made the first concession in the 'negotiation' that has already begun, leaving them vulnerable to subtle, and potentially expensive, demands for reciprocity. Each, ignorant about the other's preferences, tries to get the other to commit first and reveal information about his likes and dislikes or, even, to suggest a restaurant. When their own adeptness at posturing frustrates these efforts, they each suggest a 'safe' alternative, chosen strategically to conceal their own preferences and appear as a concession to the other. This dance ends when they finally agree on Baxter's Bistro and then find themselves eating bland fare from a standard menu in a 'generic USA' ambiance.

That night, they both check in with a mutual acquaintance, Pat, about how it went and Pat chides each of them, essentially: 'Why in the world did you go *there*? Chris, you love good seafood. Max, you love a good view. You could have taken an extra ten minutes to get to Kilgore's – and you'd have both loved it – far more than Baxter's.'

We have all been in Chris and Max's position, whether as Christine or Christopher, Maxine or Maxwell. We've made agreements based on sketchy information because we thought it too risky or expensive or inconvenient to learn more. We've made agreements in relationships because we set our sights, our aspirations, more narrowly than we needed to. Sometimes we're lucky enough to have learned that we could have done – and might still do – better; often we never know. But our example suggests that sometimes 'third parties' like Pat can help, not only after, but especially *before* negotiators come to the point of making decisions or agreements.

Notice of course that in our restaurant example, Chris and Max did less well than they could have in terms of their own interests and values. Strategically, neither did well, but, ethically, they also failed to maximise the welfare that was available. The ethical force of this may seem to some less than compelling when we are talking about two businessmen, but we could just as easily be describing two parties in an emerging political or organisational relationship, as we shall see.

Pat might have helped Chris and Max with their problem in several ways. First and most obviously, Pat might have simply expanded the space of possibilities that Chris and Max considered. Second, Pat might have enhanced the quality of information they had: passing along a recent review of Kilgore's from the press, passing along personal experience of eating there, sharing information about the menu or the decor or the location, and so on. Third, Pat might have helped them set a tone or precedent for their developing relationship. Fourth, Pat might have helped them learn about one another, recognise and appreciate aspirations or sensitivities in the other that they might not have gained so easily otherwise. Fifth, Pat might have helped them both to spend their resources more wisely than on rubber chicken in a 'generic USA' decor. Sixth, and as significantly, Pat may well have helped Chris and Max make a decision that will make them look good and not lead either of them to look back and wonder, 'What was I thinking?' Pat may have listened and informed their possibilities, and still left Chris and Max to make their own decision, their own agreement.

So in a micro-political sense, Chris and Max had a relationship to build a negotiation to develop and an outcome to achieve. Pat (had Chris and Max consulted him or her early on) could well have functioned as a planner-mediator: fostering and empowering a well-informed, wise use of resources. Notice again, Pat might have played this role without any formal authority, and even without much trust (Chris or Max might have checked Pat's information independently). So in what follows, let's broaden our view a bit to consider how the mediators of public disputes might, similarly, help community stakeholders to negotiate their own agreements, make their own decisions, in ways that can be better informed, more stable, more productive (in their terms), and more inclusive than if those stakeholders were left to their own negotiating devices (perhaps defensive, perhaps posturing, perhaps exaggerating, and so on). In doing so, we can also see what place ethics takes in this development.

We can explore a naturalistic research ethics of community planning – and public dispute mediation – by considering several of the considerations that a third party planner will face as he or she tries to work with and in between interdependent and thus negotiating community stakeholders, be they adjacent neighbourhood residents, rival or just distinct community organisations, or neighbourhood residents with distinct commitments: to environmental quality, peace and quiet, spaces for youth activities, good transportation, safe streets, as well as to concerns about how they treat each other in the context of the negotiation relationship. The planner or mediator's work in between multiple stakeholders becomes one of 'dealing with differences'. In the face of strongly articulated differences, where practical or even 'theoretical' agreements between stakeholders are never guaranteed beforehand, their work becomes a very practical 'drama of mediating public disputes' (thus the subtitle in Forester 2009).

Note that resolving the bargaining problem illustrated above by Chris and Max's initial effort to agree on a restaurant, in which strategic concerns produced outcomes that disadvantaged both parties (and thus violate utilitarian ethical imperatives), has only been 'solved' by approaches that embed strong ethical content. Howard Raiffa, for example, while starting from a view of social actors as 'cooperative antagonists' hinges their ability to achieve efficient outcomes on their joint ability to open a process of 'full, open, truthful exchange' (FOTE) (Raiffa et al. 2007).[1] In *Getting to Yes*, Roger Fisher, Bill Ury, and Bruce Patton (1991) couch their account of how negotiators might do better in language that has strong ethical resonances.[2] Kelman, similarly, ties problem solving in negotiation to ethical practice via the centrality of perspective taking (Kelman 1996).[3]

But what, one might ask, does research ethics have to do with mediation and community planning? The answer will depend on the very applied – situated and not abstract, specific and not general – problems of what planners and mediators need to learn in order to do their work. Only if a planner-mediator needs to learn

---

1   'Joint decision making emphasizes direct communication of interests, aspirations, expectations, beliefs, visions of the future, and so forth. This contrasts starkly with the uncooperative game-theoretic perspective of simultaneous choices and no preplay communications. Negotiations bent on squeezing out joint gains through collaborative decision making may wish to exchange their most intimate secrets in hope of maximizing joint gains. [We] have a great deal to say about this under the rubric of Full, Open, Truthful Exchange (FOTE)' (Raiffa et al. 2007, 83).

2   For example: 'It is not enough to know that they see things differently. If you want to influence them, you also need to understand empathetically the power of their point of view and to feel the emotional force with which they believe in it. It is not enough to study them like the beetles under a microscope; you need to know what it feels like to be a beetle. To complete this task you should be prepared to withhold judgment for a while as you try on their shoes' (Fisher, Ury and Patton 1991, 33-34).

3   Kelman (1996, 101) describes negotiation as an 'interactive process', a 'joint effort, in which parties work together to generate ideas for a solution that meets both of their needs. The hallmark of social interaction is that each participant tries to enter into the other's perspective and take the other's role, thus gaining an understanding of the other's concerns, intentions, and expectations. This empathetic process, in turn, allows the parties to influence each other's behaviour to their own benefit by being responsive to each other's needs. When negotiations are truly interactive in this sense, parties make an active effort to find solutions that maximize not only their won benefits, but also the benefits of the other – in other words to find ways in which both parties can win.'

nothing – if the parties to disputes were not only fully rational, fully informed, but fully forthright as well – would those in mediating roles have little research to do, and research ethics might matter even less. But if every case of conflict or dispute that mediators engage, however, presents particular, case-specific, distinct claims, demands and strategic moves by those involved, then mediators and planners cannot even begin to act without learning about the particularities and specificities of this case before them, so they might have some inkling of what they might do that will not blow up in their faces, and how to extend their learning to the parties who own the dispute.

So the more that mediators and planners, working between multiple and different stakeholders need to learn about those stakeholders, about the issues at hand, about the processes through which the stakeholders might interact and, in turn, learn, the more that those mediators and planners must do applied, case-specific practical research. What new information might better inform the participants here? Which of their claims might be strategic, a bluff, and which are deadly serious? Have the parties ever met face to face, or have their impressions of one another been mediated through the press – or both? The more those mediators and planners have to learn in order to understand a dispute in the first place, and the more they must then learn to gauge how they can best intervene, the more those same planners and mediators face a series of questions of research ethics – questions involving respect, critical probing, evaluations of possible outcomes and more – whose answers will shape what they can learn in real time in real cases.

To understand the sequence in which such learning develops, let's take a hypothetical case of a land use planning conflict, much like the one Lisa Beutler mediated in California between off-highway vehicle enthusiasts and environmentalists (Forester 2006). The environmentalists want the motorcycle riders to leave the State park lands alone; the off-roaders want to enjoy the outdoors with their children and families. One wants to leave 'nature' alone; the other wants the State and tree-huggers to leave them alone.

Consider the initial research issue – and ethical considerations – that would confront the mediator (or, by extension, the planner) in such a case, well before he or she ever meets with representatives of these (and other) parties or brings them together in the same room at the same time. How does a planner or mediator make a well-informed judgment about whether it's a good or a crazy idea to bring the parties to a nasty dispute together face to face?

This initial question reflects the practical work that mediators often refer to as 'assessing' a conflict. The mediators want to know, for example, if a range of mediation, facilitation, or consensus-building processes might even be appropriate in the specific case at hand. To make that judgment, 'Yes, mediation might be promising here' or 'No, mediation's hopeless in a case like this', the prospective mediators need to learn about much more than 'what the parties want' in the case at hand. They must learn, for example, about how the parties feel about the status quo (how badly do the parties want to change the current situation?); about how the parties *perceive* their future options (do they have influential friends in the

184   *Ethics and Planning Research*

Governor's office? a deep legal staff ready to go to court?); and about the parties' willingness to pay the costs of those strategies – in adverse publicity, dollar cost, or time costs. The mediators might try, too, to gauge what some independent but well-informed observers perceive as the likelihood of different strategies paying off: 'Do you think you'll win in court because you're in the right or because you have reliable legal advice telling you that?' Finally, if they understand their relationship to the parties in ethical as well as practical terms, they must find ways to involve the parties in the learning they initiate.

To begin to learn in these ways, mediators and planners typically interview a wide range of parties, some directly involved 'stakeholders' and others who might be insightful observers. The work might look like simple interviewing, but there's little simple about the challenges here (Forester 2006).

So if the mediators have a good deal to learn, if they must do careful research on the job to know if mediation might even be appropriate in a given case, how do questions of research ethics arise? We can explore this question by asking it this way: How might mediators *fail ethically* as they try to do the research they need to do? We can consider several sources of ethical failure that threaten mediators in their research endeavours. Each turns on contrasting a thin and a thick view of ethical obligations. The practical responses that mediators have to this challenge provides lessons on how to understand research ethics in practice.

Table 12.1   Research ethics in practice

Thin and Thicker Stances Toward Ethical Issues	Trust	Respect	Representation
Thin	A matter of coordination; Minimally, don't offend	Gullibility: Taking others at face value; Naïve, reducing values to tastes	Agent loyally mirrors principal's preferences
Thick	Appreciation and development of our interdependence	Probing deeper interests and preferences	Agent challenges and promotes the principal's preferences

The Challenge of Trust

The exchange of information and the development of understanding that learning involves put parties in a negotiation at risk, in the position of being, or at least feeling vulnerable. In order to meet the demands for openness that learning creates, mediators may seek to build confidence and trust by avoiding signs of bias. They want to avoid being perceived as judgmental, sexist or racist, or otherwise so preoccupied with some concern of their own that the parties to a given dispute wish to have nothing to do with them. They avoid wearing the Chamber of Commerce's lapel pin that might not endear them to community activists and the Greenpeace t-shirt that is unlikely to inspire confidence during an interview with a local developer.

Such efforts to present themselves as non-threatening, as 'neutral' with respect to the parties and the issue in dispute constitute what we would call a thin view of trust. They may avoid attributions of bias and create a limited, if not negligible, ability to coordinate action and exchange information. They will likely leave the parties with a *modus vivendi*, however, but stop well short of creating the conditions in which a serious and instructive conversation – empathetic but not sympathetic, and more humble than righteous – is possible. It is equally unlikely to create conditions that might extend to the parties relations with each other, or enhance the reflexivity about their own positions and practices that would be necessary for a more 'studied' and robust form of trust that could cope with the uncertainties, ambiguities, cultural differences, misunderstandings and other disruptions that will inevitably be part of the implementation of their agreements and their longer term relationship (Fuller 1971; Sabel 1992).

The Challenge of Respect

In the effort to develop trust and create conditions for learning, mediators face fascinating problems of respect. Respect, plausibly, can mean taking what the parties report about their ambitions, needs – their interests in the terms of the trade – at face value. Respect in such terms – that tastes are not to be disputed and people are the best judge of what they like and what is more and less important to them – can leave mediators open to two problems. It raises the early danger, particularly for novice mediators, that they can fail to give parties anything more than the superficial respect involved in earnestly noting what these parties report at the time of the interview. Second, aside from their personal interests and concerns that can get in their own way, mediators can make a mess of the interview conversation itself (for an extensive discussion, see Forester 2006). They may be, curiously, too believing for their own good. They can fail to probe beyond sound bites or quick summaries, fail to get to the point, as one mediator explained, 'after the first fifteen minutes', when the canned summaries trail off and the more detailed and instructive, if complicated or even contradictory, facets of people's stories emerge. Here mediators' or planners' failure to listen deeply, to explore ambiguity as fertile rather than as merely confusing ground, can be seen as an ethical failure or shortcoming. Taking people to mean just and only what they say – as if that showed respect to them – not only leaves the mediator, and the parties, with far more superficial information than they all often need, and often with far more superficial information than the parties would actually be perfectly willing to share, were the mediator only willing to stay around for a while and listen.

A thicker view of respect would start with respect for the parties' abilities to reflect in light of practical problems, to learn about their own interests and priorities, and to empathise with the views and needs of the other. It would acknowledge the very real fears and constraints (see Chris and Max above) that may initially limit their willingness to share information, the effects of prior framing that may shape and limit the terms in which they see the current situation, and the tacit character of understanding that may initially make important information and insights difficult to access. Experienced mediators know how to work from a thicker understanding of respect that embraces parties' abilities to empathise with the other, to reflect on their own situation and the interdependence that shapes their ability to act, and to revise their views in light of new information and insights. They understand how to use the interview setting, as well as later deliberations and negotiations, to prompt the deeper consideration of facts, future, and other that they know the parties are capable of. Mediators working from a thicker view of respect would also manage the temptations they face to put themselves at the centre of the 'magic of mediation,' as rewarding as it might be to hear parties say of creative outcomes and productive agreements, 'It's as if it were magic'. Such characterisations certainly highlight the power of the initial blinders that often constrain parties' consideration of possible options. Yet mediators know that the ability to move beyond initial positions to surprising outcomes is not based in some magic they have wrought, but in the hard work of the parties and their real capacities for learning, for expanding considerations and inventing of new options, and for negotiating practical agreements. These capacities lie with the parties themselves. Mediators may help to mobilise them, but they remain, practically and ethically, rooted in the actual capacities of the parties themselves. Respect for this autonomy and capacity for growth demands the expression of a thicker view of respect that will help the mediator challenge the initial statements of parties and probe more deeply into the details of the situation and the understandings of the parties.

The Challenge of Representation

Finally, mediators face a set of ethical challenges around issues of representation. This starts with the basic ethical question, 'Who's affected here and who deserves to be part of the planning discussions at hand?' In practical terms this becomes a question of whether the mediation process will assure those 'affected stakeholders' adequate practical representation. In planning and public policy discussions more generally, this is the abiding question, of course, of 'Who's the relevant affected "community"?'

In their initial assessment work, mediators typically try to interview both immediately affected and more distant parties and ask: 'Who's affected by the issues at hand? Who needs to be at the table? Who might make any claims later about being left out or excluded if they are not represented in any negotiations that might soon take place?' Their professional ethical concerns are likely to

Toward a Naturalistic Research Ethic 187

prevent them from going ahead with a process were it to exclude parties or if they would suspect the mediation process to be merely a guise that will provide opportunities for participation that have less than 'fair value'. On ethical as well as practical grounds, they will seek to avoid overly narrow representation that threatens to exclude deserving and affected parties. Mediators use versions of practical snowball sampling methods to meet the ethical challenge of identifying parties who should be represented and practical skills and influence to ensure that opportunities are provided to these groups.

This is just the beginning, however. They then need to address the practical challenges of choosing 'good representatives' and working with these representatives that arise once the question of 'who are the affected and relevant parties?' has been settled. A thin view of representation may lead mediators to accept the parties' choice of representatives (extending the thin respect discussed above) and risk ending up with 'a bull in the china shop', who can't listen to women or is virulently homophobic (and so on). The resulting process can be needlessly chaotic, or worse. Such a resolution of representation challenges can create problems in the future that will have ethical as well as practical dimensions. Representatives who cannot listen and learn, who see it as their job to stake out and hold positions, and who may throw stones and insults in defending their positions, may see themselves as being true to their role. In a thin view, they are loyal agents who remain true to the assignment given by the principals they represent. In doing so, however, they may compromise just the kind of ethical considerations described above for efficient agreements, for the trust needed to negotiate and implement such agreements, and for respect that goes beyond acceptance of initial statements to engage parties' capacity for listening, learning, reflection, and development.

A thicker view of the principal-agent tensions that characterise representation is needed to avoid the traps and pitfalls that make mediation necessary in the first place. Even at face value, 'a good agent does not antagonize his opposite number, is at pains to stay on good terms with him' and a fruitful process will 'require a degree of trust and mutual respect between the...negotiating agents' (Fuller 1971, 323). Moreover, if these agents are to learn, and, as we have stressed above, if this learning is central to their joint ability to meet the needs, priorities, and interests of the parties they represent, then these agents cannot be bound by a thin view of the principal-agent relationship. A responsible, even ethical, agent would need to extend their own learning to the parties they represent and help them to 're-orient' themselves toward the other parties and 'achieve a new and shared perception of [these] relationships, a perception that will redirect their attitudes and dispositions' toward the others (Fuller 1971, 325). In this respect, agents working on a thick understanding of the ethics of principal-agent relations will work in relation to their principals in a fashion that is in important respects analogous to the way mediators relate to the parties.

So mediators start by searching for representatives who have the strength to make strong arguments and to listen to others' strong arguments without being flustered, distracted, annoyed, or so personally put off that they cannot deal with the real issues at hand. They initiate a process that, on the one hand engages these representatives' abilities to learn, teach, invent, and develop and, on the other, upholds their right to stick to their interests and defend their concerns and which ensures that this occurs in the context of regular consultation with the parties they represent (for striking examples in California water disputes, see Fuller 2005). Mediators end by helping these agents extend the practical and ethical foundations of their relationships with the mediator and with one another to their relationship with the principals they represent. Here, as above, good practice, the kind we have suggested as instructive, can reconcile the practical and ethical demands that in lesser hands create tensions that may appear irresolvable.

Conclusion: The Challenge of Assessing 'Good Agreements' (What's Good Enough?)

To conclude, we turn to consider yet another ethical challenge that mediators face as they seek to learn, to do applied research, as they work on real cases. Just as more traditional academic researchers must worry about biased samples or the systematic exclusion of data, so mediators must worry too about sources of corruption that might render public agreements illegitimate, flawed, or 'agreements' in name only. Susskind and Cruikshank (1987) argues that mediators ought to pay attention to four characteristics that define 'good agreements' – fairness, efficiency, stability and wisdom (e.g. the quality of being well informed). These four characteristics in turn suggest ethical challenges for ethically responsible mediators: a) mediators should assure fairness by attending to adequate representation of affected parties having access to the same opportunities to present their interests, to learn about issues, to invent options together; b) mediators should assure efficiency by working to maximise joint gains, to enable parties to trade across differing priorities rather than 'to split differences' which will involve the parties in efforts to understand one another through empathic processes like perspective taking that have direct ethical implications (see footnotes 2 and 3 on page 182); c) mediators should resist premature and hasty agreements and anticipate possibilities for renegotiation and adjustment if a given agreement becomes less workable over time than expected; and d) mediators should assure that parties take advantage of, or have access to, the best available scientific and technical information relevant to the case at hand. We see that these are matters of research ethics when we consider the failures we witness when these four challenges are not met: we see, respectively, exclusion of affected parties and their concerns; waste and missed opportunities; instability of a supposed 'agreement', and wilful ignorance if not actually negligence.

In all these ways, mediators who work on real cases face ethical challenges if they are to learn what they need to learn to act effectively. These ethical challenges of learning in practice represent naturalistic – i.e. situated in real cases – challenges of research ethics. If the ethical challenges go unmet, research in real cases suffers. We see, as a result, that in the world of planning and public policy practice, we separate the realms of epistemology and knowing from the realms of ethics and acting only at great risk. If we are blind to ethics, we may well not learn very well. If we are blind to epistemology, we may well not act very well.

In their own practice in the face of conflict, astute mediators might teach us how to integrate ethical sensitivity and epistemological insight, how to do right and learn well, how to appreciate the contributions of research ethics to good practice.

References

Fisher, R., Ury, W. and Patton, B. (1991), *Getting to Yes* (New York: Penguin).

Forester, J. (2006), 'Making Participation Work When Interests Conflict: From Fostering Dialogue and Moderating Debate to Mediating Disputes', *Journal of the American Planning Association* 72:4, 447–56.

Forester, J. (2009), *Dealing with Differences: Dramas of Mediating Public Disputes* (New York: Oxford University Press).

Fuller, B. (2005), 'Trading Zones: Cooperating for Water Resource and Ecosystem Management When Stakeholders Have Apparently Irreconcilable Differences' PhD diss., MIT Department of Urban Studies and Planning.

Fuller, L. (1971), 'Mediation – Its Form and Functions', *Southern California Law Review* 44:2, 305-339.

Kelman, H.C. (1996), 'Negotiation as Interactive Problem Solving', *International Negotiation* 1:1, 99-123.

Pyke, F. and Sengenberger, W. (eds) (1992), *Industrial Districts and Local Economic Regeneration* (Geneva: Institute for Labour Studies).

Raiffa, H. et al. (2007), *Negotiation Analysis: The Science and Art of Collaborative Decision Making* (Cambridge: Harvard Belknap Press).

Sabel, C. (1992), 'Studied Trust: Building New Forms of Cooperation in a Volatile Economy', in Frank Pyke and Werner Sengenberger (eds).

Susskind, L. and Cruikshank, J. (1987), *Breaking the Impasse* (New York: Basic Books).

Chapter 13

Knowledge, Power and Ethics in Extraordinary Times: Learning from the Naples Waste Crisis

Laura Lieto

Relations between planning research and ethics can be heavily biased by power, especially when it is exerted beyond the ordinary procedural frame. The common aspiration of planning researchers to make their scientific production as equitable and reliable as possible according to different social claims and needs is always to be contextualised into concrete and specific power relations, which make this aspiration not just a rhetorical claim based on transcendent principles, but a challenge to practical handling, and therefore even into ethical terms.

This chapter will focus on the relations of planning research, ethics and power assuming that, in the absence of universal principles of truth, equity and reliability of scientific knowledge, planning research is constantly challenged by opposing political claims and power injunctions, and thus compelled to take charge of its ethical responsibility in the face of (sometimes) harsh conflicts rising from concrete situations. To develop this argument, the chapter will grasp some critical issues from a specific case, the waste crisis which exploded in Naples at the end of 2007, which will be regarded not so much in terms of its local implications (even if the particularity of the case means it would not be neglected in methodological terms), but rather as an 'extreme case' which is worth seeing as emblematic of much more diffuse problems common to many big European cities: the role public policies play when dealing with 'wicked planning problems', the ambiguity of scientific knowledge as a support of hard political decisions, the critical ineffectiveness of scientific and intellectual claims in public debates, are just some examples of such a problematic frame.

These issues have significant ethical implications for planning culture and practice. Moreover, the waste crisis is the core of a long-term phase of extraordinary urban and regional government (begun in 1994 and still going), and it can be used as an opportunity to explore in more depth the general issue of power/knowledge as a matter of professional and research ethics, since in this frame, knowledge – here inferred as a synthetic formula standing for *planning research* as a particular form of *search for/about knowledge* – is overstressed by concentrated power and therefore some critical issues can be highlighted more clearly.

Among European countries, Italy retains primacy in terms of environmental and social catastrophes, which a long-term case history of natural and human hazards shows quite well, as does a legal and political framework developed in the wake of these major issues. Earthquakes, floods, industrial accidents and landslides are a large part of a national 'geography of risk' which covers the whole territory, especially the South.

Dealing with territorial emergencies, from a public policy perspective, requires special procedures of intervention, usually defined as 'extraordinary government': this expression means that ordinary government standing orders are temporarily replaced by extraordinary ones, typically based on a strong concentration of power within a restricted arena of institutional actors, aimed at coping more efficiently and rapidly with situations of extreme danger and social emergency.

In times of emergency, ordinary frames of relations between power and knowledge change dramatically as well: they are more asymmetrical than usual, inasmuch as power gets more concentrated and therefore closer to an authoritarian, disciplinary model. From such a perspective (following Foucault 1976), knowledge can be regarded as a function of power, keeping asymmetries and impeding forms of reciprocity which can be a 'menace' to its disciplinary asset.

Besides all sorts of significant implications which this relation of functional subordination brings about in terms of ancillary reduction of knowledge in the service of disciplinary power, the Foucauldian perspective may help to raise some ethical issues related to the exercise of knowledge as public discourse in a restricted and authority-oriented power domain as well.

To give my argument a theoretical framework, I shall conceptualise the 'extraordinary government' as a specimen of the so-called 'state of exception' conceptualised by Carl Schmitt (1922) and further developed by Giorgio Agamben (1995). A parallel focus will be the relation between ethics and knowledge as a critical bound of freedom, trust and truth (Galimberti 2007) which should be guaranteed and supervised by public institutions and politics.

Following these two theoretical strands, I shall highlight some critical issues concerning professional ethics, specifically referring to planners both as experts and public officials cooperating with political decision-makers to cope with 'malign problems' in the case of major environmental and social disasters. The case of the Naples waste crisis (whose most striking aspects will be briefly summarised) will offer hints for the development of such a discussion, working as a background narrative in each and every part of the text (and not as a true case study).[1]

---

1 At present, a good amount of 'scientific' literature on the Naples waste crisis is still not available, whereas an almost immense volume of news remains the main source of information, together with official acts and decrees.

Extraordinary Government as a *State of Exception*

Christmas 2007 was approaching. But it was not going to be the usual mass-consumption feast, with people crowding the streets of the city centre. It was not even going to be a popular event, in the spirit of the ancient local tradition of rituals and street festivals. The city was literally invaded, from the centre to the outskirts, by mountains of solid urban waste. The regional disposal system had collapsed, dumps had run out, no effective separate collection policies had been implemented. Media all over the world diffused the image of Naples drowning in garbage.

Meanwhile, riots were getting fiercer in the popular neighbourhood of Pianura, in the western metro area: as an extraordinary measure proposed by local governments (region and city) with the consent of central government, Pianura's old waste disposal (shut down years before because of saturation, and afterwards included in a new plan for a metropolitan park all around the Naples central area) was to be re-opened to provide some extra space for solid waste abandoned in the streets. Residents strongly opposed this measure, supported by some local representatives and groups of environmental activists: it was not just a case of NIMBY syndrome (even if the old waste disposal was located right in the middle of the neighbourhood), but also a strong, collective call for public health defence against toxic materials illegally stocked (better say 'buried') in the waste disposal for a long time.[2] Fierce clashes between police and residents occurred in a chaotic and dramatic context: newspapers denounced the presence of agents of local organised crime (camorra), who infiltrated the grass-root movement to turn its pacific demonstration into a violent revolt.

The Christmas disaster was just the dramatic peak of a long-term crisis that local institutions and central government had been trying to address with procedures of extraordinary government and management of urban solid waste in the metropolitan area since 1994, when the first 'extraordinary commissioner' for solid waste management in the Campania region was appointed by national government. Despite all efforts to cope with such a complex problem, a 14-year extraordinary government of waste emergency has not turned out to be effective, rather it could be labelled as a 'planning disaster'. To investigate the reasons for this is not the aim of these few notes; but some aspects of this complex framework are worth discussing in terms of power, knowledge and professional ethics, since this kind of relation would be interesting to focus according to the 'disaster model' here mentioned.

---

2   Public health data started circulating at that time: the statistical incidence of cancer, in the western area, was very high, far above the national average; whereas no official data were available on illegal waste stocking, just direct testimonies and rumours. But it was enough to unleash a strong popular call for the protection of public health and better environmental quality of the neighbourhood.

Among the critical issues to be highlighted from this perspective is the figure of the extraordinary commissioner, a relevant start to sketching a particular arrangement of power, knowledge and ethics.

Such a figure was first designed, in Italy, by a law of 1970 (nr. 996), in the aftermath of the Arno river flood and the earthquake in the valley of Belice in Sicily (Laino 2007). It has undergone a long juridical evolution since then, assuming, as a model of reference and guide, the role of the National Service of Civil Protection (instituted by Law nr. 225/1992) in cases of environmental catastrophes and social emergencies.

The extraordinary commissioner – as a juridical figure – is provided with two major means to cope with situations of extreme danger: the severe restriction (if not suspension) of public freedom and some constitutional guarantees, on the one hand; and the by-passing (if not the violation) of the principle of separation between ordinary public authority and military power, on the other. The extraordinary commissioner is 'a juridical body allowed to substitute, on a territorial basis, all territorial institutional bodies whose ordinary action is operative on that level and is therefore provided with extraordinary power'.[3] On the basis of a resolution approved by the Council of Ministers formally stating the 'state of emergency', the commissioner is appointed by the Prime Minister, who establishes the duration of his/her mandate, means and extraordinary powers. More than a physical person, the extraordinary commissioner, in this context, is intended as a power structure, whose main feature is the straight relation between central government and local contexts, with no intermediate relations with other institutional bodies.

In the case of the Campania Region, tasks and powers of the extraordinary commissioner for waste emergency – as per the latest law decree concerning this matter[4] – basically concern the location of waste disposals and related sites of operation;[5] the expropriation for public utility of areas and buildings for new waste infrastructures; the full collaboration of state military forces to secure construction sites and guarantee public security.[6] Furthermore, any extraordinary measure

---

3   Italian Parliament's Commission of Inquiry about Waste Emergency in Campania Region, Session Report of 17 February 2002, p.10.

4   By decree (DL n. 90, 23 May 2008), the Council of Ministers appointed the current State Under-Secretary (G. Bertolaso, chief of the National Service of Civil Protection) as extraordinary commissioner for waste emergency in the Campania Region. This figure – at the highest level of central state administration – comes after a long series of commissioners (and failures) and therefore is provided with powers even stronger than before.

5   On such a matter, the law states – in the specific case of the localisation of a waste incinerator in Naples metro area – that the Mayor has to make a decision about it no later than 30 days after the approval of the decree itself. If the deadline is not respected, the Mayor is relieved and the decision is in the hands of the Prime Minister.

6   Collaboration with the Army basically concerns checking access and exit from waste disposals and related operation sites, prosecuting all those who are not formally allowed to enter special sites or impede the implementation of the waste emergency plan, providing public security in case of violent protest.

should be adopted to implement fully the extraordinary waste management plan; it would be taken as a dispensation from a long list of national and regional laws (see art. 18) if not compatible with ordinary procedures and rules.

The outcomes of a long-term process, such as the 14 years of extraordinary government of waste management in our city-region, have not proved as positive and decisive as hoped for, and the reasons for that are manifold and worthy of investigation. One critical issue that can be discussed in more depth is government with a permanent exemption from ordinary practices, which – even if (mostly rhetorically) justified as a measure to cope with exceptional circumstances requiring quick decisions and efficiency – has become a millstone in the long run, as a structural substitution of the 'ordinary' by the 'exceptional'. This switch besides all modest outcomes achieved until now looks dubious even for some negative *structural* effects it plays on the local context (on actors, behaviours and planning practices), as it tends to reduce dramatically participation and public deliberation within decision-making processes, and therefore over-exposes knowledge to a risk of self-reference and ineffectiveness, which occur when no public validation of scientific work is necessarily required. This critical issue, in my view, is a matter of 'state of exception'.

According to Carl Schmitt, 'exception has no reference; it escapes from general hypotheses, but at the same time discloses with absolute purity a formal element which is specifically juridical: the decision' (Schmitt 1988, 39). In this definition, we see the main difference between norm and exception, whereas – according to Schmitt – the latter's main function is precisely to disclose the intrinsic nature of the former. The norm, in order to function, needs a 'homogeneous, average situation', since it cannot 'be applied to chaos'. In other words, a juridical order has to be settled first, as a necessary base on which norms can work. The juridical order is established by the Sovereign State, the only kind of authority provided with the monopoly of the 'ultimate decision', the essence of state power. Here the difference between norm and decision is clarified through a paradox: the Sovereign State has no need for Law (norm) to create Law itself (decision). As Schmitt (1988, 41) argues, 'exception is much more interesting than the normal case. This doesn't prove anything, whereas exception proves everything: it doesn't just confirm the rule; the rule itself exists as long as the exception does as well'.

Through the state of exception, the Sovereign State creates the basic condition for Law to exist and function. The Law is general by nature, it must be applied regardless of singular cases: this condition is possible only if the exception is included (and excluded at the same time) in the structure of Sovereign power. This condition of inclusion/exclusion is typically a suspension, a *threshold of indifference* between nature and law, culture and violence; it is based on the assumption that the 'primal performance' of the Sovereign power (the source of political power) is the production of the 'bare life', a kind of human life which 'can be killed and cannot be sacrificed' (Agamben 1995, 92). This means that life, as it is 'captured' by the Sovereign power in the state of exception, is indifferent to any order (religious[7] or political) and – because of that – guarantees the existence of a 'zone' of power which is excluded by the Law, some kind of 'free and legally empty space' (Agamben 1995, 43) which is the essential requirement for juridical generality to exist.[8]

This conceptualisation is mostly driven by the research of Michel Foucault on *bio-politics* (Foucault 1976 and 2004b), i.e. the growing implication of biological life and phenomena of population within technologies and strategies of political power in modern western states.[9] Bio-power has been essential to the development of capitalism, as a form of 'controlled introduction of bodies into the apparatus of production and a way to adapt phenomena of population to economic processes' (Foucault 1976, 124 in the Italian edition).

It would be pointless trying to develop, in short, such a theoretical debate:[10] in the more restricted context of my argument (the parallel between state of exception and extraordinary government), it would be worth focusing just on a few issues emerging from it.

The typical condition of extraordinary government – as illustrated above – is the temporary suspension of ordinary norms in favour of a stronger role assigned to centralised 'decisions'. In a long-term case such as the 14-year extraordinary government in Naples, this suspension becomes generalised, weakening its provisional character and becoming somehow permanent.

This time issue is relevant, as long as it actualises the condition of suspension, making the exception the rule. According to Agamben (1995), in order to keep the norm active, the state of exception (as a threshold of indifference between violence and law) must be kept like a 'hidden core' inside the Sovereign power. But when it becomes actual and somehow generalised, it spreads its effects on life, which tends to turn 'bare', 'sacred'. In other words, life becomes a political stake: nothing more pertinent to the waste crisis in Naples, with all its adverse effects on public health.

One sort of counter-proof of life turning *bare* is, in the Neapolitan case, the prohibition of public participation in critical decisions concerning the transformation of local contexts (such as the location of waste disposals, as in the

---

7   Agamben (1995) defines bare life also as 'sacred life', according to the archaic structure of *sacratio* as it was conceived by the Romans. This structure was based on two main features: the non-punishability for killing and the exclusion from ritual sacrifice of the so-called *homo sacer* (sacred man). The sacredness of life – like its transcendent nature – is something which is subjected to the total power of death, beyond any human jurisdiction.

8   Bare life as the primal performance of political power is – according to Agamben (1995) – the main political stake of totalitarian regimes of the 20th century (Nazism and Soviet Union), the most extreme experiments of bio-politics in the West until now.

9   Nevertheless, in Agamben's work, it is developed in a different direction, focusing on totalitarian regimes and assuming the 'camp' as the basic spatial arrangement of this political 'capture' of human life into power mechanisms.

10   For an overview, see Foucault's courses at the College de France (*Sécurité, territoire, population*, 1977-1978; *Naissance de la biopolitique*, 1979).

case of Pianura) in the face of major risks to the population whose elements are still very hard to assess.

What is in question, in such cases, is not just a deficit of communicative action, of 'disabling and distorted claims' (Forester 1989) standing in the way of wide participation of residents and other social actors in planning decisions on tough problems. This does not mean that this issue is out of the picture (I will develop this argument afterwards as well), only that it is more 'collateral' than other, more compelling problems.

This deficit, in the extraordinary government context, mostly deals with the reduction of 'life' (here grouping different meanings, like public health, environmental quality, landscape preservation, food quality, etc.) to a 'bare' condition, highly exposed to serious risks really hard to control and prevent (here is the parallel with the philosophical expression *a life that can be killed*) but, nevertheless, unable to defend its rights and take direct charge of them *in the first person*, because of its exclusion from the decision-making arena, which can be paralleled to a position 'out of the ritual' of democracy (what, in philosophical terms, Agamben 1995 defines as the *ritual of sacrifice*).

One ethical issue rising from such a framework – as it may concern planning researchers in their role as 'experts' – is the controversial relationship between their knowledge and the kind of centralised and authoritative power the extraordinary government wields.

The lack of public participation in decision-making processes is not just a means to implement decisions rapidly and efficiently, bypassing usually conflictual and time-consuming procedures; it is also a pre-condition for knowledge to function in a particular way, without providing some crucial resources for public dialogue (synthesis, reciprocity, accountability), and therefore assuming a role of 'fragmentation technology', whose main function is 'training' (bodies, masses) through 'separation', enforcing asymmetry at the expense of reciprocity and synthesis (Foucault 1975).

In a situation of extraordinary government, expertises and technicalities are usually more in demand than forms of knowledge as narratives or framework analyses – more comprehensive, communicative and integrated. This is not just a matter of 'wicked problems' (Rittel and Webber 1973) requiring highly specialised professional competencies to be treated properly (which is not obvious at all, but still a habit in public administration and professional circuits[11]), but also because

---

11 As Rittel and Webber argued more than 30 years ago, planning problems, conceived as 'wicked problems', cannot be solved (at best they can be 're-solved' over and over again), 'mimicking the cognitive style of science and the occupational style of engineering' (1973, p.160). Nevertheless, confidence in specialisms and technicality is still common sense, especially in times of social and political crisis, when it seldom works as a rhetorical device covering up political and professional deficiencies. Planning problems are 'wicked' (malign, tricky, aggressive) as long as they constantly challenge our theories of forecasting, our expertises, the ways we describe these problems in the wider context

the more fragmented it is, the more effective knowledge can be, supporting power to develop its action and spread its effects in space and society.

Fragmentation of knowledge – to some extent – is here regarded as a function of domination, specifically as a 'masking device': the more specialised and technical a branch of knowledge is, the more 'disinterested' and somehow 'neutral' it claims to be. Beyond the cloak of conformity, this can be regarded as a typical mechanism of ideology, which is occluding conflicts and contradictions created by 'the utmost interested use of an apparently disinterested knowledge' (Lefebvre 1974, 33 in the Italian edition).

In these terms, the ethical dilemma – for experts in the planning fields, professionally and morally engaged in the public domain – is how to be liable (for the consequences of their actions over living spaces), moving on uncertain terrain where political stakes (social consensus, stability of political coalitions) and social demands (for environmental quality, public safety, health) clash and conflict, this terrain being riven by major problems such as environmental and social emergency, public order, national or European government sanctions, etc. No expertise can solve or bypass the ambiguity and the multiple causal relations of which wicked problems are made: planners are not just experts, but 'players in a political game' (Lefebvre 1974, 169 in the Italian edition), coping with different issues and values, between control and reform (Yiftachel 1998).

Truth and Freedom as 'Intractable' Collective Claims: Ethics vs Technique

The old mantra of planning as an active component of politics comes back to the forefront of contemporary planning, as the Naples waste crisis case shows quite well. Wicked problems hardly challenge the applicability of general principles to unique situations, and planners are compelled to make decisions case by case: in ethical terms, this behaviour can be labelled as the 'ethics of the wanderer' (Galimberti 2007), inspired by Aristotle's concept of *phronesis*: without maps, the wanderer faces difficulties from time to time, as they occur and by means at hand.

What matter, in the present discussion, are means and the way they are defined and used, i.e. professional knowledge applied to specific problems/situations perceived as crucial by most parts of society. The waste crisis case – in its exceptionality – helps learning: in part, it is a case of 'wandering', since, in many critical situations, technical analyses and reports are used as a scientific support for different political claims and planning decisions have been carried out running after urgency, in an ever-changing frame of reference; in part, it is a case of giving up general, understandable principles and values, to go along with technicalities and specialisms (i.e. fragmentation of knowledge), at the expense of public rights of information, liability and accountability of scientific knowledge as a support for political decisions.

---

of social and political pluralism. From this perspective, dealing with wicked problems is inherently a matter of constantly re-defining knowledge boundaries.

In May 2008, a national government decree (DL nr. 90, 23 May 2008) establishes, among other things, the location of ten new sites for waste disposals all over the region, distributed by province. The waste situation, at the time, is still highly critical and new sites are necessary, according to the new Berlusconi government (just elected after the two-year Prodi government), to cope with the emergency effectively and rapidly, in the absence of a regional industrial system of waste stocking and recycling, still far from being completed. By the same decree, the chief of the National Service of Civil Protection is appointed as extraordinary commissioner in charge as sub-secretary of the President of Ministry Council. Last, but not least, a good part of the political campaign of the right-wing coalition has been focused on solving once and for all the Naples waste crisis, regarded as a national – if not international – issue, and not just a local problem.[12]

As for the Naples province, the new waste disposal is located in the old, brownfield quarry of Chiaiano, a popular high-density neighbourhood in the Northern metro area.[13] *Protests were heard right away, even more violent than the Pianura episode, at the end of 2007.*

The quarry is zoned by decree as a site of 'national strategic relevance', and is to be managed and secured by military forces. Fierce clashes between residents and the army dramatically occur in those early summer days; environmental and radical activists occupy the quarry and some come under legal sanctions, as foreseen by the new decree (up to five years' imprisonment for those who enter the site without official permission). As usual, rumours (reported by the media) say that camorra agents infiltrated local social movements, barring both civilians and public officials. Residents, mostly organised into peaceful protest groups and committees, keep asking for reliable information about the feasibility of the new land use and for guarantees about public health. The rivalry between different experts (some appointed by local committees, some appointed by the extraordinary commissioner) begins, and no re-composition of different theories and analyses seems possible, even now.[14]

---

12 Naples has been playing a major role in Berlusconi's propaganda drive in the latest electoral campaign. The massive waste crisis occurred in one of Italy's biggest cities, long governed by left-wing coalitions (since 1993, after the new Law instituting the direct election of Mayors), and has been easily turned into the media emblem of the decadence of a whole ruling class born out of the old Communist Party in the 1970s. Antonio Bassolino, former Regional Secretary of the PCI, has been the first demo-elected Mayor of the City and, after two mandates (and a brief break as Minister of Employment in the Dalema left-wing national government), has been elected Governor of Campania Region. As governor, he has also been in charge as extraordinary commissioner for waste emergency and is currently involved in a judicial investigation about the waste crisis, with other public officials.

13 The neighbourhood's area is 9.67 square km, the population is 23,045. Chiaiano is part of the VII Municipality of Naples, together with two other neighbourhoods (Scampia and Piscinola), with a total population of 92,626. The health care pole of Naples city-region is just a few kms south-east.

14 For an overview, see <www.chiaianodiscarica.it>, <http://napoli.indymedia.org>.

On one side, there's the ordinary planning policy the local left-wing governments have been supporting since 1994, when the new master plan-making process started (the plan – Piano Regolatore Generale – was conclusively approved in 2004). The old quarry is located in the Wood of Chiaiano, 'the largest urban forest in the whole Campania Region', which is part of the open space metropolitan system (the Hill Metropolitan Park distributed all around the city centre[15]), zoned in the master plan as a large conservation area, for innovative and environmentally compatible activities and functions (multi-functional agriculture, agritourism, public parks, etc.). According to the risk zoning map of the City of Naples (included in the Master Plan), the area is rated as a 'very high hydro-geological risk' zone.[16]

On the other side, the decision made by the extraordinary commissioner to include the quarry in the list of new waste disposal sites is officially supported by scientific analyses which justify the new land use disposition and support the project for the waste disposal released immediately after the national government decree. These scientific elaborations (not published until now[17]) don't carefully consider – according to the experts appointed by the local communities – the specific, and environmentally fragile, conditions of the site.[18] Moreover, several irregularities are highlighted in the project methodology, as well as in the whole

---

15   The Hill Metropolitan Park has been institutionalised as a new regional park on the basis of the Naples Master Plan's zoning map. For further information, see <www. parcodellecollinedinapoli.it>.

16   See the risk rate zoning map of the urban territory in <http://www.comune.napoli. it/flex/cm/pages/ServeBLOB.php/L/IT/IDPagina/1023>.

17   The elaborations here mentioned basically concern the work of environmental impact assessment commissioned from the Regional Agency for Environmental Protection (ARPAC) by the extraordinary commissioner, and the project of the new waste disposal, designed by a private engineering company (Ad Acta Projects srl) appointed by the extraordinary commissioner as well. These materials have not been published (this is also because of the 'strategic national relevance' status of the site they concern), but given confidentially to the consultants appointed by local committees and by the Municipalities of Marano and Mugnano (two high-density towns close to Chiaiano). These consultants have joined a 'bi-partisan' technical board (composed of experts appointed by the extraordinary commissioner and experts appointed by local committees) in order to cooperate with the government 'by the side' of citizens. Unfortunately, no 'big results' have been achieved from such 'cooperation', as repeatedly reported by the media in these past months.

18   In the scientific report by three different experts (two geologists, one engineer, all university professors) appointed by the Municipalities of Marano and Mugnano (included in the latest Conference of Services scheduled by the Extraordinary Commissioner in August 2008 as a restricted public audit on the waste disposal problem), a lot of data and assumptions both in the government decree and the waste disposal project are contested. First of all, they say none of these documents is based on reliable, preventative geo-technical, geological and urban planning and mobility analyses, and therefore they are wrong from a procedural and methodological point of view. Second, the quarry is totally inadequate to host a 700,000 ton urban solid waste disposal, because of severe problems of stability of the tufa round walls (slits and subsidence), high risks of landslide and flooding of the quarry's

location procedure followed by the extraordinary commissioner. Basically, none of these documents is based on a reliable preventative scientific analysis.

In the middle of such a 'knowledge dispute', people keep claiming their right to public health, environmental and landscape quality, decent property values. These claims are as socially pervasive and dramatic as the answers which the 'professional discourse' about 'what-ought-to-be-done' has been giving till now are uncertain. The scientific background concerning health risks from the proximity of a large population to a waste disposal is very confusing and does not provide any 'public truth' to calm down people's fears of biased opposition.[19] No clear compensation measures have been defined by the central and local governments to make people accept a land use of the quarry different from a public park, as addressed in the Master Plan and in the project of the Metropolitan Hill Park. Not to mention the inevitable decrease of property values close to an 'unwanted infrastructure' such as a waste disposal.

In the course of modernity, technique (a general term here referring to expert/ professional knowledge) has been considered no longer a means but 'a universal condition to achieve any goal' (Galimberti 2007, 37). In these terms, technique is itself a goal, an end, aiming at its own strengthening; and politics, to achieve its goals, must rely on technical apparatus, which is not just support for decision-making, but tends towards a non-finalised making (its own strengthening). I would assume this position is more of a rhetorical device than an effective and substantial mechanism, at least in planning terms,[20] since this may work as an interesting corollary to the idea of knowledge fragmentation discussed above.

This non-finalising mode of knowledge becomes a common trait in situations where fragmentation and proliferation of different specialisms and positions are the rule – as in the Naples case. This is a critical factor inasmuch as it affects at

---

base, and low depth of ground water. See F. Ortolani, G.B. De Medici, A. Spizuoco <http://www.comunemarano.na.it/index>.

19   In research commissioned by the National Service of Civil Protection (of which the extraordinary commissioner is the Chief) from the Office of Environment of the World Health Organization it is stated that, in an area of 1 km from urban solid waste disposals in the provinces of Naples and Caserta, the mortality rate for cancer (liver, lung, stomach) and the rate of congenital malformations are 12 percent higher than national averages (see <http://it.wikipedia.org/wiki/Crisi_dei_rifiuti_in_Campania#cite_note-igiene-12>).

20   Driving these assumptions to their logical, extreme consequences – as Galimberti does – means attributing technique an overall function 'confused' with power, assuming that no power (least of all, a form of concentrated power) can dominate technique, since 'the technical apparatus – as the sum of multiple apparatuses – is definitely superior to all competencies' (Galimberti 2007, 471). In planning terms (even – as in the present case – in a condition of extraordinary government, where technicalities get stronger than ordinary, more inclusive procedures) technique is not in 'full command' to understand and describe problems, nor to conceive solutions, since planning – dealing with societal problems – remains a political activity, always coping with power.

least two crucial ethical relations: the relation technique/freedom ('I can make a choice (the right one) only if I'm technically competent') and the relation technique/truth ('Truth is what affects, what produces effective outcomes'). When Chiaiano residents protest against the government, they are just asking questions like: *will our children be safe from cancer risks? will the ground water of the quarry be safe from toxic percolation? how can we accept a different land use? who guarantees that the project of the new waste disposal has all normative and technical requirements to be safe for public health?*

These relations are crucial in ethical terms inasmuch as, on one side, they express the social belief in the 'makeability' of perceived problems by means of expert knowledge; on the other (with the backdrop of 'wicked planning problems') they deal with the uncertain status of research competencies (who's competent? what are the effects of her/his making? on behalf of whom are competencies exerted?) and the way they are exerted practically, in any case.

The double, and mostly intractable, dimension of these relations clearly rises from an ethical vision of (search for) knowledge in terms of accountability: following Max Weber (1919), 'we don't have to focus on men's intentions, but on the effects of their actions'. In such a context, though, Weber specifies that, in order to assign an ethical value to the effects of technical actions (in terms of practical responsibility), these effects *must be predictable*. Such an assumption leaves unpredictable outcomes out of the picture, whereas these are commonplace in practical knowledge fields, like planning and governance. This is a political matter.

Acting Ethically *and* Politically

In the Chiaiano case, the difficulty of residents in making a choice – i.e. accept/ refuse hard decisions such as locating a waste disposal in the middle of their neighbourhood 'for public interest's sake' – is not just the NIMBY syndrome, but the practical impossibility of subscribing to or contesting on a reliable base (of data, theories, models, opinions, etc.) decisions they are not competent to judge. In other words, they are not free to choose because they do not know where the (public) truth is. Therefore they are compelled to play – in Lacanian behavioural terms – the social role of the Hysteric, whose 'underlying truth is one of anxiety, uncertainty, or confusion' (Hillier and Gunder 2003, 236). Residents' challenge to experts is: 'Prove your knowledge is true!' and, since this proof is hard to accomplish (if not impossible), any answer experts provide is always unsatisfactory and therefore 'mistrust increases, which may result in either heightened resistance or dejected exit' (Hillier and Gunder 2003, 236).

In the Naples waste crisis case, technique seems quite weak and subordinate to power. Perhaps the most relevant issue this experience raises – at least in terms of planning research ethics – is that knowledge (as fragmented and contradictory as it appears in the course of this long crisis) can be a masking device covering the 'pathetic' face of politics. Having lost its main role as 'locus of decisions', politics asks knowledge to cope with hard decisions as a substitute, a surrogate.

But this does not produce encouraging outcomes, least of all a 'domain of experts' over politicians, or similar techno-utopias: in specific historical contexts – Southern Italy, in this case – some sort of 'anthropological remnants' of politics are still very resistant, which means that the relation power/knowledge would never turn into a domain of experts but would always be biased by socio-political 'wobbling modes' (i.e.: 'Power strengthens knowledge here and weakens it there'), in a sort of zero-sum game where neither technical nor political domain is fully achieved.

In this framework, the controversial relation between knowledge and freedom, or knowledge and truth, becomes even more critical, somehow detached from how the 'real world' of planning practices really works: in this world 'the aim is not to find the truth, but to improve some characteristics of the world where people live' (Rittel and Webber 1973, 167). Otherwise, the only thing left to do would be to draw truth and freedom from the media!

There is no well-defined way to cope with all these difficult issues planning 'wicked problems' raise: no universal principle of the Common Good, no rooted Public Truths available to address planners' theories and practice, in such a way that they can be safe from non-ethical drifts, producing outcomes which can be harmful to the community they are engaged with as public officials.

The only, essential, condition one can claim is that politics would be back at the core of planning practice, as a terrain where different and even conflicting options and values concerning the future of communities, neighbourhoods and territories could be assessed and confronted openly. Without a full acknowledgement of the democratic dialogue the figure of the planner as a 'dialogue enabler', 'organizing and shaping hopes' (Forester 1989) within inter-subjectivity spaces, seriously risks weakening (if not losing) his ethical credibility, which is the *raison d'être* of such an ideal type.

This is a major challenge for planning research at present, dealing with increasing social demands of public treatment of issues related to space and place, usually polarised into circuits of stakeholders operating on a large scale and communities mobilising to defend local interests.

Conclusions

As extreme as it may appear, the Naples waste crisis case can be a good story to learn about planning ethics in general terms.

The condition of extraordinary government – regarded as a specimen of the state of exception theorised by philosophers and theorists of the State – bears mechanisms of the relation power/knowledge that otherwise, in 'ordinary' conditions, would not emerge with the same clarity.

One major issue stemming from it is the fragmentation of knowledge as a means of power to affirm and reproduce itself. This form of domination is based on the reduction of 'life' to a *bare/sacred life*, which means assuming it as a political stake, and not as a major part of a societal body responsibly involved in the political deliberation processes.

Another theme is the critical relation between experts/researchers and citizens, especially when social claims to truth and freedom in public decisions become more acute and polarised. In such cases, this relation becomes a sort of vicious circle, where institutional crisis factors are intertwined with the decline of 'public truth', until a typical social, asymmetrical relation between master (official knowledge, experts) and hysteric (residents, activists, etc.) becomes a rule in social behaviours.

In ethical terms, this means for planning researchers 'in the public domain', working in public administration as well as in civic organisations, a constant – sometimes very hard – task of assessing and questioning their own work in the face of clashing political claims, in the absence of clear frames of reference for scientific knowledge assessment, under the pressure of political agendas, on one side, and urgent social problems, on the other.

Technicality is no escape from such a dilemma, even when requested by all parties to cope effectively with urgent problems such as environmental and social catastrophes. As the Naples story shows, inclusive forms of knowledge are still a relevant requisite to 'improve the world where people live'.

Most importantly, technicality is way to justify a subordinate position of knowledge 'in the face of power', since this would immediately reveal a 'masking device' which is not acceptable in ethical terms. On the contrary, 'planning is political. We know that quite well by now. We really need less often to keep re-discovering politics and power and more often to carefully assess specific types of vulnerabilities, for only where dominating power is vulnerable is critical resistance possible. Presumably, enhancing such critical resistance is the point of critical theories of space and planning' (Forester 2000).

References

Agamben, G. (1995), *Homo Sacer. Il Potere Sovrano e la Nuda Vita* (Milan: Einaudi).

Forester, J. (1989), *Planning in the Face of Power* (Berkeley: University of California Press).

Forester, J. (2000), 'Conservative Epistemology, Reductive Ethics, Far Too Narrow Politics: Clarifications in Response to Yiftachel and Huxley' <http://www.people.cornell.edu/pages/jff1> – section *Recent Writings.*

Foucault, M. (1975), *Surveiller et Punir. Naissance de la Prison* (Paris: Gallimard) it. trans. *Sorvegliare e punire. Nascita della prigione*, 1993 (Torin: Einaudi).

Foucault, M. (1976), *La Volonté de Savoir* (Paris: Gallimard) it. trans. *La volontà di sapere*, 1999 (Torin: Einaudi).

Foucault, M. (2004a), *Sécurité, Territoire, Population. Cours au Collège de France 1977-1978* (Paris: Seuil-Gallimard) it. trans. *Sicurezza, territorio, popolazione. Corso al Collége de France 1977-1978*, 2005 (Milan: Feltrinelli).

Foucault, M. (2004b), *Naissance de la Biopolitique. Cours au Collège de France 1978-1979* (Paris: Seuil-Gallimard) it. trans. *Nascita della biopolitica. Corso al Collége de France 1978-1979*, 2005 (Milan: Feltrinelli).

Galimberti, U. (2007), *Psiche e Techne. L'Uomo nell'Età della Tecnica* (Milan: Feltrinelli).

Hillier, J. and Gunder, M. (2003), 'Planning Fantasies? An Exploration of a Potential Lacanian Framework for Understanding Development Assessment Planning', *Planning Theory* 2:3, 225-248.

Laino, G. (2007), 'Per una Razionalità Plurale, Ibrida e Contingente, Responsabile e Accurata. La Crisi dei Rifiuti a Napoli', *CRU – Critica della Razionalità Urbanistica* 20-21, 65-84.

Lefebvre, H. (1974), *La Production de l'Espace* (Paris: Editions Anthropos).

Rittel, H.W.J. and Webber, M.M. (1973), 'Dilemmas in a General Theory of Planning', *Policy Science* 4, 155-169.

Schmitt, C. (1922), *Politische Theologie, Vier Kapitel zue Lehre von der Souveränität* (München-Leipzig) it. trans. *Le categorie del politico*, 1988 (Bologna: Il Mulino).

Weber, M. (1919), *Politik als Beruf* (München-Leipzig) it. trans. 'La politica come professione' in *Il lavoro intellettuale come professione*, 1971 (Torin: Einaudi).

Yiftachel, O. (1998), 'Planning and Social Control. Exploring the Dark Side', *Journal of Planning Literature* 12: 4, 395-406.

Chapter 14

Ethical Awareness
in Advocacy Planning Research

Giovanni Attili

We all think that we know how to ask questions and talk to people, from common everyday folks to highly qualified quantophrenic experts. Yet to learn about people, we must treat them as people, and they will work with us to help us to create accounts of their lives. So long as many researchers continue to treat respondents as unimportant faceless individuals whose only contributions are to fill more boxed responses, the answers the researchers will get will be commensurable with the questions they ask and the way in which they ask them. As researchers, we are no different from Gertrude Stein, who, while on her deathbed, asked her lifelong companion Alice B. Toklas, 'What is the answer?' When Alice could not bring herself to speak, Gertrude asked, 'In that case, what is the question?'

Fontana and Frey (2005, 722)

The Collingwood Neighbourhood House Research Project

In recent years, Leonie Sandercock and I have been developing a particular stream of research focused on the immigration challenges that shape our *mongrel* cities (Sandercock 2003): the cohabitation of ethno-diverse subjectivities, the fear of the cultural-Other, the disempowerment and the discrimination of marginalised communities. These are key challenges for planners whose goal is to build cross-cultural cities: a leap of the imagination as well as a necessity which cannot be postponed.

But how to nurture this leap of imagination? There are multiple ways of addressing this objective. Among these, stories and storytelling can play an important role. Nowadays a significant number of scholars are investigating the important relationship between story and planning, critically scrutinising the so-called 'story turn' in planning theory (Forester 1989; Mandelbaum 1991; Eckstein and Throgmorton 2003; Sandercock 2003). They highlight how planning is performed through stories, how rhetoric and poetics become crucial in interactive processes, how the communicative dimension is central to planning practices, how a story can awaken energies and imaginations, becoming a catalyst for an involving urban conversation.

Our first research project was the attempt of narrating the inspiring story of a local institution of Vancouver: the Collingwood Neighbourhood House (CNH), a locally-based organisation which developed dramatic achievements for its community over a period of 20 years. The mission of the CNH is to create and maintain 'a place for everyone' (Dang 2002, 73), welcoming and supporting a wide range of immigrants. The delivery of an enormous variety of services according to perceived local needs is only a part of the work of this organisation. The CNH's real purpose is to build a community where it didn't previously exist, through intercultural and diversified approaches: empowering local leaders, emphasising the role of arts as community connector, developing inclusive planning processes, transgressing language and cultural barriers, building anti-racism education programmes. Engaging diverse people in common activities, the Collingwood Neighbourhood House became over the years a significant urban bonding agent: the incubator of new socialities, the gathering place for an increasing number of immigrants as well as 'oldtimers', the place where strangers can become neighbours (Sandercock and Attili 2008).

Ethical Issues in Qualitative Research

We decided to explore this powerful reality through a series of in-depth-interviews. This qualitative methodological approach was used to capture a plurality of voices, perceptions, stories connected with the experience of the CNH. This method has to be understood as an interpretative practice whose aim is to make the world visible, making sense of phenomena in terms of the meaning people bring to them (Denzin and Lincoln 2005). It is an activity based on a deep interaction with people who are invited to express themselves and their worlds. It is an involving process that invokes a series of important ethical issues regarding the construction of the interviews and the use of the collected information. In general: subjects must agree voluntarily to be interviewed as a result of full and open information about the project; the relationship between interviewer and interviewee must be built with no deceptions; confidentiality and privacy of interviewees must be preserved; the interviews must be accurately transcribed without omissions or fraudulent interpretations; a particular care must be taken to assure no dangerous consequences for the life of the interviewees. All these issues have been faced historically by social scientists through the formalised definition of ethical codes and protocols. In many countries review and monitoring organs (such as the Institutional Review Boards, IRBs) have been established to control how this kind of human research responded to universal ethical standards. The assumption was that social research was based on a value-free perspective and its ethical dilemmas had to be addressed through positivistic and standardised procedures. The result was a bureaucratic *gamesmanship* (Blanchard 2002, 11) with severe structural deficiencies: an approach characterised by the rationalist presumption of canonical ethics which was destined to be progressively challenged by new and emerging epistemological consciousnesses.

Situational Ethics

Nowadays the regulatory systems built to monitor the ethically sensitive issues of social research are increasingly deconstructed in favour of a different approach to knowledge: the research cannot be considered a value-free inquiry formalised through objective rules, rather a contextualised activity in which values and moral assumptions play a significant role. Moreover researchers and communities cannot be considered as separated and hierarchically organised monads: they are connected by a mutual, collaborative and pedagogical relationship. In this respect, 'participants have a co-equal say in how research should be conducted, what should be studied, which methods should be used, which findings are valid and acceptable, how the findings have to be implemented and how the consequences of such actions are to be assessed' (Denzin 2003, 257). This reflects a different commitment of the researcher, who is no longer subjected to a 'remote discipline or institution but to those he or she studies' (Denzin 2003, 258). This approach implies a constant redefinition of what needs to be done to address ethical challenges in social research projects. The universal basic moral standards (such as respect for people, beneficence and justice[1]) established by monitoring organs or institutions need to be shaped according to the different contexts, situations and embodied relationships that embrace the research participants. From this perspective the research cannot be seen as a pre-established or pre-approved set of procedures. It cannot be guided by a monocultural ethical rationalism. Rather, it needs to be built in collaborative ways through a mutual learning process: the different subjects who are part of this process have a co-responsibility in defining the proper strategies to deal with ethically sensitive issues. This approach is particularly relevant in multicultural contexts characterised by a plurality of ethical perspectives, values and views.

In the Collingwood Neighbourhood House project, we couldn't escape the formalised ethical review process which characterises every academic research involving human subjects. Nevertheless this kind of process seemed insufficient to achieve an ethically responsible social research. In other words, we were not convinced that all that was necessary was to fill out and follow a codified protocol in order to protect and respect the interviewees and their stories. What appeared necessary was an evolving and adaptive ethical awareness and practice: the willingness of cooperating with the members of the community to find original and contextualised ways to build the research itself.

In this process we asked, and were taught, how to deal with specific interviewees, how to report some of the information we collected in order to preserve the safety of the interviewees themselves, how to address some potentially conflicting issues. It was not only the researchers' ethical perspective, nor just the one of the community: it was a research path that emerged in a co-learning environment where researchers were 'led by the members of the community to discover them' (Denzin 2003, 243). This approach transgresses pre-codified procedures based on

---

1   As outlined in the Belmont Report (1978).

rational validation and opens up unexpected synergies that inform the research. The caring values are still central but need to be reshaped according to the specificity of the contexts and of the people involved.

The cooperative mutuality of this approach deconstructs the non-contingent cosmology of universal ethical values in favour of a *situational ethics* rooted in a cooperative and contextualised relationship. What does need to be acknowledged is that the relation between researchers and respondents is not completely symmetrical, contrary to Denzin's argument (1997).

There are power positions that cannot be ignored or blurred; rather they need to be recognised through a responsible ethical practice that is rooted in an 'asymmetrical reciprocity' (Young 1997).

The Power to Narrate

In our research experience we were really conscious about a power of ours: the power to narrate. Our goal was to tell the story of the Collingwood Neighbourhood House. But how to do this? What kind of structure or plot did we want to portray? What sort of audience did we want to address? What messages did we need to spread? How to use the multiplicity of stories that emerged during the interviewing process? What 'language' (academic, popular, journalistic) did we want to use? And why?

Nowadays there is a widely recognised consciousness about the impossibility of an objective and neutral account of the reality researchers want to investigate. Every description is necessarily partial, opinionated and value-driven, and therefore political. We constantly apply filters to make sense of the world: we use a cone of light to illuminate what is relevant to us, through judgments and moral assumptions. From this perspective the story we wanted to narrate couldn't be conceived as the transparent revealing of an ontological reality that existed independently from us. We needed to abandon the obsession with a mimetic representation in order to experience a significant metaphorical shift: from discovery and findings to constructing and making. The story of the Collingwood Neighbourhood House had to be built. In this construction process we had a lot of options: we could have told significantly different stories of the same reality but we ended up creating a story whose intention was to advocate for this organisation. We dismissed the presumptuous clothes of neutral observers and donned the garments of committed agents of change. We performed a political act, supporting this local institution and its achievements. We used the power we had to narrate a story: the one of the CNH, but even our story. In each story, in fact, before narrating the others, we narrate to ourselves and we narrate ourselves, disclosing invisible threads which hide a desire or its opposite: a fear.

Our story wanted to celebrate the achievements of the CNH for two main reasons: first of all to disseminate an inspiring narrative that was potentially able to motivate and encourage other communities struggling with immigration challenges. Secondly to support the CNH in its financial crisis due to increasingly severe budget cuts. In order to achieve these goals we decided to narrate the story of the CNH through the construction of a documentary (Attili and Sandercock 2007), mobilising the potentialities of filmic codes, expanding the horizons of planning languages, creating a communicative tool that is now widely recognised to be more accessible, inclusive and not confined within technical or expert spheres.

The intention was to disseminate the documentary in different places and contexts as an inspiring tool and as a catalyst for interaction (as outlined in the next section). Moreover, the CNH could potentially take advantage of the documentary to show its story and build new fundraising strategies.

Disseminating the CNH Story

For one year now we have been showing our documentary to different audiences in different parts of the world, in diverse academic and professional settings[2] as well as at several international film festivals[3] where the documentary was awarded an honourable mention (International Federation of Housing and Planning, International Film and Video Competition, Geneva, September 2006) and a special mention (Berkeley Video and Film Festival, October 2006). Social issues, immigration policies, planning themes, media and communication topics became objects of intense discussion in the different places where we showed the film. This variety of issues is due to the complexity of the story that we narrated as

---

2   Among these: City of Vancouver, Department of Planning, Central Area division (Vancouver, British Columbia); City of Vancouver, Department of Planning, Social Planning Division (Vancouver, British Columbia); Immigration and Canada's Place in a Changing World, national conference (Metropolis, Vancouver, British Columbia); Narrative Matters, international conference (Arcadia University, Nova Scotia); Eyes on the City, international conference (International Visual Sociology Association, Urbino, Italy); Paths and Crossroads: Moving People, Changing Places, international conference (Metropolis, Lisbon, Portugal); Borders and Cores. What is Planning in the New Era? Conference (American Collegiate Schools of Planning, Fort Worth, Texas); Sustainable Urbanization: Turning Ideas into Action, World Planning Congress (Canadian Institute of Planners and the Planning Institute of BC, Vancouver, British Columbia); Urban Futures, Continuities and Discontinuities, World Congress (International Federation for Housing and Planning, Rome, Italy); and Global Studio Workshop (Vancouver, British Columbia). In addition, we decided to use the film as a catalyst for discussion in different architecture and planning schools (School of Community and Regional Planning, Vancouver, British Columbia; Engineering Faculty of La Sapienza University, Rome, Italy; Architecture Faculty of 'Roma III', Rome, Italy; Planning Faculty of IUAV, Venice, Italy; Architecture Faculty, Alghero, Italy; and the Architecture Faculty of Politecnico, Milan, Italy).

3   New York International Independent Film and Video Festival (2006), Los Angeles International Independent Film Festival (2006), Toni Corti Indipendent Video Festival (2006), Berkeley Film Festival (2006).

well as to the wide range of communicative impulses that characterise this film, a multiplicity of narratives and languages which are simultaneously interwoven on the screen, going beyond the traditional documentary format.

Moreover we ended up building an educational package including a community development manual to complement the film. Both film and manual were taken to a series of workshops held in strategic locations throughout Canada.[4] By documenting the twenty-year achievement of Vancouver's Collingwood Neighbourhood House, the workshops' goal was to illuminate some of the factors that shape public attitudes about immigration and can lead to a sense of welcome and inclusion. These workshops were the occasion to ask what lessons can be learned from an institution such as CNH, which has developed positive practices related to the diversity of its work force, its volunteers, and its clients. They were an occasion to reflect on how citizenship can be actively constructed through community development, so long as this is underpinned by an intercultural philosophy of the kind that continues to inform the work of CNH.

By showing the documentary and using the complementary manual, each workshop was shaped according to the topics and themes identified by the participants and relating to the lessons of the CNH experience. Many people attended the workshops from federal, provincial and local governments, as well as from various immigrant and refugee serving organisations, from the arts sector, and from universities. The response was again extremely positive. In a follow-up evaluation, a remarkably high percentage (90 percent) of attendees rated the workshops in the top category. In addition, an interesting dynamic emerged in the course of these workshops as people working in the same field and in the same city discovered each other for the first time, thus establishing new networks concerned with the social integration of immigrants.

Advocacy Awareness

As previously outlined, our research was intended as an advocacy strategy to support the CNH. The story we documented through the use of film languages has been built in an extremely partial way and in favour of a specific subject. But this kind of choice again provokes fundamental ethical questions.

If we look back at the traditional advocacy planning stream first theorised by Paul Davidoff (1930-1984), we need to acknowledge a revolutionary historical shift in planning practice: planners finally became part of the realm of politics, explicitly working for traditionally excluded groups. In the advocacy perspective, planners had to dismiss their distancing attitudes to play a key role in addressing

---

4 This stage of our work was funded by a RIIM Metropolis grant which allowed Leonie Sandercock and Paula Carr, executive director of CNH, to use the Metropolis Research Network and take advantage of its Centres of Excellence in four Canadian cities: Edmonton, Halifax, Moncton and Toronto.

a 'just democracy', reconciling professionalism and political engagement, deconstructing the neutrality chimera and working for an inclusive and plural citizenship. Despite several criticisms (e.g. the hierarchical relationship between planners and planned) this revolutionary movement deeply affected planning history and still survives today, revisited and reshaped, both in planning practice and research.

The CNH project is an attempt to embody a new form of advocacy planning research. As planners, we made some political choices about for whom and for what, to work. 'These choices reflect our values, our notions of justice, of what matters: that is, they reflect us as ethical beings' (Sandercock 2005). We decided to advocate for an organisation struggling for its economic survival. There is no way of avoiding being political: the question is not whether we should take a position, rather which position we want to take, since it is not possible to prevent this choice. The documentary and the story we portrayed were the result of this choice.

The problematic element is when a potential audience confuses the story we built with the reality itself: when the political act is misinterpreted and the documentary is mistaken for an exhaustive and objective account of the story of the CNH. We built a representation of this organisation: an emotional and political portrait which resulted from a complex setting of filters and choices. The representation of the CNH was deliberately partisan, in accordance with our goals and our identified audience.

Framing the Story

To avoid misinterpretations, lack of understanding and ambiguity it was necessary to make these political assumptions explicit. In other words, it was necessary to frame the representation we built. Metaphorically, the frame helps the potential spectator in contextualising the image s/he is observing. It determines the grammar and the pragmatics of the eye which scans the representation. Just like the frame of a painting, it works like a deictic: a sign which shows, indicates, exhibits. A sign which separates the painting from the world. A sign which directs the vision of the spectator, transforming the painting into an object which can be envisioned and interpreted. To frame a representation means to enact a significant shift: from the vision of the 'aspect' to the interpretation of the 'prospect' (Poussin 1995, 30-31), from the eyesight to the deeper understanding.

In our case, building the frame (or context) of the CNH story involved writing a book to accompany the documentary. In this book (Sandercock and Attili 2008), we set out our position and outlined as transparently as we could the process of building the research itself. We portrayed a sense-making narrative of the path we followed: an inside view of the different stages, the challenges and the goals which constantly accompanied and shaped our inquiry. The book reveals the *hows* and the *whys* that made us choose to tell our specific story of the CNH: the language we used, the ethical dilemmas, the contents we portrayed. It is a fundamental interpretative tool which potentially helps the spectator to contextualise the documentary, situating the CNH story and its genesis, adding informative layers and analytical suggestions.

Marin (2001) suggests that each representation is characterised by two basic and interconnected dimensions: transparency and opacity. The first dimension is a transitive one: the act of representing something. The second dimension is reflexive: the act of presenting one's self in the process of representing something. In other words, each representation is not only the attempt to more or less mimetically describe something, but it is also the result of a situated subject, of an embodied view that makes the representation itself more opaque, or perhaps, densely layered. Bateson (1991) would say that the map is not the territory: the map is not the passive and accurate photograph of the world, rather the reinterpretation of it. This assumption reveals an important shift: from the world as it is, to the world as we know it. In this process there are no veils to tear in order to get in touch with a noumenal or objective reality which would exist outside ourselves. Representing something means being part of a process that connects subject and object through an aesthetic relationship, an allusive transposition, a redundant translation (Nietzsche 2006). Framing a representation means creating a space to make sense of this process, transforming its opacity into an object of interpretation.

In our case, framing the CNH story meant making our advocacy project explicit. A way to ethically address the potential confusion connected with the concept of storytelling itself. We told a story: one among the many others that could have been told. The frame is the compass that can be used to orient the comprehension of it; to understand why that specific story and not another one; to avoid the risk of being shipwrecked in the ocean of relativism, in the chaos of different representations – stories that cannot be fully understood if their genesis process is not readable, if their goals are not understandable, if their questions are not examinable.

Different Kinds of Frames

As previously outlined, we decided to frame the Collingwood Neighbourhood House video-story through the writing of a book (Sandercock and Attili 2008). But why did we decide to use a different medium, abandoning the filmic codes in favour of a written language? The choice of writing a book was made for three main reasons.

First of all, we decided to adopt a complementary language to expand the communicative horizons of the research project and to capture more diversified potential audiences. The idea was to build a package (book+dvd) which could widely disseminate the story of the CNH and be used in flexible ways within different communities. And we were particularly concerned to provide a comprehensible context, regarding the Canadian political and institutional system, for European audiences.

Second, framing the Collingwood Neighbourhood House story meant meticulously taking into account: a multitude of political and historical context factors; further elements of the story of this local institution which were not told in the video-narrative; a detailed video-making process description; and an accurate portrayal of the research stages. All these elements couldn't have been accurately and analytically expressed within the original film or through a second enclosed film of reasonable length.

Finally, we wrote a book to specifically target the academic world which traditionally seems to give legitimacy only to specific forms of written texts. The CNH advocacy documentary cannot be recognised as a conventional and legitimated University product. It can be compared with other academic qualitative researches based on the involvement of other subjects. But it's rather different in its expressive and communicative dimension. It has different rules of argumentation, dissimilar expressive codes, diverse rhetorical mechanisms compared with academic written rationality. In that respect, the idea of writing a book attached to the video project represented the attempt to start a dialogue with the discipline we belong to. It was the means through which we build the chance to express the reasons which stand beyond such an advocacy video research project, addressing its fecund possibilities and its significant repercussions in the urban planning field.

Hopefully in the future, the academic world (specifically the urban and regional planning discipline) will be more and more open to diverse research products which are based on a plurality of different languages, and written texts will be only one of the possibilities to be academically legitimised. The CNH research project wants to be a forerunner in this direction: a project characterised by a helpful blurring of languages and types of research.

Our next project will take a further step in emphasising the role of filmic languages. We are currently working on a video-research called 'Finding our way: the journey from colonisation to partnership in Native/non-Native relations in Canada', the story of two First Nations Bands, in the community/region of Burns Lake (northern British Columbia, Canada). In this project, the documentary will be framed not only by a book, but also by a specific video section: we will create a self reflexive video chapter as part of the dvd menu. In this video chapter we will outline the frame of the research project, placing ourselves in the process of the construction of the story, addressing the ethical issues as part of the narration. This time, the risk is to express the frame in the same language as the research itself.

Speaking for Others

The frame of a research product helps to read what is beyond the visible part of it: the process and the involved subjectivities. It's the means through which it is possible to measure the credibility of the research, its situational ethics and its asymmetrical reciprocity. In this respect there is a further consideration that needs to be developed: namely, the ethical complexity of the very idea as well as the act of advocating for someone else. That is traditionally seen as the act of 'speaking for others'. Planning is historically imbued with this sense of assuming the needs of others, of claiming to understand others. Advocacy planners exalt this mission, traditionally working for marginalised communities and expressing their needs 'in a language understandable to his client and to the decision-makers he seeks to convince' (Davidoff 1996, 307).

Nevertheless this assumption is questionable. As bell hooks outlines: 'No need to hear your voice when I can talk about you better than you can speak about yourself. No need to hear your voice. Only tell me about your pain. I want to know your story. And then I will tell it back to you in a new way. Tell it to you in such a way that it becomes mine, my own. Rewriting you, I write myself anew. I am still author, authority. I am still colonizer, the speaking subject, and you are now at the center of my talk' (hooks 1990, 343).

Speaking for others is not an obvious operation. First of all it requires a definition of *other* vs *self*: a definition that constantly shifts according to the position of the central subject. Moreover the *other* and the *self* are changed in the mutual knowing process. Second, the art of speaking and listening is 'politically constituted by power relations of domination, exploitation, and subordination. Who is speaking, who is spoken of, and who listens is a result as well as an act of a political struggle' (Alcoff 1995, 105).

To avoid this, the planner should be part of the community he/she wants to speak for. But this solution seems not to be the proper answer because there is no way to change the 'outsider-ness' of the planners themselves. As Stieglitz (1999) acutely observed, what needs to be transformed is the patronising role traditionally embodied by advocacy planners, looking for a more balanced relationship between community and planners: 'a strategic game between power liberties' (Foucault cit. in Hindess 1996, 99).

These considerations have important implications in the planning theory realm: the advocacy planning paradigm represents a historically disruptive shift which was able to integrate the political dimension and the partiality in the work planners do. Nevertheless it appeared shackled by a certain naïvety in failing to address classic distributional and power issues as well as the core of the relationship between the so called 'planners and planned'. Assuming a renewed ethical consciousness connected with the concept of asymmetrical reciprocity, nowadays advocacy planning practice can redefine itself in new ways: as a contextualised and situational practice in which planners and communities co-develop strategies to address shared values and needs.

In the CNH research project we tried to involve members of the organisation in the process of building the documentary, not only by listening to their voices but also working through their research inputs. Our intention was to eliminate the 'unjust equation whereby the community is the passive object of research by knowledgeable outsiders who devise expert solutions' (Stieglitz 1999, 61). In order to achieve this goal we developed a cooperative model, requiring the active participation of the community. The different stages of the construction of the documentary were carefully examined by members of the CNH, whose suggestions helped in shaping the final plot.

Unavoidably, we had the final say in the definition of the story, thereby embodying that asymmetrical reciprocity previously outlined. But we tried our best not to 'speak for others' but rather to 'speak with others', expanding planning languages, creating a communicative and empowerment tool, spreading an inspiring narrative to those communities struggling with immigration challenges. Our voices intermingled with the ones coming from the CNH: a polyphonic multiplication of the skills, stories and languages of all the people involved in the same research process.

References

Alcoff, L.M. (1995), 'The Problem of Speaking for Others' in: Judith Roof and Robyn Wiegman (eds).

Attili, G. and Sandercock, L. (2007), *Where Strangers Become Neighbours*, DVD (Ottawa: National Film Board of Canada).

Bateson, G. (1991), *A Sacred Unity: Further Steps to an Ecology of Mind*, (ed.) Rodney E. Donaldson (New York: Macmillan).

Blanchard, M.A. (2002), 'Should All Disciplines Be Subject to Common Rule?', Human Subjects of Social Science Research Panel, US Department of Health and Human Services. Retrieved from: http://findarticles.com/p/articles/mi_qa3860/is_200205/ai_n9076777/pg_1.

Campbell, S. and Fainstein, S. (eds) (1996), *Readings in Planning Theory* (Malden, MA: Blackwell).

Davidoff, P. (1996) [1965], 'Advocacy and Pluralism in Planning', in: Scott Campbell and Susan Fainstein (eds).

Denzin, N.K. (1997), *Interpretative Ethnography: Ethnographic Practices for the 21st Century* (Thousand Oaks, CA: Sage).

Denzin, N.K. (2003), *Performance Ethnography: Critical Pedagogy and the Politics of Culture* (Thousand Oaks, CA: Sage).

Denzin, N. and Lincoln, Y. (eds) (2005), *The Sage Handbook of Qualitative Research* (Thousand Oaks, CA: Sage).

Eckstein, B. and Throgmorton, J. (2003), *Story and Sustainability: Planning, Practice and Possibility for American Cities* (Cambridge MA: MIT Press).

Ferguson, R. et al. (eds) (1990), *Out There: Marginalization and Contemporary Cultures* (New York: The New Museum of Contemporary Art and Cambridge, MA: the MIT Press).

Fontana, A. and Frey, H.J. (2005), 'The Interview. From Neutral Stance to Political Involvement', in: Norman Denzin and Yvonna Lincoln (eds).

Forester, J. (1989), *Planning in the Face of Power* (Berkeley: University of California Press).

Hindess, B. (1996), *Discourses of Power: from Hobbes to Foucault* (Cambridge, MA: Blackwell).

hooks, b. (1990), 'Marginality as Site of Resistance', in: Russel Ferguson et al. (eds).

Mandelbaum, S. (1991), 'Telling Stories', *Journal of Planning Education and Research* 10:1, 209-14.

Marin, L. (2001), *Della Rappresentazione* (Rome: Meltemi).

Nietzsche, F. (2006) [1873], *Su Verità e Menzogna* (Milan: Bompiani).

Poussin, N. (1995), *Lettere sull'Arte*, (ed.) D. Carrier (Cernusco: Hestia Edizioni).

Roof, J. and Wiegman, R. (1995), *Who Can Speak? Authority and Critical Identity* (Urbana: University of Illinois Press).

Sandercock, L. (2003), *Cosmopolis 2: Mongrel Cities of the 21st Century* (London, New York: Continuum).

Sandercock, L. (2005), *How far can/should planners go? A planning imagination for the 21st century*, Planning Institute of British Columbia – PIBC Conference 'Live on arrival. The art of making plans happen', Victoria, BC, 22 April 2005.

Sandercock, L. and Attili, G. (2008), *Where Strangers Become Neighbours: Integrating Immigrants in Vancouver, Canada* (Berlin: Springer).

Stieglitz, O. (1999), 'Advocacy Planning and the Question of the Self and the Other', *Critical Planning* 6:1, 57-62.

Young, I.M. (1997), *Intersecting Voices: Dilemmas of Gender, Political Philosophy and Policy* (Princeton NJ: Princeton University Press).

Chapter 15

On Having Imperial Eyes

Libby Porter

Introduction

It's easy convincing yourself that you're different. In deciding to pursue a PhD research project that investigated the highly contested relationship between Indigenous people and environmental planners in Victoria, Australia, I'd underpinned my whole research approach with a very seductive myth. It went like this: 'I am going to do research *with* (not on) Indigenous peoples, I will be ethically sensitive and culturally aware, I will make a significant contribution to the people who are involved, and I will certainly not pursue research patterns of the not-too-distant past where knowledge and artefacts were routinely stolen from Indigenous people in the name of scientific interest and the personal gains of academic researchers. No, I'll be quite different from *that* kind of researcher.' Myths repeated become pretty convincing. It took me a long time to see that I, too, have 'imperial eyes' (Smith 1999, 42).

This chapter is a narrative about the discovery of my 'imperial eyes', much too late in the project to really do anything about them in a methodological sense, and what that meant. I synthesise my research experience through two specific themes, in order to reflect on what ethics means for planning research in contexts structured by postcolonial identity politics. The first theme concerns the positionality and power of the researcher in cross-cultural research settings, and in particular postcolonial settings where Indigenous people are the objects of a white social scientist's research interest. The second theme concerns the life of research findings beyond the project itself, and what this means for ethics in planning research. Before I turn to these, here's some background on me and how the project came about.

A Positioning

I'm a white, middle-class woman and I grew up in rural Australia with literally no knowledge of the history of relations between Indigenous and white Australians, and certainly no appreciation that my own privilege was entirely constructed from the dispossession and oppression of Indigenous peoples. As a child in rural Victoria, I was taught the perniciously racialised version of Australian history where Indigenous people were invisible in Australian history and society. Oh, except when we did 'ancient history' at school which taught us that there was a time, long ago, when strange dark people roamed Australia looking for food. As I became more conscious of the presence of Indigenous people in Australia through my teenage years, I began to wonder whether things were not as I was taught. Getting involved in a 'faith and culture' exchange programme took me and a bunch of other, rather earnest, young white Australians to visit Indigenous communities in far north Queensland where the inaccuracies of my education and the full extent of my own racism were finally exposed.

For a white, educated woman like me a typical response to that experience was to want to 'work in the field', to contribute something in order to undo the basis of those privileges. Such was my coming to the PhD research programme, where I could get to fulfil those socially progressive desires (as well as get a learned title and a good career). In the early stages of the research, I spent hours in the library poring over the texts that would help me do these socially progressive 'good works' through research. Here was my myth-making in progress. The literature taught me about reciprocity and 'giving back' to participants (Hammersley and Atkinson 1983; Maxwell 1993), about the problems of doing research on sensitive topics and how to approach this (Lee 1993), and on the nature of the ethnographic encounter and its textuality (Clifford 1986). On reflection now (and it is literally only now as I sit and write this paragraph that I'm learning this) the literature, all of it written by whites, was teaching me how to be a 'good white woman' (see Nicoll 2000; Haggis and Schech 2000) without ever having to unravel my own racism and theorise my own privilege.

Then I had to leave what felt like the safe confines of the library and actually 'enter the field', as they say in anthropology. For me, 'the field' was in two places: a large national park in Western Victoria and a much smaller state forest in the north of the state. In both places, Indigenous people were asserting recognition of the right to use, control and manage their own native lands. My idea was to look at how the negotiation of those rights claims by Indigenous peoples was going to work itself out in the context of planning and land management decision-making. Given that all the planners and policy-makers involved were non-Indigenous, I was curious about how a system of governance that values land as a commodity was going to accommodate the seemingly different relationship with land claimed by Indigenous groups.

The reflections I offer here are based on those I recorded at the time I undertook the fieldwork (between 1999 and 2003) in a series of research journals. They are of course only my voice, another instance of the privilege I gain in reporting experiences through publication. Re-reading my journals gave me access to those experiences but how I feel about them now and the way I re-present them here seems to differ greatly from how I remember myself at the time.

Resolving Whiteness

Much has been written on 'doing research in cross-cultural settings' both within and outside the ethnographic literature (Agar 1996; Clifford 1988; Geertz 1973; Cushner and Breslin 1996; Stanfield and Dennis 1993). This usually means that the researcher is from a different cultural background from those she is 'researching', although the definition has been extended to researchers who enter research settings where fundamentally different social rules and values operate. There's a general presumption in the literature that the researcher's cultural position is dominant to that of the researched: white researchers in field settings of 'ethnic minority' groups, for example; or educated, employed researchers in settings where participants are from unemployed and underskilled groups. And so on.

A significant literature is also developing concerning contemporary environmental and land-based questions in postcolonial settings, which can assist our reflection on the relationships between researchers and Indigenous peoples, especially where those two are from different cultural backgrounds (Jacobs 1994; Yiftachel and Fenster 1997; Howitt et al. 1996; Birch 1997; Lane 1997 and 2000; Langton 1998; Rangan and Lane 2001; Stevens 1997; Jackson 1997; Carrick 1999) and a critical literature on a range of questions about cross-cultural research with Indigenous peoples (Moreton-Robinson 2000; Smith 1999; Nicoll 2000; Sonn 2004; Ishtar 2005). There is also a good deal of literature on the importance of 'reflexivity' in the research process (Denzin 1997; Guillemin and Gillam 2004). I'm not going to rehearse these literatures here, but my own research trajectory was shaped by it, and the reflections offered here might contribute to it.

The most obvious aspect of these ethical questions for me was in my own position as a white researcher approaching the field as a doctoral candidate. I was quite conscious of the fact of my colour and cultural background. At the time, I was conscious of it in the sense that it advertised my privilege, and that it might, quite reasonably, make the Indigenous people involved in the research suspicious of me. I was also conscious that my whiteness advertised my ongoing privilege: it was me, the white woman, who would get the PhD, the title, the good job, the publications. So, this research activity I was undertaking was very directly building my own future privilege on the back of a (willing) participation by Indigenous people. Moreover, the research agenda, the fact that it could exist as a set of research questions, was entirely underpinned by the persistent fact of dispossession of lands by my people from Indigenous people. Dispossession is the foundation of my academic career. This is a deeply uncomfortable fact: I'm squirming as I type it here, though as Nicoll (2000, 380) shows, 'coming out as a white woman' can also be quite liberating.

But let me return to then. Back then, I hadn't come out yet. I was still figuring out the methods of becoming a 'good white woman researcher'. One of my journal entries is especially telling on getting through all these complex 'positionality' questions. In it, I urge myself to stop 'navel-gazing' and just get on with it: 'don't let yourself get seduced and consumed by all this endless theorisation of positionality', I wrote to myself. There was a research project to get on with, there wasn't space and time to ask these much harder questions about why and how it was possible for a white woman to be doing this kind of research, and whether it was ethical anyway. No, I needed to get on with the practical work of figuring out a way through these issues. My attention was turned, then, to some much easier, more procedural (Guillemin and Gillam 2004) ethical questions (though they felt hard at the time) like how to negotiate access, and confidentiality of participants' data.

In this regard I was fortunate to have, as supervisors and mentors, people who were both open to the ethical dimensions present and oriented to their practical negotiation. A first practical step in that negotiation was to develop a 'code of conduct' that would govern my own research practice with Indigenous participants specifically. The question of whether that code should also govern my conduct with non-Indigenous participants (who constituted about half of my research group) was a difficult one. What did it mean to have a code of research conduct that only applied to half the participants in a project?

Again, much anguished reflection ensued. Indigenous people in Australia, as elsewhere, have been the subject of research since British invasion. Much of that has resulted in theft from Indigenous peoples: theft of knowledge, resources, and artefacts. Very little of the privilege of research findings and their outcomes has benefited Indigenous communities. Quite the opposite: Western scientific research has been routinely used to underpin oppressive and paternalistic modes of governance. Perhaps the best examples are the eugenics movement, which became influential in Australian public policy to justify an attempt to 'breed out' Indigenous bio-physical characteristics. It was also responsible for the plundering of Indigenous graves, and the theft of remains and other artefacts. In more contemporary terms, social science and anthropological research continue to have a reputation of thievery and deception amongst Indigenous communities to the extent that the activity of researchers within Indigenous communities is viewed with considerable suspicion.

In addition, a very great power differential existed in my *specific* research setting between Indigenous and non-Indigenous participants. All of the non-Indigenous participants were employed in government departments working in fields such as environmental planning, national park management, forestry, and protected area policy development. Their status within the research as a 'title' of this kind added a different kind of quality to their involvement: they were protected by their posts, the institutional setting in which they worked and the privileges it afforded. The information they gave me was not 'their own': it stemmed from their position as officers in government. Most (but not all) of the Indigenous participants had no such institutional setting from which they worked, and where they did, it was not usually a government institutional setting but either a community organisation or collective. It seemed to me, then, that these were qualitatively different positions from which to participate in a social research project, with qualitatively different potential outcomes. My decision was to extend the code of conduct only to the

Indigenous participants. The code thus expressly addressed issues relating to the cross-cultural and historically-constituted relationship between the researcher and the researched in a postcolonial setting.

Covering aspects such as confidentiality, management of the research, reciprocity, approval before publication of findings, and reporting to participants, the code went some way beyond the University's Ethics committee requirements. While I appreciated its importance in academic terms, it wasn't until I got into the field and used the code as the basis of first discussions with each research participant that I realised how powerful a tool it was. When one particularly cautious and 'prickly' Indigenous participant (I interpreted this at the time as displaying a deep suspicion of me) suddenly visibly relaxed during a detailed discussion of the code, I realised that maybe it was possible to address some of these procedural ethical dilemmas. Articulating the presence of historical injustice in our relations seemed to offer some kind of pathway. Actually acknowledging the politically sensitive nature of the topic, the historical use of social research in the oppression of Indigenous peoples, but recognising the small ways that such problems can be addressed enabled *me* very significantly in being able to undertake the research. I continue to follow that code even now, five years after the fieldwork was completed, because I had committed to supplying the participants with copies of publications and other material that came out of the research. Yet I'm circumspect now as to whether that instrument really enabled anybody else other than me. I return to these questions in a moment.

Get Real, it's Real: Research as a Material Practice

A PhD research project, perhaps because it is an 'academic' project in the many senses of that word, can easily seem removed from the real world; from material realities and lived consequences. The sheer number of hours spent in a university library has a tendency to remove one's sense of grounded reality, that the things one 'does' in research actually have any impact. I mean here those consequences beyond the immediate, procedural ethical issues of confidentiality and 'user participation'.

For me, this question arose in relation to the position of my research in the wider context of Indigenous land rights claims being fought, at the same time I was undertaking the research, in courts and tribunals. Obvious procedural ethical questions arose from undertaking research in this kind of context. One was confidentiality and intellectual property rights, issues I have touched on already. Another was the use of the data and my interpreted findings. It took some hard talking from an Indigenous academic and mentor very near to submission of my thesis to get me to see the importance of this question of how my findings might get used.

The background here was the Australian High Court's finding in *Mabo v Queensland [No.2] (1992) 175 CLR 1* which found that a form of title, that became known as 'native title', survived colonisation by the British (see Butt and Eagleson 1996, and Stephenson and Ratnapala 1993 for an overview). The statutory framework that was subsequently enacted provided a legal mechanism by which Indigenous groups could have ownership of their traditional lands recognised. Much writing has been devoted to the profound limitations of the approach embedded in the Native Title Act not to mention the whittling back of rights under the conservative Howard Government's rule (Beckett 1996; Choo and O'Connell 1999; Dodson 1996; Riley 2002; Weiner 2002; Strelein 2003). What is important to understand here is that Indigenous people claiming native title rights had to prove the existence of those rights to a tribunal judge. The 'proof' came in the form of demonstrating that the claimant group had maintained a connection to their country. Indigenous people not only had to prove their clan membership and the country belonging to that clan, but also that a connection had been maintained with that country over time. For Indigenous people living in densely settled parts of Australia, such as Victoria, where dispossession was virtually complete, this proved an extremely formidable and profoundly unjust burden of proof. Nowhere is this better seen than in the decision in the Yorta Yorta people's case. Here, the Native Title Tribunal decided (upheld by the High Court on appeal) that the Yorta Yorta people's connection to their country had been 'washed away by the tide of history' because that connection to country could not be demonstrated in a form that the courts recognised as 'traditionally' Aboriginal (see Strelein 2003; Atkinson 2002).

The evidence base for proving native title claims of course lay in two sources: early anthropological accounts of kinship groups and territorial connection, and contemporary anthropological research into ongoing connections to place, use of land and resources. My own research, which claimed to report on Indigenous relationships with and knowledge about place, belonged in this latter domain, though this was never my intention. I didn't think of myself as 'doing' native title research. Despite this, my thesis would ultimately contain information carrying the status, whether deserved or not, of scientific authority simply because it was produced by someone (more particularly a 'white social scientist someone') in a university. Given that the research was undertaken in two case study areas with live native title claims (many of the research participants were claimants), the question of how to manage the future use of my research findings was very pertinent. Perhaps most concerning was the distinctly possible prospect that my findings might be used *against* native title claimants.

After long discussions with mentors and research participants about this problem, I eventually had to fill my thesis with qualifying statements, which highlighted that I was not an anthropologist, and that the data was not collected in a manner amenable to drawing conclusions either about specific native title claims or native title more generally. Now being 'out of the field' in a methodological sense, and a long way from the field geographically, I have little sense of the impact or justness of this approach. That experience, however, highlights to me the importance of seeing research as a real practice in the real world, with actual material implications that may lie well beyond the researcher's intent or even the field itself. There is, of course, no real way to control for this. Like publishing, our words and ideas can be used in ways we never intended, because they are accessible (sometimes) to a wider community of potential readers and users. This, however, does not obviate the responsibility we have for the production of those ideas and the integrity of the thinking and research that sits behind them. When real materialities might be impacted by our work, then that work must be subject to critical scrutiny. In the case of PhD research, in planning and geography schools for example, it highlight the very great importance of supervision and that students have access to a wide community of mentors and scholars to expose those issues and guide their resolution.

Coming Out: Reclaiming my Whiteness

Solutions to the ethical problems present in my research, including positionality effects, confidentiality, and the use of the findings beyond the field were found in relatively established procedural rules for research ethics. In many senses they were satisficers for the problems I encountered. Yet, solving procedural ethics issues as if they are solely procedural problems and using the accepted rules of research ethics is problematic in this context. I want to look now more critically at the tools I employed to try and reclaim, in a critical and exposing sense, the fact of my whiteness.

My code of conduct was deeply circumscribed by the Western culture that was its author(ity): while intellectual property was addressed, it was attributed to the 'provider' of that information in an individual sense (participant x said this..., participant y said that...). Individualised notions of knowledge and property were intrinsically instilled into the ethical framework (see Smith 1999 for a discussion on this).

Given its attention to procedural problem, my code failed to address, or acknowledge, those much deeper ethical quandaries that were always present in the research and which I alluded to earlier. Even the most reflexive and sensitive ethics protocols cannot remove the fact that research done by whites on Indigenous folks is exactly that: Indigenous people are the object of white folks' social-scientific endeavour (see Smith 1999, 118, also Moreton-Robinson 2000).

This is perhaps best explicated in the notion that the code only governed the research practice and not its design. This is where my myth really began to unravel. After an extended period of time 'in the field', and lots of discussions with supervisors and lots of reflective writing, I began to admit to the really rather obvious fact that this was my research, my design, my world view. It wasn't in the slightest bit collaborative, or participatory, or 'grassroots'. Research subjects were not involved in the design of research questions, or the methodological approach: it was instigated, designed, implemented and analysed entirely by me. As a result, my research design was like all other research designs: structured by the researcher's epistemological and ontological position. It is impossible to escape being what you are. My whiteness was an 'inescapable aspect of [my] conversation cross-culturally' (Haggis and Schech 2000, 389).

It seems self-evident now, but it was really not until I neared the end of the fieldwork that the full implications of this became apparent. While I have written about this elsewhere (see Porter 2004), it is worth reflecting on again here. The core research question I had developed in the project concerned the 'spaces of inclusion' available within planning systems for Indigenous people to express knowledge and aspirations about land and its management. A set of assumptions were operating in this approach that took me a long time to see. The experience of fieldwork began to both answer as well as critically review my research agenda. The idea of 'inclusion' became increasingly problematic as the research and analytical work progressed. It became apparent that I had assumed that Indigenous people would desire a greater 'inclusion' of their aspirations and knowledge within the dominant land governance system. Such an assumption failed to appreciate Indigenous sovereignty (see for example Dodson 1994; Langton 1994; Dodson and Pritchard 1998; Langton 2000 and 2002), a domain that I had never appreciated and of course can never fully know, and how this might affect my fieldwork. Indigenous people might seek to achieve their aspirations through the development of quite separate – sovereign – systems of Indigenous governance, for example, which rendered my research questions rather ridiculous.

Latent theories underpinning my idea of 'knowledge' were also exposed during the fieldwork and analysis. What constituted 'Indigenous knowledge' and how would I know it when I saw it? How would it be identifiably 'Indigenous' knowledge, as opposed to some other kind of knowledge? Further, by linking knowledge and aspirations together I had built into the research agenda the implicit assumption that to have aspirations, Indigenous people must first have knowledge (of a kind that I could recognise and claim as 'Indigenous') about country. I began to see not only how I had identified and reified an Indigenous 'other' in Victoria, different from me, but assumed that knowledge of this otherness would (and should) be available to me as the analyst. It was a double-act of whiteness and further evidence that I was just like *that* research: the style I'd decided to loathe. Indigenous difference was firmly and centrally the object of my white social-scientific gaze.

This shook me. It meant two things most importantly: first, that the very design of the research, the questions I'd asked, the way I'd framed the problem to be answered, was deeply imperialist. This was confronting given that the project emerged from my desire to expose the persistence of the colonial project in Victoria. Well, I guess in the end it did – but it was far more personal than I'd ever anticipated. Second, I had undertaken most of the fieldwork looking for things that might not exist in a form that my 'imperial eyes' would recognise. It was too late to redo the fieldwork, and too late in effect to redesign the research questions. Abandoning the project was never a serious option (you don't just 'give up' because of a little methodological hitch, I told myself). Getting a PhD required reconciling this problem.

I decided to resolve it by approaching the analysis of the field data in an entirely different way. Instead of coding for 'aspirations' and 'knowledge' (which was my original plan) I repeatedly read transcripts, fieldnotes and observations until patterns emerged about the inter-lacing of knowledge and power in particular concrete decision-making moments. Perhaps most importantly, I began to look much more closely at the way the non-Indigenous participants in the research constructed those very issues (Indigenous knowledge and aspirations) and used that as an analytical tool to deconstruct not just my own research agenda, but the policy approach I had set out to research. In this sense, I tried to de-centre Indigenous difference as the object of study and position 'my own' (whites, planners) there instead. Studies of whiteness, and theorisations of whiteness, are (not uncritically) assuming an increasing importance in human geography literatures (see Moreton-Robinson 2000; Shaw 2007; Morrison 1992; Pulido 2002).

Perceiving this problem also meant I saw differently the implications of how my findings might be used. I could now see that putting knowledge and aspirations for country together caused deep philosophical problems. But how could that coupling be used in, for instance, a native title tribunal hearing? Potentially with devastating consequences, particularly where I had not represented, for my own analytical reasons, particular people's knowledge/s and stories. Their absence might easily misguide, or worse provide 'proof' to someone seeking to undermine native title claims. How I constructed the thesis, the arguments I used and the way I wove them together suddenly had far greater implications.

Unlearning Knowledge, Learning Positionality and Power

Is it ethical for white people to undertake research on (with, including) Indigenous people? If all these ethical dilemmas are so utterly entrenched in the first place, and so profoundly difficult to shift, what real positive effect can research ever have? Or as Haggis and Schech put it: 'This leaves the question what IS an acceptable form or framework of help which does not ignore or take for granted existing relations of power?' (2000, 393, original emphasis). There are real and urgent issues faced by Indigenous people, in Australia as elsewhere, that need research and policy attention. None of those issues, not one, is an 'Indigenous issue'. They are all the product of historically constituted racial relations. Non-Indigenous people are implicated always and everywhere in the contemporary material realities of Indigenous people's lives. This is especially so in the field of planning (see Porter 2007, 2006a and 2006b; Jackson 1997 and 1996). To choose to walk away from these difficult, often painful ethical dilemmas because (if we are white) we are 'too positioned' fails to acknowledge that responsibility. The question for me, then, is more accurately: is it ethical for white people to choose *not* to undertake research on (with, including) Indigenous people? Choosing not to be involved is a privilege of whiteness.

For those, like me, with imperial eyes, we assume that the world is open to us as knowing subjects, that we can make the world knowable to us through our own empirical endeavours. Learning is our privilege, knowledge of the world virtually a right. Research in settings and situations where postcolonial politics will structure the relationship between researcher and researched must be present to this dilemma and undertake to properly conceptualise what that means for the research. That it is possible to be in the 'us' position, observing 'them' in that position over there, must be recognised as a construct of historically constituted social relations. The naturalness with which researchers with imperial eyes assume that position must continuously be the subject of analysis. In that sense, we unlearn (following Spivak see Landry and MacLean 1996) the right to our own knowledge and newly learn the fact and the implications of our positionality. We expose our deployment of an 'invisible standpoint' (Nicoll 2000, 371) from which we construct our knowledge of the world.

But what does all that actually do for planning research generally, or a research project specifically? To be honest, I'm not really sure. Recognising privilege, acknowledging that you have imperial eyes, doesn't remove your eyes, or shift racialised relations of power. It doesn't even do anything to shift the location of power from which I, and you, can produce knowledge about Indigenous Others as 'experts in the field'. It doesn't open more university careers to Indigenous people, or steer research funding directly to Indigenous communities. The reality is there is no comfortable place from which to undertake research practices, no safe or ethically-bounded place from where we can wait for an acceptable model. It is as Nussbaum (1990) observes: we can choose to treat philosophical and methodological problems as insuperable, but we do so at enormous cost.

References

Agar, M.H. (1996), *The Professional Stranger: An Informal Introduction to Ethnography* (San Diego: Academic Press).

Atkinson, W. (2002), 'Mediating the Mindset of Opposition: The Yorta Yorta Case', *Indigenous Law Bulletin* 5:15, 8-11.

Beckett, S. (1996), 'Workability in Whose Interest? The Native Title Amendment Bill 1996', *Aboriginal Law Bulletin* 3:84, 4-7.

Birch, T. (1997), '"Nothing has changed": The Making and Unmaking of Koori Culture', in Gillian K. Cowlishaw and Barry Morris (eds).

Blunt, A. and Rose, G. (eds) (1994), *Writing Women and Space: Colonial and Postcolonial Geographies* (New York: Guilford).

Butt, P. and Eagleson, R. (1996), *Mabo: What the High Court Said and What the Government Did*, 2nd edn (Sydney: Federation Press).

Carrick, C. (1999), 'Indians, Planning and Political Change: Environmental Conflict in British Columbia's Coastal Forests', *Plurimondi* I:1, 175-202.

Choo, C. and O'Connell, M. (1999), *Historical Narrative and Proof of Native Title* (Canberra: Australian Institute of Aboriginal and Torres Strait Islander Studies).

Clifford, J. (1986), *Writing Culture: The Poetics and Politics of Ethnography* (Berkeley: University of California Press).

Clifford, J. (1988), *The Predicament of Culture* (Cambridge MA: Harvard University Press).

Cowlishaw, G.K. and Morris, B. (eds) (1997), *Race Matters: Indigenous Australians and 'Our' Society* (Canberra: Aboriginal Studies Press).

Cushner, K. and Breslin, R.W. (1996), *Intercultural Interactions: A Practical Guide* (Thousand Oaks: SAGE).

Denzin, N.K. (1997), *Interpretive Ethnography: Ethnographic Practices for the 21st Century* (California: SAGE).

Dodson, M. (1994), 'Towards the Existence of Indigenous Rights: Policy, Power and Self-determination', *Race and Class* 35:4, 65-76.

Dodson, M. (1996), 'Power and Cultural Difference in Native Title Mediation', *Aboriginal Law Bulletin* 3:84, 8-11.

Dodson, M. and Pritchard, S. (1998), 'Recent Developments in Indigenous Policy: The Abandonment of Self-determination?', *Indigenous Law Bulletin* 4:15, 4-6.

Fetterman, D.M. (ed.) (1993), *Speaking the Language of Power: Communication, Collaboration and Advocacy (Translating Ethnography into Action)* (London: Falmer Press).

Geertz, C. (1973), *The Interpretation of Culture: Selected Essays* (New York: Basic Books).

Guillemin, M. and Gillam, L. (2004), 'Ethics, Reflexivity, and "Ethically Important Moments" in Research', *Qualitative Inquiry* 10:2, 261-280.

Haggis, J. and Schech, S. (2000), 'Meaning Well and Global Good Manners: Reflections on White Western Feminist Cross-cultural Praxis', *Australian Feminist Studies* 15:33, 387-399.

Hammersley, M. and Atkinson, P. (1983), *Ethnography: Principles in Practice* (London: Tavistock).

Howitt, R., Connell, J. and Hirsch, P. (eds) (1996), *Resources, Nations and Indigenous Peoples: Case Studies from Australasia, Melanesia and Southeast Asia* (Melbourne: Oxford University Press).

Ishtar, dé Z. (2005), 'Striving for a Common Language: A White Feminist Parallel to Indigenous Ways of Knowing and Researching', *Women's Studies International Forum* 28:5, 357-368.

Jackson, S. (1996), 'Town Country: Urban Development and Aboriginal Sea Rights in Australia', in Richard Howitt, John Connell and Philip Hirsch (eds).

Jackson, S. (1997), 'A Disturbing Story: The Fiction of Rationality in Land Use Planning in Aboriginal Australia', *Australian Planner* 34:4, 221-226.

Jacobs, J.M. (1994), 'Earth Honouring: Western Desires and Indigenous Knowledges', in Alison Blunt and Gillian Rose (eds).

Landry, D. and MacLean, G. (1996), *The Spivak Reader: Selected Works of Gayatri Chakravorty Spivak* (New York: Routledge).

Lane, M.B. (1997), 'Aboriginal Participation in Environmental Planning', *Australian Geographic Studies* 35:3, 308-323.

Lane, M.B. (2000), 'Difference, Civil Society and the State: Indigenous Interests in Natural Resource Planning', paper presented to the Association of Collegiate Schools of Planning, Atlanta, Georgia, US.

Langton, M. (1994), 'Self-determination: Overhauling the Administrative Practices of Colonisation', *Surviving Columbus*, 132-141.

Langton, M. (1998), *Burning Questions: Emerging Environmental Issues for Indigenous Peoples in Northern Australia* (Darwin: Centre for Natural and Cultural Resource Management).

Langton, M. (2000), 'A Treaty between Our Nations?', *Arena Magazine* 50, 28-34.

Langton, M. (2002), 'A New Deal? Indigenous Development and the Politics of Recovery', Dr Charles Perkins Memorial Oration, University of Sydney, Sydney, 4 October.

Lee, R.M. (1993), *Doing Research on Sensitive Topics* (London: SAGE).

Maxwell, J.A. (1993), 'Gaining Acceptance from Participants, Clients and Policymakers for Qualitative Research' in David M. Fetterman (ed.).

Moreton-Robinson, A. (2000), *Talkin' Up to the White Woman* (St Lucia: University of Queensland Press).

Morrison, T. (1992), *Playing in the Dark: Whiteness and the Literary Imagination* (Cambridge MA: Harvard University Press).

Nicholl, F. (2000), 'Indigenous Sovereignty and the Violence of Perspective: A White Woman's Coming Out Story', *Australian Feminist Studies* 15:33, 369-386.

Nussbaum, M. (1990), *Love's Knowledge: Essays on Philosophy and Literature* (New York: Oxford University Press).

Porter, L. (2004), 'Unlearning One's Privilege: Reflections on Cross-cultural Research with Indigenous Peoples in South-East Australia', *Planning Theory and Practice* 5:1, 104-109.

Porter, L. (2006a), 'Planning in (Post)Colonial Settings: Challenges for Theory and Practice', *Planning Theory and Practice* 7:4, 383-396.

Porter, L. (2006b), 'Rights or Containment? The Politics of Aboriginal Cultural Heritage in Victoria', *Australian Geographer* 37:3, 355-374.

Porter, L. (2007), 'Producing Forests: A Colonial Genealogy of Environmental Planning in Victoria, Australia', *Journal of Planning Education and Research* 26:4, 466-477.

Pulido, L. (2002), 'Reflections on a White Discipline', *Professional Geographer* 54:1, 42-49.

Rangan, H. and Lane, M.B. (2001), 'Indigenous Peoples and Forest Management: Comparative Analysis of Institutional Approaches in Australia and India', *Society and Natural Resources* 14:2, 145-160.

Riley, M. (2002), *'Winning' Native Title: The Experience of the Nharnuwangga, Wajarri and Ngarla People* (Canberra: Australian Institute of Aboriginal and Torres Strait Islander Studies).

Shaw, W. (2007), *Cities of Whiteness* (Carlton: Blackwell).

Smith, L.T. (1999), *Decolonizing Methodologies: Research and Indigenous Peoples* (Dunedin: University of Otago Press).

Sonn, C.C. (2004), 'Reflecting on Practice: Negotiating Challenges to Ways of Working', *Journal of Community and Applied Social Psychology* 14:4, 305-313.

Stanfield, J.H.I. and Dennis, R.M. (1993), *Race and Ethnicity in Research Methods* (California: SAGE).

Stephenson, M.A. and Ratnapala, S. (eds) (1993), *Mabo: A Judicial Revolution: The Aboriginal Land Rights Decision and its Impact on Australian Law* (St Lucia: University of Queensland Press).

Stevens, S. (1997), *Conservation through Cultural Survival: Indigenous Peoples and Protected Areas* (Washington D.C.: Island Press).

Strelein, L. (2003), *Members of the Yorta Yorta Aboriginal Community v Victoria [2002] HCA 58 (12 December 2002) – Comment* (Canberra: Australian Institute of Aboriginal and Torres Strait Islander Studies).

Weiner, J.F. (2002), *Diaspora, Materialism, Tradition: Anthropological Issues in Recent High Court Appeal of the Yorta Yorta People* (Canberra: Australian Institute of Aboriginal and Torres Strait Islander Studies).

Yiftachel, O. and Fenster, T. (eds) (1997), *Frontier Development and Indigenous Peoples*, Progress in Planning Series (Oxford, UK: Pergamon Press).

Chapter 16
Multiple Roles in Multiple Dramas: Ethical Challenges in Undertaking Participatory Planning Research

Francesco Lo Piccolo

All the world's a stage,
And all the men and women merely players;
They have their exits and their entrances,
And one man in his time plays many parts.

William Shakespeare, *As You Like It*, act 2, scene 7, 139-142

Introduction

The chapter will explore some ethical issues which arise when undertaking research with minorities (ethnic groups, children, poor people) within participatory processes in the case of an uncollaborative planning context. There are important ethical issues that have to be carefully considered when undertaking research with any people, but particularly when these people are marginalised or excluded by wider society; as a consequence, they are seldom given the opportunity to voice their experiences, stories, needs and desires, due to multiple factors of mainstream disengagement, which are social, economic, linguistic, cultural and spatial (Olufemi and Reeves 2004). In brief, their knowledge is marginalised.

If this is accepted, some questions arise. How are we supposed to consider planning researchers – understood as immersed in the policy process – as moral/political agents, given their political commitments? What is a 'significant' knowledge? Which sort of knowledge is not 'recognised' and consequently excluded by Institutions? And what obligations does a researcher have in relation to the power relations assumed and supported by answers to these questions? In which way could the researcher 'carve out room for manoeuvre' (Thomas 2005, 241) and still maintain intellectual independence and integrity? Finally, and in order to provide shared benefits (Reason and Bradbury 2007), how can we develop projects in which the researchers are not the sole beneficiaries? In other words, what do we owe and what could we appropriately offer to research participants? What kind of research relationships could we or, better, should we form?

234   *Ethics and Planning Research*

Thomas (2005) fully describes how planning researchers have to face (and even negotiate) a complex moral landscape, which is subjected to potentially morally compromising possibilities. These compromises are essentially due to:

- The subjective status of the researcher which depends on access, cooperation and even (financial) support from powerful (political) institutions;
- The unpredictable exploitation or (mis)use of research findings;
- The direct interest and (consequent) pressures of funding institutions on the research areas.

Here there are both general ethical issues and specifically research ethical issues: the chapter will stress the perspective of the researcher, although a strict and rigid distinction does not entirely apply to the case, given the context which will be described.

The central purpose of this chapter is to raise and illustrate some ethical dilemmas due to the ambiguous role of action-researchers whose aims and attempts are those of pushing forward a collaborative planning approach in a rather uncollaborative place, such as Palermo. The uncollaborative nature of our society and institutions in relation to planning is well described by Brand and Gaffikin (2007). In some local contexts (as the ones here described) there are further elements (due to the characteristics of the political regime as well as of the structure of the society) which deepen the uncollaborative nature of planning policies. The following considerations, even if nurtured by the described case studies of the Palermo context, may be applied to other, more general, cases. In fact, how many places and arenas in the world show now divided and fragmented societies in comparison with an (abstract?) rhetoric of cohesion, solidarity and inclusivity? What is the role, and the consequent ethical challenges and implications, of the planning researcher in such contexts?

The stage is the city of Palermo, and *dramatis personae* are City Council Institutions (the Housing, the Environmental and the Planning Departments), (plural) residents, (few) local associations, school teachers and students, university students and the author, who plays multiple roles in (multiple) dramas.

Prologue: Participatory Processes, Inclusionary Research Agendas and Ethical Challenges

I had previously framed some of these questions and the following reflections in the light of communicative rationality and ethics (Lo Piccolo 2008). Forester (1989 and 1999) faces the issue of communicative ethics and further elements of reflection are developed by Healey (1997 and 1998) regarding the inclusive process of communicative ethics. Also in Innes (1995 and 1996) and Innes and Booher (1999) the concept of communicative rationality, as described in Habermas (1981 and 1989), gives an epistemological and ethical framework for guiding and constructing consensus building, where it is defined as 'an array of practices in which stakeholders, selected to represent different interests, come together for face-to-face, long-term dialogue to address a policy issue of common concern' (Innes and Booher 1999, 412). In this framework, rationality and ethics rely on accuracy, integrity, accountability and sincerity of what participants say in communicatively rational discussions, and on a planner's duty of responsibly constructing dialogues (and knowledge) according to truth and rigour.

In order to re-shape planning practices on the base of an inclusionary approach, also Healey (1997) considers the Habermasian communicative ethics a valuable conceptual resource, which implies the ethical challenge of building up inclusionary processes. In other words, the ethical commitment to enabling all stakeholders to have a voice is a way forward in realising the practical meaning of participatory democracy in pluralist societies (Healey 1997, 5), but also a recognition and a call to harness the heterogeneity of knowledge. In epistemological terms, while collaborative planning recognises that there are different types of knowledge and places of its production (including the tacit and experiental knowledge of local inhabitants), what is a 'significant' knowledge for an inclusionary research agenda? Which sort of knowledge is not 'recognised' and consequently ignored and excluded by institutions, representing the unofficial, and therefore invisible (Sandercock 1998) side of the story?

In this theoretical framework, the ethical principle of inclusionary communicative ethics (in practice as well as in research) is strictly linked to the issue of consensus building, no matter if it is interpreted in a strictly institutional or radical way, and however stakeholders could be selected and involved. Recent literature has in many ways questioned this (Brand and Gaffikin 2007; Watson 2006). On the other side, reviews of some of these critiques and replies to various criticism are, for example, in Healey (2003) and Innes (2004), while assessments of positive outcomes of collaborative approach and citizen involvement are, for example, in Burby (2003) and in Gunton et al. (2003). I raised a question (Lo Piccolo 2008) on an issue that appears to be neglected or only partially considered by such recent planning debate: how to apply principles (and practices) of communicative ethics when and where planning processes do not have consensus building as a priority in their agenda? The case studies described below are to be ascribed to this precise context, and the chapter tries to face some ethical challenges which are (also) due to the nature of the political regime and planning context. Given the absence of any collaborative approach from the local institutions, which are indifferent to either the issue of inclusion or consensus-building, how to construct and apply any form of communicative ethics? How to conduct an 'inclusive' research in such a context, starting with contradictory (or weak) request by either institutions or disadvantaged groups, being involved only on the account of and consequently exploiting just our own academic role? These statements and context can explain the reasons of the indeed ambiguous nature of the below described experience, which is both an educational and a research action, in the stream of some more challenging and intellectually stimulating others, as that one described in Reardon and Forester (2008).

If the practice of collaborative planning is also characterised by a reconception of conflicts as 'creative tensions' (Brand and Gaffikin 2007, 288), what about those contexts where conflicts are eluded, implicit or drained (that is, devoid of their oppositional power)? The stories which will be narrated in the chapter show such a context, where deprived and minority groups (immigrants and local poor, children and young people) have passively accepted policies which confirm their inferior status or the absence of public policies in favour of de-regulating and privatising the public realm, without expressing any particular form of protest and/or conflict. Even when some conflicts arise (as it is happening in the case of the ZEN housing neighbourhood in recent times), they appear as occasional forms of protest, which are almost ignored by institutions, and which – consequently – extinguish in a short amount of time, due to their unstructured nature and the weak status and organisational capability of their participants.

From this, further questions arise. If we consider planning researchers as moral/political agents, in the light of their political commitments, does not this moral and political commitment interfere with objectivity and the very nature of a scientific method? On the other hand, do the competitive pressures on academic research affect the researcher's agenda and way of conduct (Thomas 2005), encouraging self-absorption and self-aggrandisement?

Healey and Gilroy (1990) focus on the critical ingredients of a people-sensitive planning; most of those considerations do apply to an inclusionary research agenda, especially in that part of the argument where different types of consciousness are identified and described. Healey and Gilroy (1990, 28) refer to: an epistemological consciousness; an ethical consciousness; a political consciousness, of the power relations embedded; a socio-psychological consciousness, of the ways our personalities affect other people and they us; a structural consciousness, of the forces which shape our societies and the way these may be manifest in our roles; a self-reflective consciousness. To be honest, most of the above mentioned types of consciousness are hard to be fully and concurrently achieved in the research work as it will be described, and they represent more an ethical ideal, or a reference-framework for monitoring and re-tuning practice, than an easily accomplished task.

Moreover, according to McClintock et al. (2003, 716), a distinction has to be 'introduced between research and researcher context, in order to appreciate "the position of the researcher" engaged in research practice [as] appreciating the position of the researcher when engaged in research practice is a necessary part of transparency' within the whole area of 'research as participative'. But, even if I agree on a general level with this statement (Lo Piccolo 2008), the below described experiences show that a firm, explicit and clear position of the researcher does not often occur. Readers will find in the chapter a continuous shifting and waving between at least three positions: researcher, activist and academic, in the attempt of introducing elements of (inclusive) collaborative discourse in practice and research.

Scene I: The Historic Centre and the Local Agenda 21 Programme of Palermo

This is an area of widespread urban decay and, at the same time, of great potential, owing to its location within the core of the city and the historical (and potential) value of its buildings. The restoration of the historic centre, connected with wider policies of urban revitalisation, is still an essential component of a strategy for the re-development of the city. In the last 15 years, several initiatives for the revitalisation of the historic centre have been undertaken: an increase in renewal interventions managed by the private sector, public interventions of restoration and renewal managed by the City Council, new commercial activities, an increase in cultural and tourist-oriented events, and a new 'nightlife' can be considered as the main elements of these changes, following the approval and the implementation of the Detailed Executive Plan (PPE) of the Historic Centre (Lo Piccolo 1996 and 2008).

The historic centre of Palermo is presently going through a highly controversial period characterised, on the one hand, by a number of forms of spot regeneration through private initiatives and local development partnership programmes and, on the other hand, by old and new forms of physical and social decay caused by both neglect on the part of public authorities and by the emergence of new problems and marginal realities. In the past years the decay of the area has brought about a decrease in the market value of property and in rents, despite its central location. History has it that immigrant communities have always chosen to settle in areas such as this exactly for reasons of low-cost housing and location, moving into long-abandoned buildings that were generally unfit for habitation, where they are still leading a precarious existence (Lo Piccolo 1996 and 2000).

In previous research (Lo Piccolo 2000; Lo Piccolo and Leone 2008) doubts are raised about the survival of the ethnic communities as well as of the autochthonous poor people. Re-development work is raising property prices with a consequent rapid loss of low-cost housing. If it is accepted that the historic centre should regain its previous residential use, the repopulation will inevitably involve either the return of the upper and middle classes living on the outskirts or the maintenance of the present ethnic and local poor communities (Lo Piccolo 1996 and 2000). If the City Council is not able to organise effective housing, implement social policies, and launch coordinated programmes for preserving and reusing its estate so as to encourage private investment and support the most disadvantaged groups, such a process is quite unlikely to start. The recent choice of the City Council administration is oriented towards the very opposite direction, being extremely supportive of private investors and neglecting social and housing public policies. According to this framework, the Local Agenda 21 is not only a tokenistic but also a deliberately ineffective process (Lo Piccolo 2008).

The LA21 project was officially launched in 2004, with some general initiatives of involvement and consultation, formally directed to all citizens, but with poor political motivation; this is proved by the slackness with which the operating unit

238   *Ethics and Planning Research*

of LA21 was created (at the end of 2004) made up of architects and planners working in the City Council Environmental Department, with no cooperation with those working in the City Council Planning Department.

It is important to remark that neither during this first stage nor during the following ones were the issues concerning the historic centre, the social marginality and related policies considered a priority within the wider schedule of LA21 (Lo Piccolo 2008). In this context, LA21 – notwithstanding its potential – is destined to play a minor role in the City Council agenda. Despite the fact that LA21, with its nature of participation and inclusionary process, is recognised as a powerful tool which can fight inequalities and discrimination, in Palermo it has assumed the characteristics of a politicised process, with scarce effects. Between 2005 and 2006, following the plenary forum of LA21, three thematic forums were created concerning: mobility; urban green areas, gardens and parks; and environmental education. Within the third (quite vague) theme, a research team from the Dipartimento Città e Territorio of the University of Palermo was involved.

Scene II: The ZEN Chronicles

Palermo's ZEN chronicles are an intriguing example of the problems affecting peripheral public housing areas in Southern Italy with respect to inclusionary and exclusionary planning practices. In fact, the ZEN[1] neighbourhood is an emblem of the marginality that characterises many public housing projects in Southern Italy.

In addition to the historical reasons and the consolidated phenomena that characterise this public housing neighbourhood, in recent years the problems have increased, with respect to, on the one hand, fertile but fragmented 'bottom-up' social practices and, on the other, the establishment of controversial forms of negotiated planning by private investors. By contrast, the municipal administration – against a general background of long-term indifference and, essentially, absence – is once again proposing initiatives that refer to the models and rationale of negotiation. They remain separate from local social and economic circumstances and prove to be inadequate and far from able to address residents' priority needs.

The illegal occupation of ZEN homes should be set in the wider context of the 'struggle for housing' in Palermo, and its evolution. This struggle began in 1968 and continued throughout the 1970s. Illegal occupation, which, in common with many public housing projects, occurred even before the homes had been completed and declared habitable, is even more significant in the ZEN neighbourhood, since it affects about 70 percent of the housing units actually built. If we take the planned number of housing units, which varies depending on the source consulted (Bonafede and Lo Piccolo 2007; Sciascia 2003), and exclude those never built at

---

1   ZEN is the acronym for Zona Espansione Nord (North Development Area), which is the 'name' of the neighbourhood.

all and those that have since been burnt down, it seems feasible to state that only about 2 percent of ZEN housing units has been allocated according to the rules.

While public housing policies in Palermo remain, worryingly, at a standstill, illegal occupation of the ZEN housing units has reached a significant level. The phenomenon should be set against a socio-demographic structure where the population is mainly of working age with high rates of unemployment, unusually high illiteracy rates and low levels of secondary education, if compared with the rest of the municipal area. At the same time the high drop-out rates in local schools, which involve the youngest age groups at high social risk (Mattina 2007), fuel a demand for personal assistance services. The deficit of services and public gathering places, along with the precarious health and sanitation conditions and the lack of primary infrastructure, undermine any – already weak – feeling of inclusion in the *civitas* that residents might experience.

The great poverty that is the distinguishing feature of the ZEN community, composed mainly of the urban sub-proletariat, and the precarious state in which they find themselves as a result of the lack of jobs and of a secure and stable housing situation and access to education and information, have produced a particularly complex relationship between social and housing exclusion (Mattina 2007).

The local political administration, contaminated by the intermediation of the Mafia, along with illegal transactions and the occupation of the homes, are some of the issues which, taken with the lack of basic facilities for the local community, have helped create highly singular living conditions here. The primary infrastructure, and most notably the water and sewage networks, is in a state of the utmost inefficiency. The illegal occupation of the ZEN housing has triggered a vicious circle of conflicts of responsibility which have been batted backwards and forwards between the Autonomous Institute of Public Housing (IACP), the public water company (AMAP) and the City Council. The 'implicit' project – in the absence of the necessary public intervention – is evident. We need only consider the arrangements for the residential water supply, notoriously 'awarded' to private companies, and the promises of jobs and 'amnesties' for people occupying homes illegally. Such promises are announced in the run-up to elections and are intertwined with acts of vandalism and illegal trafficking, of which sub-renting and the purchase and sale of public property by private parties are not unusual (Bonafede and Lo Piccolo 2007).

With respect to the lack of services and to residents' unexpressed demands, local associations and institutions, which have recently joined an Inter-Institutional Network (Italian acronym RI), have set up programmes which generate new social and cultural activities. The associations and the numerous local public operators reflect the fragmentary social nature of the neighbourhood. While they tend to follow a common plan, leavening – in as yet uncertain form – the inhabitants' demand for deliverance from cultural stereotypes and standardising development models, they inevitably address each other – and the problem – starting from completely different reference values and ideas of society and citizenship. Their working methods too are often conflicting, as often happens in social learning practices (Forester 1999). As such, their initiatives are transformed into actions of delegitimisation, concentration or manipulation of information, and occasional coalitions amongst members. In the absence of mature and direct participation by residents in the debates, such tendencies reveal that the network's organisational ability is still immature and easy to exploit, also from within, by the power of the elites (Bonafede and Lo Piccolo 2007).

While fragmentary but fertile social initiatives link up unexpected forms of solidarity through innovative methods, at the same time the ambiguous public policies propose traditional models of urban marketing – camouflaged by participative values – that tend to frustrate the possible inclusion processes of the most vulnerable and at-risk population groups. The opening of negotiating practices focusing on the ZEN neighbourhood dates back to 1999, when Palermo's City Council Planning Department, with the consultancy of Ecosfera, drew up a Local Development Partnership (known in Palermo as an Integrated Intervention Programme, PII) under Law 179/1992. Its declared objective was to address, as its priority task, the elimination of conditions of physical, planning and social decay in the public housing area through a programme divided into four objectives.[2] In spite of this, and notwithstanding its declaration in principle of a priority role for public initiatives, in its slow and only partial implementation the PII essentially favoured a number of private initiatives on the periphery of the neighbourhood. It failed to tackle or in any way resolve its state of marginality and decline and its impossible living conditions.

As far as the public PII initiatives are concerned, the situation is moving at an irreversibly slow and inefficient pace. And although the PII's report, and presentations in public debates by technical experts from the administration, refer frequently to vaguely defined participatory practices, the actual planning content of the programme, which is scarce in quantity and slim in content, has been criticised and contested by numerous associations operating in the neighbourhood.

Rehearsals: Past Educational Experiences as Reasons for the Involvement of the Research Team

The reasons for our involvement in both the described contexts relate to previous activity carried out at the Dipartimento Città e Territorio and at the School of Architecture and Planning of the University of Palermo: this activity concerns and combines field research and teaching at University. The double goal is to introduce university students to participation in a practical way, and take the opportunity to carry out on-the-spot research even where there is no interest whatsoever on the part of the city administration. Moreover, the aim (and related methodology) is

---

2   In fact these are not actual objectives so much as wide-ranging, vague thematic areas, little more than slogans, as can be deduced from the language used: the use of the everyday; civil life; urban and environmental quality; urban dignity and recognisability.

Multiple Roles in Multiple Dramas 241

to develop a research environment that would allow marginal people to engage honestly and openly with the research (Lo Piccolo 2008; Lo Piccolo et al. 2008).

The stages of investigation and identification of actions and procedures were carried out in the local district communities (the historic centre and the ZEN neighbourhood) and by actively listening to, understanding and mediating the emerging needs of community groups with a view to making use of shared technical and non technical skills in the creation of plan processes, in order to 'develop the capability to enter into the "assumptive worlds" of those with whom they interact, and to make their own "world view" available to those with whom they relate' (Healey and Gilroy 1990, 27). Where 'weak' and 'minority' social groups were involved, such as the groups of immigrants in the historic centre or the poor inhabitants of the ZEN neighbourhood, a participatory approach was encouraged in order to ensure social equity and community-oriented choices.

Participants were informed from the beginning that they would take part in nothing but a simulation and that it was a mere university initiative. Despite this, many people participated very actively and, probably thanks to the very nature of the activity, participation seemed not to be overwhelmed by the predominance of self-interests. The representatives of local communities openly recounted their personal stories, experiences and problems; this generated a richness and depth of research material that may otherwise not have been available. It is important to highlight the 'diversity' – compared to the standards commonly adopted – of a large part of the needs expressed. These needs are related to the specific character of the residents in the areas, and an analysis carried out from an external observation point would have difficulty identifying them.[3]

Even though the experience described above was only academic research and students' exercise, without any commitment of the public administration whatsoever, good results emerged for both the educational and the research purposes. Being involved was crucial for the socialisation and integration of participants in terms of development of social skills and self-confidence; the opportunity to discuss their problems, needs and expectations; learning about the places in which they live. Further analysis of the experience allowed students and researchers to discuss the concepts of community and 'minorities', and implicit potentials of their involvement and role within planning practices. Seeing things through 'different' eyes gave them the opportunity to consider in a unconventional way the principles of active citizenship, collective and shared creation of spaces and policies, and democratic participation (Lo Piccolo et al. 2005), nurturing their ethical as well as political consciousness.

Following this research and some other research projects led by my colleague Ignazia Pinzello with a number of neighbourhood schools (Pinzello and Quartarone 2005), we were asked by the City Council administration to be involved in the

---

3 The 'anomalous' percentage distribution of the different age groups, the particular structure of a large part of the families, the 'contradictory' role of women and the cultural and religious traditions all emerge as significant factors.

LA21 programme. As previously remarked, the city administration very lazily and unwillingly carried out the opening stages of LA21. As a matter of fact, the interaction efforts were solely aimed at achieving social consensus and formally carrying out the actions and measures required by the programme structure: a typical and significant case of priority of motives of (formal) effectiveness versus justice and equity.

In the meanwhile, since the Inter-Institutional Network (RI) of associations was set up in 2005 in the ZEN neighbourhood, the need has emerged, within the network itself, to establish effective listening and interaction practices with the residents' community and with the social forces operating in the neighbourhood. This was in order to help re-define and up-date the old PII, with a view to drawing up a plan (with related actions) that would be able to respond effectively to social demands and real needs. This request, formally granted by the Mayor of Palermo in July 2006 but essentially disregarded (and perhaps also misunderstood) as the situation evolved,[4] should have been formalised in a neighbourhood workshop. This, to date, has not taken place, in spite of the numerous preparatory meetings and an initial involvement of the School of Architecture and Planning of the University of Palermo: an involvement that has never been formalised and whose tasks have never been clearly identified.

Act I: Looking for Residents and Working 'With' Them

Many scholars such as Lindblom and Cohen (1979), Schon (1983), Innes (1990 and 1998), Healey (1997) and – also in the Italian planning context – scholars such as Magnaghi (1991 and 1998), Paba (2003) and Attili et al. (2007) highlight that citizens possess – and are able to use – 'ordinary knowledge' that is crucial in order to ensure that plans and policies reflect local conditions and values.

Being well aware of all the above, the research team, at the stage of the research projects' definition and negotiation with the City Council administration, tried to broaden the scope of the research in order to direct the administration's efforts and hit the target of a wider and more effective involvement of various strata of the population, particularly minorities and weak groups. In the case of LA21, the City Council administration partially and formally agreed; in the case of the ZEN neighbourhood, and despite many meetings, no formal agreement with the administration occurred.

This shows the city administration's predominant interest in keeping the residents of the ZEN in a permanent state of exclusion. At the same time, the municipal administration's declared intention of opening a negotiating table with

---

4 Recent developments in the situation seems to be pointing to a workshop, over a limited timescale, for the purpose of a planning tender/competition. This is difficult to view as consistent with the need expressed for listening and interaction practices for a community that has been scarred by high degrees of marginality and social decline.

the RI betrays, rather, its intention to obtain consensus to open negotiations. This would be publicised in the media and disguised by participatory values, and would run counter to fertile experimentation practices that could give rise to inclusion processes in the most vulnerable and high-risk segments of the population. We are therefore witnessing a failure to fulfil social and political obligations with respect to one of the most fragile and disadvantaged areas of the city. Once again, and in spite of the initial involvement of Palermo City Council and the RI, the research working group has ended up assuming an autonomous, independent role, with the involvement of students, residents, and some associations (Lo Piccolo et al. 2008).

In both cases, most of the initiatives were carried out independently with the support of a network of local associations. These associations have been working for years mainly with children and young people by organising a number of play and extra-school formative activities to limit and prevent school drop-outs and fight effects of social marginality on young people.

In the case of LA21, two forums were opened: the first in S. Anna social centre (City Council premises) and the second in the headquarters of the associations (S.A.L.I. Network in Tavola Tonda square). The forum held in the City Council premises was not publicised nor did the City Council administration support its organisation: it was held only thanks to the personal interest and passionate drive of a very active City Council social worker acting in the area. The forum held in the headquarters of the S.A.L.I. Network of associations in Tavola Tonda was attended by more people and far better structured thanks to the efforts of some members (Lo Piccolo 2008). In the case of ZEN, one forum was opened in the *ZEN Insieme* (Zen Together) social centre, where it was possible to organise a successful *Planning for Real* exercise. Despite the limited attendance (just women, children and a small number of young people), residents participated very intensely in all the occasions, because of the issue that were to be dealt with (unemployment and very poor housing conditions, above all).

One critical element which is worth stressing is the poor attendance especially during the closing stages of the forums. What Matthews (2001) underlined about young people can be extended within our case studies to most of the inhabitants: people lead busy lives and, as forums demand a long-term commitment, membership is often difficult to sustain. Moreover, the absence of the city administrators on the one hand made attenders' speeches more genuine and sincere, but on the other hand further weakened the general motivation: participants clearly did not consider themselves in positions of power or authority and this also affected their involvement.

Then, we have to remark the very poor attendance of young people, as amongst them there are characteristics that inhibit their willingness to participate: some because they are not interested, some others because they are not confident and many others because of cynicism towards the opportunities as presented. In our specific case, we must add the indirect effect of the Mafia control on some of them, considering that civic participation is often seen as an 'act of betrayal'. The experiences described above testify that forums are inappropriate participatory devices to involve young people, especially those who are traditionally hard to reach (Matthews 1998) and, in more general terms, that 'the role of the traditional planning meeting as a consultation model is recognised as only partial to any broad participatory strategy' (Finney and Rishbeth 2006, 30). Consequently, we developed alternative ways for engaging young people and children in the projects.

Act II: Workshops at Schools

This initiative is also related to another previous activity carried out at School of Architecture and Planning of the University of Palermo: again, the activity mixed field research and teaching at University. The aim is to introduce students to the themes of participation with a specific social sector: primary and secondary school pupils (aged from seven to nine and from ten to fourteen). Most of these pupils belong to the lowest social classes: a significant number of them are at risk of failing at school and experiencing in the near future unemployment and social marginality; sometimes they also risk being involved in illegal activities or even crime. In such a context, as was highlighted by Skelton (2001), formal inquiries or interviews do not seem to address the aim of a proper understanding of young people's perspective and living. Following other research (Valentine et al. 2001; Skelton 2001; Finney and Rishbeth 2006) and previous experiences carried out by some colleagues of ours, we decided to establish a more interactive approach, supporting Sandercock's (2003) assertion of the shared benefits of creative approaches in research, pedagogy, education and practice.

In the school workshops, the technical expertise of university students coped with the common knowledge of local children and young people, applying a Socratic approach to an interaction method which involved also playing, drawing and manual and creative capabilities in general of children: starting from that, discussions and reflections were raised around key institutions, places and problems which formed part of their everyday geographies (school, home, streets and squares, sports and holidays, green spaces, mobility). Children (even the most 'problematic') were involved widely and successfully: it was important that they felt they were active participants in something and enjoyed themselves (Lo Piccolo et al. 2005 and 2008).

As regards methods, it is worth underlining the importance of the active involvement of university students in workshops at schools. 'Using' students as young planners and facilitators in the interaction with children is very effective because this reduces the age gap and creates complicity between the two groups: university students illustrate their activity as 'school' practice, similar to children's activity, and ask for the collaboration of children in order to better carry out their 'school work'. This 'call for help' avoids lack of trust, and nurtures interest and attention on the part of children (Lo Piccolo 2008).

In this sense, the people involved in the project can be said to have been 'exploited' or 'instrumentally used' by my colleagues and I in our double role of educators and planning researchers (whose research agenda was so far from the institutional one): involvement of school children not only aimed at letting marginal people's voices be heard, but also at 'exploiting' the opportunity to give more weight and credibility to researchers (and consequently trying to re-balance the power imbalance with institutions). The exploitation of the university students was strategic for two main reasons: first, to bridge the gap between adults and children; second (but not less significant), to give independence and intellectual autonomy to planning researchers in the face of (institutional) power.

With regard to this, along with above-mentioned actors (planning researchers, City Council planners, politicians, university students, school pupils) also school teachers took an active part in the project. If the teachers' role from a methodological point of view was intentionally limited (in order to prevent them from influencing children's answers and interfering in the children's interaction with the university students), from an organisation point of view, their role was essential. This added elements of complexity and even contradiction to the whole process and particularly to the power relationship with political actors and critical reflexivity (Lo Piccolo 2008).

Off Stage: Reflections on Ethical Dilemmas

All the experiences described above originated from an idea which was very much in favour of an inclusionary approach: according to this idea ethnic minorities, poor people, children and young people should be valued and acknowledged as social actors, competent individuals and key participants in all aspects of the projects. This assumption is largely described by many scholars with reference to collaborative planning practice (see for instance Innes and Booher 1999; Gunton et al. 2003). Most of those considerations also apply to planning research, including the critical aspects of power-imbalances, vulnerability and manipulation of the weakest sectors of civil society.

This inclusionary approach clashed with two ranks of problems: a. despite the formally collaborative nature of the processes, the City Council administration considered these research activities as 'collateral' and consequently did not acknowledge the inclusionary approach itself; b. the risk of an inaccurate critical selection of information and incorrect 'translation' of non technical knowledge on the part of researchers (even through the mediation of university students and associations), within a more general concern about misinformation as described by Forester (1989, 41-42). However, the planning context Forester refers to is in any case a (even formal) discursive context, where consultation (however it is organised and manipulated) is a significant part in the process. In the absence of an inclusionary, collaborative planning context, as well as of an explicit advocacy request expressed by any disempowered group, how should we construct an inclusionary knowledge? In order to build up an inclusionary research agenda, the described activities were undertaken as the only ones able to achieve significant (and not conventional) findings. All this must be extended also to the role and potential of university students involved, as educational commitment, in order to help them to change their own perspective in the process, and consequently being capable of assuming others' perspectives. Even with many compromises and hesitation, our effort was to build up an attitude of respect for others as a central moral quality to be actively developed through education and civic involvement.

A number of ethical dilemmas stem from the experiences described above, starting from the one posed when adults work with children and young people. If stressing this aspect may sound paradoxical, consequently getting to the extreme conclusion of dismissing such attempts of interaction with children and young people (Matthews and Limb 1999), the need for critical reflexivity is highlighted by many authors (Cloke et al. 2000; Matthews 2001; Valentine et al. 2001; McClintock et al. 2003) and emerges from our experience. The lesson learnt is that reflexivity should be adopted at all stages of the research process, locating and deconstructing the positionality of the researcher and the situatedness of knowledge. In fact, both researchers and researched are positioned simultaneously by a number of 'fields of power', including gender, age, class, ethnicity, race, sexuality and so on, combining with our research status, so that 'the facets of the self (…) are articulated as "positions" in a multidimensional geography of power relations' (Rose 1997, 308), which are partly due to the roles and rules which set the context, and partly to the 'power of personality' which everyone has. This requires researchers to be aware of the nature of the knowledge they use, how it relates to the knowledge used by others, and what kind of 'validity claims' are brought forward (Healey and Gilroy 1990, 26).

Moreover, as previously said, besides the power imbalance in the adult–child relationship we had to face the power imbalance in the researchers–politicians relationship. Furthermore, if we look at the activity carried out with immigrants and ZEN inhabitants, a similar power imbalance emerged in the local groups–researchers interaction; in that case, however, the ethical dilemma was mitigated by the very nature of the experience: from the very beginning, the experience was illustrated as being a mere activity contributing to teaching methods and university research, a voluntary activity with a free and independent call for help and cooperation. Despite that, the risk of using people in the research as 'guinea pigs' still remains.

From the very beginning the research team was well aware of how fragile the projects were because of the policy followed by the municipal administration and lack of experience of local planners in carrying out participation projects. The research team was also aware that City Council planners were weakly motivated: they did not 'trust' their political representatives since they were aware of the simply rhetorical and instrumental nature of the entire process. Thomas (2005, 239) reminds us there are 'good reasons for wanting to "stay close" to practice, but staying close carries with it a danger of "going native"' and we were precisely in the position of running that risk. So, why did we accept?

What was said above shows that we were aware that politics might exploit the entire project and thus put it into jeopardy; in other words, we were perfectly conscious that options for constructive engagement were anyway limited. Despite all this, what pushed us to carry out the project was the will to 'give a say' and 'raise the consciousness' of all the people involved, helped and supported by other actors (school teachers, welfare workers and associations). Our motivation relied on the assumption that any sort of collaborative planning research agenda (notwithstanding its potential misuses and distortion) will produce significant additional 'social capital' benefits such as improved knowledge (Gunton, Day and Williams 2003) that can be considered as a step towards emancipatory knowledge. Even if all the conditions as described in Innes and Booher (1999) to define emancipatory knowledge did not occur in our cases (due to – for example – the lack of mutual trust or the unequal level of respect and access to information), a step forward was undertaken. If we agree with Innes and Booher (1999, 418) when they remind us that 'communicative rationality represents an ideal, rather like that of scientific rationality, which is never fully achieved in practice, though it is a goal or template against which to judge research or communicative practice', and that 'what is mostly missing from the evaluation [of consensus building outcomes] is an assessment of the long-term effects, whose importance is just beginning to be evident' (ibid., 420), these arguments can explain and justify our decision of accepting the risks of the described research projects.

Epilogue

The ethical theory we assumed in our research experience was inspired – as stated in the first section of the chapter – by the communicative ethics of collaborative planning, despite the difficulties of applying such a theory in our context, as in many other 'uncollaborative places'. The principal question raised from this chapter is, in fact, how to assume the inclusive process of communicative ethics (Forester 1989; Healey 1997) in planning research. The experiences described in the chapter show attempts to face this issue in an uncollaborative context, where the main lesson learned regards the need and constraint of assuming as researcher an ambiguous role, which is neither 'with' (on the side of) institutions nor 'against' (in the face of) them, exploiting the educational role in order to carry on somehow an inclusionary research project.

In this sense, the notion of ethics is closely related to the idea of a real possibility and, particularly, of the possibility of acting (Tagliagambe 2000). So ethics refers to an active capability that develops a willing to act, that is *practice*. As a metaphor but also as a practical example, some Italian radical planners like Scandurra (2000) suggest the adoption of Socrates' model, walking along Athens' streets, interviewing himself and others on what it is right to do, continuously re-discussing the present laws and political system, developing a collective quest for truth. In this interpretation of intellectual/reflexive action, the (planning) researcher does not claim to be speaking on behalf of the city, but just as 'one voice' of the city, holding 'a moral conversation in which the capacity to reverse perspectives, that is, the willingness to reason from the others' point of view, and the sensitivity to their voice is paramount' (Corbridge 1998, 46). Posing questions on the destiny of the city, of its laws regulating the life of the community, he/she poses questions on the *ethos* of the *polis* (Barcellona 1995), with no gap between theory and practice, knowledge and action.

A similar approach can be found in the thought of the US pragmatists, and in particular in John Dewey's writings, where the development of knowledge of the world and acting in the world belong to the same process of learning and researching through experience. In her review of the influence of US pragmatist philosophy on the development of theories about the nature, purpose, ideals and methods of planning, Healey (2008) highlights that 'the core of this "unique method" was the habit of questioning and exploring, testing answers and discoveries in relation to empirical evidence of one kind or another.' In all those approaches – no matter if influenced by the Socratic model or the pragmatist philosophy – the role of critical inquiry is essential, as testified even by our experience, in order to develop and support democratic polities, or at least inclusive and progressive research agendas.

This value-driven approach can privilege – from time to time – concepts like equity and justice, sustainable development and human rights, inclusion of excluded minority groups and defence of disadvantaged people. If this value-driven approach has been theorised, and even applied in practice, in the research field a contrast between a researcher's value-driven perspective and a research's rigour and (presumption of) objectivity can occur. In such a radical approach – as well as in the discursive ethics of collaborative planning – there is an epistemological conflict that remains as one of the more unsolved problems in the research field: how to conciliate the value-driven approach of the collaborative – as well as radical – planning theoretical framework with the overall duty of rigour and objectivity in research?

Mazza (2002, 15) questions '*how* planners must develop their political function', raising doubts 'whether it is just and useful that planning theory pursues and defines a clear moral purpose and a progressive political ideology. (…) In other words the question is *how* planners must develop their political function'. While Mazza puts emphasis on the (proper) professional duties of planners, which are rooted in a somehow 'pure' technical ground, he notes that 'on the contrary, the conscious or unconscious will of considering planning as "the fourth branch of government" is still very strong within planners of various political and technical ideas – e.g. participation supporters and technocrats, loyal and adverse to ideological claims to objectivity, etc. – and it is often linked to the belief that it is possible to pursue a clear moral aim and a progressive (or conservative) policy without assuming a partisan stand'.

If we move from the theoretical level of planning practice towards the epistemological level of planning research (and its ethical challenges), the relationship (in the form of opposition) between a moral and partisan stand is overlaid by the relationship (in the form of potential contradiction) between rigour and objectivity on the one hand and value-driven knowledge – and even ideology – on the other. If this potential contradiction is anytime present in the research agenda and it also comes up from many experiences reported in the chapter, the claim for a pure, neutral and consequently 'problem-solving' technical knowledge is not the solution in the field of planning research.

Despite the intriguing reflections on the (potential) role of the formalised technical knowledge which are illustrated in Mazza (2002), in the light of the described experiences the opposition technical-common knowledge does not occur and it is substituted by a more fragmented, articulated – and even controversial – system of relationships: there is no 'one' monolithic, common knowledge (and it does not coincide – as stated in Mazza (2002, 18) – with the political discourse knowledge), but a plural, sometimes conflicting, puzzle of common knowledges, which are undoubtedly difficult to fit with each other, or to be used in the construction of an overall picture.

As McClintock et al. (2003, 723) highlight, there are a number of options to cope with these complex dilemmas, from the 'neutral' position of assuming 'objectivity' as an ethic, up to the possibility of considering an ethic of 'responsibility', based on self-reflection and the awareness of possible positions for a researcher. If we do so, embracing dialogic and reflexive approaches to research, standard approaches to ethical research practice become increasingly complex and open to negotiation (Cloke et al. 2000). In our experiences, we tried to put this approach to an empirical test always falling into contradiction and ambiguity. Taking into account what we have learned from our experience, reflexivity does not dissolve ethical tensions but 'opens up possibilities for new ethical and moral maps with which to explore ethical terrains more appropriately and more honestly' (Cloke et al. 2000, 133).

Indeed, the principles of rigour and objectivity come from the positivist research tradition, which has been developed in a Western epistemological framework. Many scholars in the fields of geography and sociology have questioned these epistemological assumptions and their ethics, for their lack of attention towards the implications of power relationships. Both critical and feminist approaches have focused on the role of power regarding gender, class, race and education, highlighting the historical role of social science research to keep and preserve dominant hegemonies. Humanistic geographers have consequently rejected the ideal of objectivity and recognised the fundamental role of subjectivity in the efforts of engaging reflexively with research. Planning researchers are as much involved with this process and they have to face the same type of challenges and dilemmas.

This critical approach involves also an attention towards the role and influence of emotions on the research process. Damasio (1999) has demonstrated the role of emotion in rational thinking. Ansell and Van Blerk (2005) argues, on the basis of their research experience, that the exclusion of emotions from most of the official research projects' descriptions does not imply that emotions are not taken into account in the design and management of research. The same arguments are provided by Finney and Rishbeth (2006) in their research story-telling on the engagement of marginalised groups, or by Laurier and Parr (2000) in their acknowledgement of how emotions and emotional exchanges can differently orientate researchers in their work. Widdowfield (2000, 200) highlights the need for researchers to engage with and reflect on their own emotions embodied in the research process, which is a two-way process whereby 'not only does the researcher affect the research process but they are themselves affected by this process'.

Even according to our experience, emotion and reason are not opposites and the role of emotion in the research activity is strictly linked to ethics, as emotion can not be ignored or denied as a part of a moral response to the world. Thomas (2005, 245) notes that 'Nussbaum (1990), for example, suggests that the development of clear moral perception involves the development of appropriate emotional and imaginative capacities, and Murdoch (1985) illustrates how a kind of re-imagining and re-thinking of what another person is can be an important moral development'.

If we look at emotion just as a purely individual phenomenon (and this perspective revolves primarily around a strong sense of the individual that has deeply influenced research), it have to be related only to a someway limited conception of ethics. But our research experience in participative processes reminds us that research is not only an individual activity, and it is the result of mutual interactions in a collective process. Moreover, as Solomon (1997, 300) argues, 'most of our emotions are social, not only in their context but in their content'. This view of emotions as social is also fundamental to the 'ethics of care' of Carol Gilligan (1982), which calls for a situational ethics, wherein relationships with others are of paramount importance (Ansell and Van Blerk 2005).

Finally, I wish to stress another implication, which emerges from our experience and which is also highlighted by McClintock and al. (2003, 723): an ethic of 'responsibility', based on self-reflection, entails removing a priori that doing research is 'a good thing'. This leads to some conclusions that have already been expressed (Lo Piccolo and Thomas 2008) in reference to the necessary distinction between scholarly and policy/governance related projects, in order to escape from the ambiguity of playing multiple (and even conflicting) roles in the attempt of 'squaring the circle' (Thomas 2005, 239) by obeying institutional requests on the one side and by writing 'shadow works' to fulfil the moral obligation of truth and rigour on the other side.

The experiences we have described emphasise this aspect and show the compromises and strategies used at least to attenuate, if not solve, this dilemma. So, this chapter has probably raised more questions than answers, and as such it represents a reflective piece rather than a guide for (research) action; but there can be little doubt that future research actions in the field will be in need of these and further reflections.

Acknowledgements

I would like to thank my colleagues Giulia Bonafede, Marco Picone and Ignazia Pinzello for their persistence – in most of the phases of our research projects – in our interaction with the City Council administration. Ideas, comments and field research were shared with Rida Berradi, Giada Bini, Davide Leone, Licia Giacopelli, Giuseppe Lo Bocchiaro and my students. I would also like to thank Leontine Regine and Sergio Lo Verde of the S.A.L.I. Tavola Tonda Network of Associations, and Bice Mortillaro Salatiello and Liliana Presti of the ZEN Insieme Association for their great support to the project. A special thank to Patsy Healey and Huw Thomas for their comments on earlier drafts.

References

Ansell, N. and Van Blerk, L. (2005), 'Joining the Conspiracy? Negotiating Ethics and Emotions in Researching (around) AIDS in Southern Africa', *Ethics, Place and Environment* 8:1, 61-82.

Attili, G., Decandia, L. and Scandurra, E. (eds) (2007), *Storie di Città: Verso un'Urbanistica del Quotidiano* (Rome: Edizioni Interculturali).

Badami, A., Picone, M. and Schilleci, F. (eds) (2008), *Città nell'Emergenza. Progettare e Costruire tra Gibellina e lo ZEN* (Palermo: Palumbo).

Barcellona, P. (1995), *Democrazia: Quale Via di Scampo?* (Molfetta: La Meridiana).

Bonafede, G. and Lo Piccolo, F. (2007), 'Cronache ZEN: La Questione Abitativa tra Assenza di Politiche Pubbliche, Pratiche dal Basso ed Arte della Negoziazione', *Archivio di Studi Urbani e Regionali* XXXVIII:90, 47-66.

Brand, R. and Gaffikin, F. (2007), 'Collaborative Planning in an Uncollaborative World', *Planning Theory* 6:3, 282-313.

Burby, R.J. (2003), 'Making Plans that Matter: Citizen Involvement and Government Action', *Journal of the American Planning Association* 69:1, 33-49.

Busacca, P. and Gravagno, F. (eds) (2005), *A Mille Mani* (Florence: Alinea).

Cloke, P. et al. (2000), 'Ethics, Reflexivity and Research: Encounters with Homeless People', *Ethics, Place and Environment* 3:2, 133-154.

Corbridge, S. (1998), 'Development Ethics: Distance, Difference, Plausibility', *Ethics, Place and Environment* 1:1, 35-53.

Damasio, A. (1999), *The Feeling of What Happens: Body, Emotion and the Making of Consciousness* (New York: Harcourt Brace and Company).

Finney, N. and Rishbeth, C. (2006), 'Engaging with Marginalised Groups in Public Open Space Research: The Potential of Collaboration and Combined Methods', *Planning Theory and Practice* 7:1, 27-46.

Forester, J. (1989), *Planning in the Face of Power* (Berkeley: University of California Press).

Forester, J. (1999), *The Deliberative Practitioner: Encouraging Participatory Planning Processes* (Cambridge, MA and London: MIT Press).

Gilligan, C. (1982), *In a Different Voice: Psychological Theory and Women's Development* (Cambridge, MA: Harvard University Press).

Gunton, T.I., Day, J.C. and Williams, P.W. (2003), 'Evaluating Collaborative Planning', *Environments* 31:3, 1-11.

Habermas, J. (1981), *The Theory of Communicative Action: Reason and the Rationalization of Society* (Boston: Beacon Press).

Habermas, J. (1989), *The Theory of Communicative Action. Lifeworld and System: A Critique of Functionalist Reason* (Boston: Beacon Press).

Healey, P. (1997), *Collaborative Planning: Shaping Places in Fragmented Societies* (Houndmills and London: Macmillan).

Healey, P. (1998), 'Collaborative Planning in a Stakeholder Society', *Town Planning Review* 69:1, 1-22.

Healey, P. (2003), 'Collaborative Planning *in perspective*', *Planning Theory* 2:2, 101-123.

Healey, P. (2008), 'The Pragmatic Tradition in Planning Thought', *Journal of Planning Education and Research* OnlineFirst, published on 8 October 2008 as doi:10.1177/0739456X08325175.

Healey, P. and Gilroy, R. (1990), 'Towards a People-sensitive Planning', *Planning Practice and Research* 5:3, 21-29.

Innes, J.E. (1990), *Knowledge and Public Policy: The Search for Meaningful Indicators*, 2nd edition (New Brunswick, NJ: Transaction).

Innes, J.E. (1995), 'Planning Theory's Emerging Paradigm: Communicative Action and Interactive Practice', *Journal of Planning Education and Research* 14:4, 183-90.

Innes, J.E. (1996), 'Planning Through Consensus Building: A New View of the Comprehensive Planning Ideal', *Journal of the American Planning Association* 62:4, 460-472.

Innes, J.E. (1998), 'Information in Communicative Planning', *Journal of the American Planning Association* 64:1, 52-63.

Innes, J.E. (2004), 'Consensus Building: Clarifications for the Critics', *Planning Theory* 3:1, 5-20.

Innes, J.E. and Booher, D.E. (1999), 'Consensus Building and Complex Adaptive Systems: A Framework for Evaluating Collaborative Planning', *Journal of the American Planning Association* 65:4, 412-423.

Laurier, E. and Parr, H. (2000), 'Emotions and Interviewing in Health and Disability Research', *Ethics, Place and Environment* 3:1, 98-102.

Lindblom, C. and Cohen, D.K. (1979), *Usable Knowledge: Social Science and Social Problem Solving* (New Haven, CT: Yale University Press).

Lo Piccolo, F. (1996), 'Urban Renewal in the Historic Centre of Palermo', *Planning Practice and Research* 11:2, 217-225.

Lo Piccolo, F. (2000), 'Palermo, a City in Transition: Saint Benedict "The Moor" *versus* Saint Rosalia', *International Planning Studies* 5:1, 87-115.

Lo Piccolo, F. (2008), 'Planning Research 'with' Minorities in Palermo: Negotiating Ethics and Commitments in a Participatory Process', *Planning Practice and Research* 23:2, 187-209.

Lo Piccolo, F. and Leone, D. (2008), 'New Arrivals, Old Places: Demographic Changes and New Planning Challenges in Palermo and Naples', *International Planning Studies* 13:4, 361-389.

Lo Piccolo, F. and Thomas, H. (2008), 'Research Ethics in Planning: A Framework for Discussion', *Planning Theory* 7:1, 7-23.

Lo Piccolo, F. et al. (2005), 'Spazi Urbani della Differenza: Ruolo delle Minoranze e dei Nuovi Soggetti nella Analisi e Definizione di Politiche Urbane Innovative nel Centro Storico di Palermo', in Piera Busacca and Filippo Gravagno (eds).

Lo Piccolo, F. et al. (2008), 'Per una Cittadinanza Attiva: Esercizi di Interazione nella Analisi e Definizione di Politiche Urbane Innovative per il Quartiere ZEN di Palermo', in Alessandra Badami et al. (eds).

Maciocco, G., Deplano, G. and Marchi, G. (eds) (2000), *Etica e Pianificazione Spaziale. Scritti in Onore di Fernando Clemente* (Milan: Franco Angeli).

Magnaghi, A. (ed.) (1991), *Il Territorio dell'Abitare. Lo Sviluppo Locale come Alternativa Strategica*, 2nd edition (Milan: Franco Angeli).

Magnaghi, A. (ed.) (1998), *Il Territorio degli Abitanti. Società Locali e Autosostenibilità* (Milan: Dunod).

Matthews, H. (1998), 'The Geography of Children: Some Ethical and Methodological Considerations for Project and Dissertation Work', *Journal of Geography in Higher Education* 22:3, 311-324.

Matthews, H. (2001), 'Participatory Structures and the Youth of Today: Engaging Those Who Are Hardest to Reach', *Ethics, Place and Environment* 4:2, 153-159.

Matthews, H. and Limb, M. (1999), 'Defining an Agenda for the Geography of Children: Review and Prospect', *Progress in Human Geography* 23:1, 61-90.

Mattina, G. (2007), *Il Quartiere San Filippo Neri 'ZEN' di Palermo* (Rome: Caritas Italiana – Edizioni IDOS).

Mazza, L. (2002), 'Technical Knowledge and Planning Actions', *Planning Theory* 1:1, 11-26.

McClintock, D. et al. (2003), 'Metaphors for Reflecting on Research Practice: Researching *with* People', *Journal of Environmental Planning and Management* 46:5, 715-731.

Olufemi, O. and Reeves, D. (2004), 'Lifeworld Strategies of Women Who find Themselves Homeless in South Africa', *Planning Theory and Practice* 5:1, 69-91.

Paba, G. (2003), *Movimenti Urbani. Pratiche di Costruzione Sociale della Città* (Milan: Franco Angeli).

Pinzello, I. and Quartarone, C. (eds) (2005), *La Città e i Bambini. Per un Laboratorio di Pianificazione e Progettazione Urbana* (Palermo: Palumbo).

Reardon, K. and Forester, J. (2008), 'Planning, Hope, and Struggle in the Wake of Katrina: Ken Reardon on the New Orleans Planning Initiative', *Planning Theory and Practice* 9:4, 518-540.

Reason, P. and Bradbury, H. (eds) (2007), *The SAGE Handbook of Action Research. Participative Inquiry and Practice*, 2nd edition (London: Sage).

Rose, G. (1997), 'Situating Knowledges: Positionality, Reflexivities and Other Tactics', *Progress in Human Geography* 21:3, 305-320.

Sandercock, L. (1998), *Making the Invisible Visible: A Multicultural Planning History* (Berkeley: University of California Press).

Sandercock, L. (2003), 'Out of the Closet: The Importance of Stories and Storytelling in Planning Practice', *Planning Theory and Practice* 4:1, 11-28.

Scandurra, E. (2000), 'Fare il Piano: Verso un Nuovo Impegno Etico', in Giovanni Maciocco et al. (eds).

Schon, D. (1983), *The Reflective Practitioner: How Professionals Think in Action* (New York: Basic Books).

Sciascia, A. (2003), *Tra le Modernità dell'Architettura. La Questione del Quartiere ZEN 2 di Palermo* (Palermo: L'Epos).

Skelton, T. (2001), 'Girls in the Club: Researching Working Class Girls' Lives', *Ethics, Place and Environment* 4:2, 167-173.

Solomon, R.C. (1996), 'Emotions, Ethics and the "Internal Ought"', *Cognition and Emotion* 10:5, 529-550.

Tagliagambe, S. (2000), 'Che Cosa Significa Etica della Pianificazione nelle Organizzazioni Complesse?', in Giovanni Maciocco et al. (eds).

Thomas, H. (2005), 'Pressures, Purpose and Collegiality in UK Planning Education', *Planning Theory and Practice* 6:2, 238-247.

Valentine, G. et al. (2001), 'The Ethical and Methodological Complexities of Doing Research with "Vulnerable" Young People', *Ethics, Place and Environment* 4:2, 119-125.

Watson, V. (2006), 'Deep Difference: Diversity, Planning and Ethics', *Planning Theory* 5:1, 31-50.

Widdowfield, R. (2000), 'The Place of Emotions in Academic Research', *Area* 32:2, 199-208.

Chapter 17
Conclusions

Francesco Lo Piccolo and Huw Thomas

This book has been, in part, exploratory. It has provided a novel space for discussions about the ways in which ethics plays a part in research in planning. It is in the nature of an edited collection, and in some ways one of its strengths, that contributions travel in various directions from their initial starting point of the editors' brief. This allows for a breadth and diversity of thought which a single-authored text would be very unlikely to have. In this chapter we do not attempt summaries of key points from chapters, nor do we impose an artificial pattern on them. We do no more than draw out some themes and issues which have emerged in the book, as a basis for future discussion.

The Variety of Planning Research

The book provides a reminder of the many kinds of planning research which are undertaken. Patsy Healey's chapter provides a typology of types of research, derived from the relationship of the research activity and output to the policy process. Each type of research involves the researcher in different kinds of relationships. There is a relationship, first, with those encountered in the research process, including people traditionally considered as 'subjects' of research. For example, is the researcher here to assist them, as in Forester and Laws' chapter; or – at least in part – to write an academic paper or thesis about them, as Libby Porter was as she began the research she describes? The different kinds of work also involve different relationships outside the immediate field of research – there are contractual relations involved in consultancy, for example; while academic researchers may find themselves in the kinds of power-networks described by Imrie and Goonewardena. As Forester and Laws remind us, ethics begins with how we treat each other, i.e. with social relations; and the various kinds of research take place on different ethical terrains.

What constitutes the 'ethical terrain' can be subject to disagreement and debate, and as Goonewardena and Verma point out (albeit in different ways) there is a real danger that ethics will be understood in a way which insulates the researcher and his/her immediate work from broader concerns, including certain sets of (possibly unjust) social relations. Some might think that commercial consultancy, as discussed in Healy's chapter, may sometimes be in danger of doing just that – defining the realm of ethics narrowly so that the broader socio-political consequences of one's actions are not subject to personal or other scrutiny. Of course, it may well be that a consultant for much of the time believes that the broader social context is essentially just, so that insulation is not problematical for her or him.

Those who are troubled by broader contexts within which planning research is conducted hold on to the thought that the ethical terrains are not immutable. For example, the nature of university life in western countries may have changed as universities respond to neoliberalism (Whiteley et al. 2008), but the details of the response can vary from place to place, and as Goonewardena points out political struggle to change universities for the better (as part of wider social change) may be the appropriate ethical action to take. Yet, even as the planning researcher engages in political struggle on a broad front, that struggle must also connect with the question of how to act here and now in the daily routines of work. At times the minutiae of everyday life as a researcher can be easily related to the broader struggle (choosing thick rather than thin ethical stances, in Forester and Laws' terminology, might be politically as well as epistemologically motivated). But many would be persuaded by the kind of arguments put forward by Taylor's chapter, and resist a crude consequentialism where all acts are judged in relation to their efficacy in bringing about longer term change. Consequences matter, but most will baulk at the idea that one kind of consequence trumps all others. How then to judge what to pay attention to…what to accord weight in…how to read the ethical terrain? The metaphor may change, but the task remains a difficult one.

The Variety of Approaches to Ethics

The book has not tried to argue a case for any particular approach to ethics, but certain shared themes emerge from some contributions. One of these themes might be characterised as a questioning of the distinction between planning and research, or more broadly between research and any other aspect of life. Planning theorist such as Schon (1983) and others influenced by American Pragmatism have emphasised that understanding the world (a broad construal of what research is about) is an activity bound up with living and acting in the world (Healey 2008). The chapter by Forester and Laws in this volume bears the influence of this tradition, where research is integrally bound up with the practice of planning. Verma, similarly, emphasises the way in which an understanding of things cannot be divorced from the broader purpose served by that understanding. An implication of this approach to research is that the researcher must not be defined simply by competence in certain techniques (though some competence may be a necessary characteristic of being a researcher); more significantly, the researcher should be certain kind of person.

What kind of person might this be? We will use a thought from Nigel Taylor's chapter as a starting point for some reflections, without wishing to impute any particular view or thesis to Taylor beyond what he has said in his chapter. It is only fair to point out that Nigel Taylor was not asked by us as editors to address the question of what kind of person a researcher might be directly, but his chapter does suggest that the researcher should have a reverence for truth. In the abstract no one is likely to disagree that a concern for truth is surely a good place to start in thinking about the ethical qualities of a researcher. Yet, one need not be a hardened post-modernist to realise that there may be more than one claim to truth in play when research in planning is involved. Without recourse to some kind of radical relativism one can make sense of struggles over 'whose truth?' in the pretty unsophisticated terms of, for example, the possibility of there being different windows on the world (the blind men and the elephant). With a little more sophistication one might argue that different frameworks for understanding people – with their associated ontologies – are compatible, but not reducible to each other (explanations in terms of intentionality/meaning and explanations in terms of neural mechanisms/or even underlying social structures might fit this bill). If one holds that there is no sharp fact-value dichotomy, that to understand the world in a certain way is to take up a moral standpoint then as one researches/experiences the world there will always be room for different ways of re-arranging/re-interpreting one's emerging, always provisional knowledge of the world along with one's ethical perspective on it. On this view, radically different kinds of approaches to economics involve differences in how people (as they are and how they might be) are conceived, for example, and that makes the choice of economic theory more than the technical choice Healy sees it as. Some of our contributors would argue different cases again, but for our purposes all that is necessary is to note that planning researchers need an ethical sensitivity which sees it as more than a personal quest for truth and understands the complexities of the circumstances under which research may be undertaken.

Some chapters investigate the ethical challenges (and consequent compromises) of inclusionary research agendas, as in the case of Australian Indigenous People (Porter), of the Vancouver Collingwood Neighbourhood House organisation (Attili) or of the marginalised groups in Palermo (Lo Piccolo). As Heron (1996) highlights, there are two orders of reasons for having people as partners in research: on political grounds citizens have a right to participate in decisions that concern and affect them, and that is the democratisation of research; while on epistemological grounds people participate in their own knowing, and that practical knowledge is the fulfilment of the knowledge quest; McClintock et al. (2003) add to these motivations Freire's interest in 'raising consciousness' (Freirc 1972). A number of ethical dilemmas stem from the experiences described in those above mentioned chapters, placing the activity of research in webs of power-laden social relations. If stressing this aspect of power imbalance between different 'subjects' of research may sound paradoxical, consequently getting to the extreme conclusion of dismissing such attempts of inclusionary research, the need for critical reflexivity is highlighted by many authors (Cloke et al. 2000; Matthews 2001; Valentine et al. 2001; McClintock et al. 2003) and emerges from the experiences of our book.

In their case studies, Libby Porter and Giovanni Attili both illustrate how their efforts to be ethical researchers involved a sensitivity to different claims to truth, and the ways that such claims (and the research that may underlie them) are bound up with the wielding of power. In these circumstances planning researchers must relate themselves and their work to the structures of power in which they are enmeshed and find a position they feel they can accept ethically. There can be many reasons why a researcher may feel uncomfortable with a research project he or she is undertaking, but to the extent that some of those reasons can be foreseen then the researcher is ethically obliged to exercise foresight. The chapters by Niraj Verma, Laura Lieto and Anthony Brinkman illustrate in their different ways how the framing of research is a purposeful activity which has ethical and political implications. Research problems do not present themselves ready framed. So, for example, framing them in ways which require certain techniques to be used is to promote change (or no change) of a certain kind in the world. Not framing certain problems, not asking certain questions – as Brinkman and Lieto show – serves a certain social purpose. We can say that it helps create a certain kind of world, and what kind of world we have is an ethical question for the researcher. Understanding this can help a researcher avoid becoming involved in a project which later throws up dilemmas which appear intractable. Prudence about what to become involved with is an important virtue for a researcher. But what constitutes virtuous prudence, as opposed for example to self-interest, is a matter resolved only by relating the virtue to its broader context. Prudence is a virtue when exercised in relation to good and just ends; but what those might be is something which a researcher must learn to be sensitive to in context.

Developing an Ethical Sensitivity

For some, there are obvious resources on which to draw when they are troubled. There may be faith communities or other kinds of communities with established sets of values, sacred texts (their sacredness will be established in relation to a socio-spiritual tradition, a kind of community) and wise people, and – sometimes – things they have written. Some may draw upon these resources as authoritative sources of advice and knowledge, which help an individual develop a particular kind of ethical sensibility (and hence a way of living in the world) which is shared by others, past and present. Others may see them as sources of ideas which an individual can evaluate in relation to the essentially personal project of living their lives. Whether any sense can be made of what such an evaluation of the latter kind involves is a difficult question, but for our purposes it is enough to note that people often seek advice and find it helpful. Some of the authors of our more autobiographical chapters (Healey, Schilleci, Lo Piccolo, Porter, Healy and Attili) discussed their work and dilemmas with others at some time or another. Patsy Healey mentions her research team; and Libby Porter makes a point of mentioning that she did seek advice and 'sounding-boards' as her understanding of the nature of her work changed. Adrian Healy has a reference point in his company's code. But overall, the sense one receives is of researchers grappling alone with these matters – buying in, or maybe shipping out, as they see fit, but essentially steering their own course. Daniela Mello's account of the PhD experience in Italy shows that this rather atomised environment can extend to the socialisation process – not only is there no systematic approach to addressing ethics in research, but it is clear that the experiences of many PhD students has left them seeing no particular purpose or advantage in thinking about ethics.

In these kinds of circumstances, introducing research protocols which demand that ethical approval be received before research can commence runs a serious risk of becoming no more than a tick box exercise of the kind warned against by both Goonewardena and Thomas. Becoming a researcher – as much as becoming a planner – should involve a further stage in the process of becoming a particular kind of person (as Thomas would put it, a virtuous person). Doing so is difficult when universities appear to value (and encourage) the kind of commercialism and competitiveness described by Imrie. First, an atmosphere is created in which the sense of a common endeavour in pursuit of something more worthwhile than self-interest finds it difficult to take root. Second, it alienates researchers from their work, as they worry about achieving their 'outputs', rather than how their work contributes to the development and flourishing of particular kinds of social relations (and how it might contribute to their own flourishing) (Valentine 2005).

Moreover, references to 'further stages' in processes assume that a process is already under way. Of course, in a sense it is, but many social theorists have pointed to what is at best a disruption or dislocation and at worst a loss of a capacity and desire for serious moral reflection and discussion in advanced capitalist countries (Fevre 2000; MacIntyre 1981). The coarsening of the terms in which morality is discussed publicly reflects particular socio-economic conditions, and the effectiveness of a specific political project in getting so many people to see the world and themselves in a certain way. It also reminds us of the lack of encouragement there often is to engage with, and the real difficulty many of us now have in accessing, conceptual frameworks which can capture the moral-psychological depths and complexities of people's lives and the challenges they bring up. For many, the great historical faiths provided sophisticated resources on which they drew; for others, literature and the arts can do so. For a variety of reasons these are not so widely drawn upon, in any social milieu. More significantly, their usefulness depends upon their contributing to, and being interpreted within, a context, a way of life, in which people can be brought to see how they have some purchase. These ways of life may sometimes revolve around employment, such as craft-working (Sennett 2008). In the context of planning research the challenge for researchers (and managers of researchers) is to create circumstances in which there is a shared sense of purpose as to the nature of the work, and an understanding (through practise) of its having a depth, complexity and significance which can only be fully appreciated through using a sophisticated set of value-infused ideas and frameworks. This can happen, arguably for example, in the case of the Chicago School (Jackson 1984). The pressures on contemporary higher education in at least some parts of the world mean that it is not easy to create such research communities, or sustain them; but we remain optimistic enough to continue the attempt, and know that many others are of the same mind. Perhaps this book will help with that task in some small way.

References

Cloke, P. et al. (2000), 'Ethics, Reflexivity and Research: Encounters with Homeless People', *Ethics, Place and Environment* 3:2, 133-154.

Fevre, R. (2000), *The Demoralization of Western Culture* (London: Continuum).

Freire, P. (1972), *Pedagogy of the Oppressed* (New York: Herder and Herder).

Healey, P. (2008), 'The Pragmatic Tradition in Planning Thought', *Journal of Planning Education and Research* OnlineFirst, published on 8 October 2008 as doi:10.1177/0739456X08325175.

Heron, J. (1996), *Co-operative Inquiry: Research into the Human Condition* (London: Sage).

Jackson, P. (1984), 'Social Disorganization and Moral Order in the City', *Transactions of the Institute of British Geographers* 9:2, 168-180.

MacIntyre, A. (1981), *After Virtue* (London: Duckworth).

Matthews, H. (2001), 'Participatory Structures and the Youth of Today: Engaging Those Who Are Hardest to Reach', *Ethics, Place and Environment* 4:2, 153-159.

McClintock, D. et al. (2003), 'Metaphors for Reflecting on Research Practice: Researching *with* People', *Journal of Environmental Planning and Management* 46:5, 715-731.

Schon, D. (1983), *The Reflective Practitioner* (London: Temple Smith).

Sennett, R. (2008), *The Craftsman* (London: Yale University Press).

Valentine, G. (2005), 'Geography and Ethics: Moral Geographies? Ethical Commitment in Research and Teaching', *Progress in Human Geography* 29:4, 483-487.

Valentine, G. et al. (2001), 'The Ethical and Methodological Complexities of Doing Research with "Vulnerable" Young People', *Ethics, Place and Environment* 4:2, 119-125.

Whiteley, R., Aguiar, L., and Martin, T. (2008), 'The Neoliberal Transnational University: The Case of UBC Okanagan', *Capital and Class* 96, 115-142.

Index

Aalborg Charter (sustainability) 47
academic research
    capital 81-5
    contractualism 74-85
    freedom 107-8
    planning 71-85, 85-9
'academic rock stars' 67
academics and consultancy 157-8
act-utilitarianism *see* classical
    utilitarianism
Adorno, Theodor 57, 67, 71, 79
advocacy planning research 207-18
    advocacy awareness 212-13
    Collingwood Neighbourhood House
        Research Project 207-17
    framing the story 213-14, 214-15
    power of narration 210-11
    qualitative research 208
    situational ethics 208-9
    speaking for others 215-17
AESOP (Association of European Schools
    of Planning) 2-3
AICP *see* American Institute of Certified
    Planners
air pollution in Los Angeles 47-8
American Association of University
    Professors (AAUP) 107
American Council on Education (ACE) 107
American Institute of Certified Planners
    (AICP) 114, 115
American Planning Association (APA) 114
American Pragmatism
    ethics 6, 42-5
    human failings 43-4
    planning 248, 256
    purposeful categories 44-5
    structural categories 44-5
An Introduction to the Principles of Morals
    and Legislation 15
APA *see* American Planning Association
Apotex (pharmaceutical company) 59

Arcades Project 57-69
Aristotle 31, 35, 49, 65, 125
Arno river flood 194
Association of European Schools of
    Planning (AESOP) 2-3
Australia and indigenous people research
    219-27, 227-8, 257
autobiographical approach 4
Autonomous Institute of Public Housing
    (IACP) 239
'auxiliary hypotheses' 50
AWAP *see* public water company
Azienda Foreste Demaniali (forestry
    agency) 138

'balance' rhetoric 47-8
Bentham, Jeremy 15, 17-18
Beutler, Lisa 183
bio-politics 196
Blackredge, Paul 65-6
book
    organisation and contents 6-9
    purpose 4-5
    summary 255-60
'bounded rationality' concept 43
'business-facing' orientation in planning
    schools 77-8

Calthorpe, Peter 47
Cameron, Ewen 57-8
Canadian Association of University
    Teachers (CAUT) 59-60
Canadian Government research councils 60
Cardiff University research ethics 158
careers in research planning practice 163-6
Carson, Rachel 49
CAUT *see* Canadian Association of
    University Teachers
'character planning' 52
Christian consequentialists 13-14
cities and social structure 1

classical utilitarianism 14-16
CNH *see* Collingwood Neighbourhood
    House
code of ethics
    consultancy 146-50
    professional conduct 114, 115
cognitive human failings 43-4
College of Physicians and Surgeons of
    Ontario (CPSO) 60
Collingwood Neighbourhood House (CNH)
    Research Project 207-17, 257
community planning and naturalistic
    research ethic 181-2
complacency in travel demand forecasts 113
conflicts of interest and consultancy 155-7
consequentialism
    classical utilitarianism 14-16
    consequentialists 13-14
    definition 13
    ethical education of researchers 25-7
    external world 141
    right action and good life 6
    truth and truthfulness 25-6
    utilitarian 17-20, 20-5, 26-7
consultancy 145-58, 158-9
    academics 157-8
    code of ethics 146-50, 157-8
    conflicts of interest 155-7
    ethics in practice 150-7
    honesty 153
    impartiality 150-2
    integrity 153
    intellectual ownership 154-5
    'is the client always right?' 152-3
    openness 154
    research methods 157
    transparency 154
contractualism and academic research
    74-85
corporate behaviour 7
CPSO *see* College of Physicians and
    Surgeons of Ontario
Crime and Punishment 24

Das Kapital 67
Department of the Environment (DoE)
    development plans 166-7, 172
    valuation/impact research 164

development
    environmental planning 124-5
    plans implementation 166-73
Dewey, John 248
dialectical synthesis 47-8
Discourse on Thinking 45
DoE *see* Department of the Environment

Economic and Social Research Council
    (ESRC) 4, 83-4, 91
ECORYS (consultancy) 145, 147-50, 158
Ecosfera (consultancy) 240
educational experiences in Palermo 240-2
Eisenhower, President 66
Ellul, Jacques 51
emotions in research 8
'end of history' concept 66
Engel 77
environmental planning
    associations 133-9
    crisis 124
    development 124-5
    ethical dilemmas 22
    ethics 126-8
    institutional approach 128-33
    Italian laws 129-31
    local development 123
    policies 125-39
    principles verification 140-2
    research 119-44, 128-33
    Sicily 120, 121, 131-3
    utilitarian consequentialism 20-5
epistemology 50
ESRC *see* Economic and Social Research
    Council
'essential tension' concept 48
ethical conduct in planning research
    57-69
*Ethical Conduct of Research involving
    Human Subjects* (policy statement)
    60
ethical injustices 61-2
ethical life (Sittlichkeit) concept 62
'ethical terrain' concept 255
'ethics of care' concept 8
'ethics of volition' concept 42
EU *see* European Union
'eudaimonic' ethical tradition 31

European Union (EU) and environmental issues 51
evaluation research 162, 164

'felicific calculus' 18
fertiliser production 49
Florida, Richard 67
Flyvberg, B. 35
Foot, Philippa 31-2
forestry in Sicily 138
FOTE *see* 'full open, truthful exchange'
Foucault, Michel 8, 81, 196
freedom and Naples waste crisis 198-202
'full open, truthful exchange' (FOTE) 182

Galileo and Roman Catholic church 21
game theory and conflict negotiation 65
Globe and Mail (Canadian newspaper) 60, 67
'good agreements' and naturalistic research ethic 188-9

Habernas, Jürgen 65
'happiness principle' 14
Hare, R.M. 17
Hegel 47, 62-6
Heidegger, Martin 45, 51
Higher Education Funding Council 72
higher education in US 37
honesty and consultancy 153
'how' research 162
human failings 43-4
Hume, David 65

IACP *see* Autonomous Institute of Public Housing
impact research 164
impartiality and consultancy 150-2
'imperial eyes'
    Australia and indigenous people 219-31, 257
    PhD research 219-20, 221, 223-8
    positioning 219-22
    whiteness 221-3, 225-7
implausability and virtue ethics 31-5
impropriety in travel demand forecasts 109-10
indigenous people in Australia 219-31, 257

Institute of Transport Engineers (ITE) 111
institutional approach to environmental planning 128-33
Institutional Review Boards (IRBs) 206
integrity and consultancy 153
intellectual ownership and consultancy 154-5
intellectual property rights (IPR) 75, 79, 82-3, 86
Inter-Institutional Network (RI) 239, 242, 243
'international development' and planning schools 61
IPR *see* intellectual property rights
IRBs *see* Institutional Review Boards
'is the client always right?' (consultancy) 152-3
Italian laws and environmental planning 129-31
Italy
    Nature Paralympics 139
    PhD training 95-7, 98-103, 103-4
ITE *see* Institute of Transport Engineers

James, William 42-3
Jonas, Hans 46, 50, 51
'just city' concept 125

Kain, John 108
Kant, Immanuel 47, 51, 65
Klein, Naomi 57
'knowledge for action in the public domain' research 162
knowledge business 71-85, 85-9
knowledge and Naples waste crisis 191-203, 203-5
knowledge transfer (KT) 83-5, 86
Kuhn, Thomas 48

LA21 *see* Local Agenda 21
Land Ethic concept 127, 142
Le Carre, John 60
Legambiente association 137-9
Leopold, A. 127, 142
Local Agenda 21 (LA21) programme in Palermo 237-8, 242
local development in environmental planning 123

Local Plans 164
logic and ethics 49-51
London boroughs planning 165
loneliness of research 141-2

Mabo v. Queensland case 223-4
McAll Smith, Alexander 119
McDowell, John 32
Madoff, Bernard 44
Mafia in Palermo 243
Marcuse, Peter 61-2
Marx, Karl
    capitalism 62, 77, 83
    contradictions in civil society 64
    dialectical synthesis 47
    Das Kapital 67
    labour alienation 80
    planning ethics 65
    politics 66
'Marxism and Ethics' 65-6
mediation research 8
mediators and naturalistic research ethic
        179-88, 188-9
Merton, Robert 74, 84
methodology in travel demand forecasts
        110-11
Mill, John Stuart 15-16, 17-18, 107, 115
minorities and ethical issues 8, 233-6, 237-
        47, 247-50
misunderstanding in travel demand
        forecasts 112-13
mongrel cities 207
moral character and virtue ethics 34
moral human failings 43-4
Morgan Cole (law firm) 78
motor cyclists, US 183
Murdoch, Iris 34

Naples waste crisis 191-203, 203-5
    ethics 202-3
    intractable collective claims 198-202
    politics 202-3
    State of Exception 193-8
    truth/freedom 198-202
NASDAQ (Stock Exchange) 44
Native Title Act 224
naturalistic research ethic 179-88, 188-9
    community planning 181-2

'good agreements' 188-9
    representation 186-8
    respect 185-6
    trust 184-5
Nature Paralympics in Italy 139
nature reserves in Sicily 137-9
Nicomachean Ethics 125
NIMBYism 49
normative premises 50
Nozick, Robert 15-16

Oliveri, Nancy 59-60, 62, 67
On Liberty 115
'on practice' research 163
openness and consultancy 154

Paba, Giancarlo 123
Palermo
    educational experiences 240-2
    housing policies 239
    Integrated Intervention Programme
        (PII) 240
    Local Agenda 21 programme 237-8
    Mafia control 243
    S.A.L.I. Network 243
    workshops at schools 244-5
    ZEN chronicles 238-40, 241-2, 243,
        246
participatory planning research 233-47,
        247-54
PhD research
    ethics 259
    'imperial eyes' 219-20, 221, 223-5, 226
PhD training 91-103, 103-6
    Italy 95-7, 98-103, 103-4
    need 98-103
    programmes 94, 99, 102
    systematic research 91-4
    United Kingdom 92, 94
philosophy and dialectical synthesis 47-8
Philosophy of Right 62-4
phronesis (judgment) 35
Pierce, Charles 42-3, 50
Planners Use of Theory in Practice 165
Planning and Compensation Act (1991) 172
planning practice 161-73, 173-5
'Planning Practice Research Network',
        US 163

planning researchers *see* researchers
planning schools *and* 'business-facing'
    orientation 77-8
Plato 34, 125
plausability and virtue ethics 31-5
'policy community' 162
politics and Naples waste crisis 202-3
Ponzi scheme 44
Popper, Karl 50
power
    Naples waste crisis 191-203, 203-5
    narration and advocacy planning
        research 210-11
pragmatic ethics 41-53
Pragmatism *see* American Pragmatism
programmes for PhD training 94, 99, 102
prudence in research 258
public perception in travel demand
    forecasts 111-12
public water company (AWAP) 239

qualitative research in advocacy planning
    research 208
questionnaires on ethics 57

radical politics 57-69
'raising consciousness' concept 257
Rawls, John 19-20, 50, 51
Regione Sicilia 137-8
representation and naturalistic research
    ethic 186-8
research
    emotions 8
    ethics and virtue ethics 29-35, 35-8
    mediation 8
    minorities 8
    planning practice 161-73, 173-5
        careers 163-6
        consultancy 157
Research Ethics Review 4
researchers
    ethical education 25-7
    planning schools 6-7
    training 8
respect and naturalistic research ethic
    185-6
'responsibility' ethic 150
rhetoric of 'balance' 47-8

RI *see* Inter-Institutional Network (Italy)
'right thing' concept 29-30
Rio Declaration 122-3
Rittel, Horst 43
Roman Catholic church and Galileo 21
rule-following in virtual ethics 32-3

S.A.L.I. Network, Palermo 243
Sandercock, Leonie 207
Savidan, Patrick 124
Schmitt, Carl 195
schools workshops in Palermo 244-5
science of knowledge 50
Seneca, L.A. 31, 34
sensitivity and ethics 258-60
Shakespeare, William 233
'Sicilian Ecological Network' 133
Sicily
    environment planning policies 120,
        121
    ethical behaviour 140
    forestry 138
    nature reserves 137-9
    planning 7
    territorial planning 131-3
    value driven approach 121-5
Sidgwick, Henry 17
Silent Spring 49
Singer, Edward 43
Sistema Gaia 142
situational ethics and advocacy planning
    research 208-9
social justice and space 5
social structure in cities 1
Socrates 247
South Staffordshire housing 168, 170
space and social justice 5
State of Exception and Naples waste crisis
    193-8
strategic themes implementation 169-70
sustainability and Aalborg Charter 47
sustainable development ethics 45-52
Sweeney, David 72
systematic research for PhD training 91-4
systemic theory of ethics 51-2

teaching ethics 104
territorial planning in Sicily 131-3

thalassemia and drug treatment 59
The Constant Gardener 60
The Future of Development Plans 172
The Methods of Ethics 17
The Rationale of Reward 15
The Republic 125
The Shock Doctrine 57
Thematic Group on 'Research Ethics and Planning' *see* AESOP
'they would say that, wouldn't they' (consultancy) 150-1
Thomas, Huw 58
Town Planning Review 7
training for planning researchers 8
transparency and consultancy 154
travel demand forecasting 107-14, 115-18
    bias 108-9
    bunker mentality 113-14
    planning challenges 115-16
    research void 109-13
trust and naturalistic research ethic 184-5
truth and Naples waste crisis 198-202

Underwood, Jacky 165
United Kingdom (UK)
    PhD training 92
    university intellectual property 78-9
    university research ethics committees 4
United Kingdom National Audit Office (UKNAO) 110
United States (US)
    19th century college system 75
    higher education 37
    'international development' and planning schools 61
    motor cyclists 183
    PhD programmes 94
    'Planning Practice Research Network' 163
    planning schools 61
    transit projects funding 108
United States Department of Transport (USDOT) 110
universities
    intellectual property in UK 78-9
    research ethics committees in UK 4

urban planning research 104
urban transportation modeling system (UTMS) 108
US *see* United States
utilitarian consequentialism
    ethical education of researchers 25-7
    ethics of scholarship 20-5
    research in environmental planning 20-5
    review 17-20
    truth and truthfulness 20-5
utilitarianism 14-16, 18
UTMS *see* urban transportation modeling system

virtue ethics
    description 30-1
    introduction 29-30
    moral character 34
    plausability and implausability 31-5
    research ethics 29-35, 35-8

Wente, Margaret 60
West Churchman, C. 43
Western epistemological framework 249
'what is going on' research 162
'what matters' concept 36
'what' research 162
whiteness and Australian issues 221-3, 225, 227
'wicked problems' in planning 43
Williams, Bernard 17, 21-5
Wilson, Charles Wilson 66
Wood, Allen 63
workshops in schools, Palermo 244-5
World Wildlife Fund (WWF)
    consensus 135
    education 136
    effectiveness 135
    environmental associations 133
    participation 134
    principles 141
    training 136

ZEN (Zona Espansione Nord) chronicles 238-40, 241-2, 243, 246